Advanced
Chain Maille
Jewelry Workshop

Advanced Chain Maille Jewelry Workshop

WEAVING WITH RINGS & SCALES

KAREN KARON

interweave.com

Editor
Marlene Blessing

Technical Editor
Pat Harste

Photo Art Direction
Julia Boyles

Interior Art Direction
Charlene Tiedemann

Cover & Interior Designer
Studio Court

Photography
Joe Coca, Ann Swanson

Photo Styling
Ann Swanson

Illustrator
Bonnie Brooks

Production Designer
Katherine Jackson

© 2014 Karen Karon
Photography and illustrations © 2014 Interweave, a division of F+W Media, Inc.
All rights reserved.

Interweave
A division of F+W Media, Inc.
4868 Innovation Drive
Fort Collins, CO 80525-5576
interweave.com

Manufactured in China
by RR Donnelley Shenzhen

Library of Congress
Cataloging-in-Publication Data

Karon, Karen, author.
Advanced chain maille jewelry workshop: weaving with rings and scales / Karen Karon.
 pages cm
Includes index.
ISBN 978-1-62033-659-5 (pbk.)
ISBN 978-1-62033-660-1 (PDF)
1. Jewelry making. 2. Chains (Jewelry) 3. Metal-work. I. Title.
TT212.K37 2010
745.594'2--dc23

2014011104

10 9 8 7 6 5 4 3 2 1

ACKNOWLEDGMENTS

Because family comes first, I will start by thanking my family for their unconditional love, support, and encouragement.

Next, I'd like to thank the people at F&W Media/Interweave, especially Allison Korleski and Kerry Bogert for their guidance and support at the beginning of the project, my wonderful and wise editor, Marlene Blessing, and illustrator, Bonnie Brooks, for her perseverance and patience.

I also wish to thank Lindsay Minihan from Metalwerx and all of the fantastic students I've had the privilege to teach there, especially the members of the "Repeat Offenders Club."

Finally, I'd like to thank all of the talented maille artisans who continue to keep the craft alive by inventing new and inspiring weaves, especially Laura Hepworth, Celeste McClain, Gary Dunham, Jessica Gump, and Louis K. Gorczyca.

CONTENTS

INTRODUCTION
- 10   How to Use This Book
- 11   Tools
- 13   Materials
- 15   Buying vs Making Jump Rings
- 16   More Complex Techniques
- 17   A Word on Safety

REVIEW MATERIAL
- 20   Through-the-Eye (TE) vs Around-the-Eye (AE) Connections
- 20   Weaving a Strip of European 4-in-1
- 22   Joining European 4-in-1 End to End
- 23   Starting Half Persian
- 26   Half Persian 3-in-1 (HP31)
- 28   Weaving Mirror-Image HP31 Chain
- 29   Weaving HP31 Edges
- 30   Chain Maille Math

PERSIAN WEAVES
- 34   Great Southern Gathering (GSG) Weave
- 38   GSG Sheet Weave
- 40   Half Persian 3-in-1 Sheet 6 (HP31S6) Weave
- 43   Arkham Weave
- 45   Arkham Sheet
- 51   Crotalus Weave
- 53   Viperscale Weave
- 56   **Project:** Two-Tone GSG Sheet Necklace
- 58   **Project:** Mixed-Metal Claspless Viperscale Bracelet

ELF WEAVES
- 62   Elfweave
- 67   Elfsheet
- 72   72Tiffany Weave
- 76   **Project:** Elfweave Loop Earrings
- 78   **Project:** Ombre Elfsheet Ring

HYBRID WEAVES
- 82   Interwoven 4-1
- 86   Interwoven Sheet
- 92   Dragonback Weave
- 96   Persian Dragonscale Weave
- 98   **Project:** Dragonback Ring
- 100   **Project:** Interwoven Stretch Cuff

SCALE MAILLE
- 104   Traditional Weaving Method
- 114   Linear Weaving Method
- 123   **Project:** Dragonback Bracelet with Scales
- 128   **Project:** Beaded Linear Scale and Maille Collar

TERMINATIONS, ATTACHMENTS, AND FINISHING TOUCHES
- 132   Termination Options for Chain Maille Weaves
- 133   Attachment Options for Findings
- 135   Termination Options for Scale Maille Weaves
- 136   Finishing Touches

- 143   Resources
- 144   Abbreviations
- 144   Aspect Ratio Charts
- 156   Imperial and Metric Conversion Charts
- 159   Index

INTRODUCTION

This book is written for those who are interested in making chain maille jewelry, are familiar with most of the classic weaves, and are looking for new weaves that will help them to expand their chain maille design palettes and perfect their skills with more challenging linkage patterns. If you've never tried chain maille before or are still a chain maille beginner, this book is NOT for you. Also, because this book is written from a jewelry-making perspective, if you're looking for tips on chain maille armor construction, this book is NOT for you.

For those who want to design with alternative materials, the chapter on weaving with scales, a current hot trend in chain maille and fashion, is sure to please. The weaves included in the book are mostly modern weaves inspired by the classics and created by some very talented members of the chain maille community. I have explored and experimented with these weaves, designing some cool jewelry and accessories along the way. This exploration has enabled me not only to write instructions for completing these weaves, but also to help you master each one. As well, I share some of the essentials I've learned, including jump ring sizing options, helpful hints, tips, tricks, shortcuts, and pitfalls to avoid.

How to Use This Book

As in my first book, *Chain Maille Jewelry Workshop*, this advanced book takes a technique-based approach and shows multiple methods to accomplish a weave. Sprinkled throughout, there are lots of tips and suggestions for alternate designs. In addition, each weave chapter includes two projects that illustrate some of the techniques learned in that chapter. You can choose to jump into whatever chapter appeals to you. The material within each weave chapter is presented in order of complexity, allowing you to build skills naturally within each weave group.

The book features a review chapter that provides refreshers on the information from *Chain Maille Jewelry Workshop* that you will need to accomplish the weaves in this new book. All pertinent information—together with some new tips and tricks—is conveniently contained in one volume. To complete your preparation, read the introductory and finishing chapters of the book first: they are full of tips and tricks that will help you complete the projects successfully. After you've warmed up with these three chapters, start at the beginning of whatever weave chapter interests you. Keep in mind that, although the weaves are presented in order of complexity, the sheet weave variations are more complex than the base weaves. For example, when working the Persian chapter, GSG is easiest, followed by Arkham, Crotalus, and then Viperscale. The sheet variations of GSG and Arkham are more complex than all of the base weaves, but they are placed in proximity to their base weaves for continuity. Before you complete a piece of jewelry, read the terminations section (page 130) to determine how to finish your piece with various clasp attachments and findings.

As in *Chain Maille Jewelry Workshop*, each weave section contains a chart that includes suggested jump ring sizes in two gauges (16 and 18) and two metals (sterling silver and bright aluminum) for each weave. The suggested silver sizes are based on the jump rings from Urban Maille, my favorite precious metal jump ring source (no affiliation, just a happy customer—see Resources on page 143). These charts have been expanded in this book. To illustrate the way jump rings can vary from vendor to vendor, I suggest bright aluminum jump ring sizes for three suppliers that I use, The Ring Lord, Metal Designz, and C&T Designs. I've also included a column showing the aspect ratio (AR) for each suggested size. The figures in the Aspect Ratio column were derived either directly from the vendors' websites where available or through calculation (in red, "Common" AR, page 31).

Note that these size recommendations are based on the simplest form, a bracelet. If you wish to make an item that needs to flex differently—for example, a collar that requires flexibility on the edges—you may need to make size adjustments to achieve suitable flex and fit.

The suggested counts for jump rings per inch for the sheet weaves are based on sheets that are sized as pictured. If you want to work wider (or thinner), you will need to estimate the number of jump rings you will require for your project. Also, these weaves tend to tighten a bit when widened: to make a wider weave, you may need to adjust the jump ring size to achieve the desired result.

Tools

For chain maille construction, two pairs of top-quality pliers are really all you need. Whether I work with large or small jump rings, I use full-size, smooth-jawed, flat-nose pliers. The straight, flat jaws cover more surface area on the jump rings than do pointed chain-nose pliers and provide a secure hold. All of my pliers have long handles, about 4" (10 cm). The longer handles provide more leverage and cause less hand fatigue.

I've been using the same two pairs of pliers for the majority of my work for years. I use my Swanstrom flat-nose pliers in my right hand: its spring mechanism gives me a wide range of movement with my dominant hand. In my left hand, I use my Lindstrom RX flat-nose pliers; they are lightweight and the handles are extremely comfortable. The bio-spring attached to each handle limits the pliers' range of movement, which is why I use this pair in my left, nondominant hand. Lindstrom and Swanstrom both make quality products. Many of my students also love their Wubbers pliers.

Lately, I have been making lots of micro-maille. Even though the jump rings are very small (2 mm range), I still prefer to work with full-size flat-nose pliers. Sometimes, it is difficult to fit the jaws of my "go-to" pliers into the tiny spaces in the micro-weave to grasp the jump rings firmly. The jaws are just a bit thick. I recently discovered Tronex short-jawed flat-nose pliers. They are full sized, with long handles, but the jaws are thinner (by just a fraction of a millimeter), allowing me easier access into the tiny spaces in micro-weaves. The Tronex pliers are also very well made, with very smooth jaws: therefore, no refining (see page 138) was necessary.

In addition to pliers, my jump ring–opening tool is an indispensable addition to my tool kit. I use thousands and thousands of jump rings, sometimes in a single piece. This little inexpensive tool makes the work of opening these thousands of jump rings quicker and easier.

The more chain maille I do, especially at the micro-level, the worse my eyes get! I cannot work without some sort of magnification. I have drugstore reading glasses, an Optivisor, clip-on magnifying lenses, and a magnifying lamp. I use these items alone or in combination, whatever it takes. Try different options and use what works best for you.

My digital calipers are extremely important. They help me determine the exact aspect ratio of the jump rings I'm using and are, therefore, an essential design tool (Actual AR, see page 31).

Jump ring–opening tool

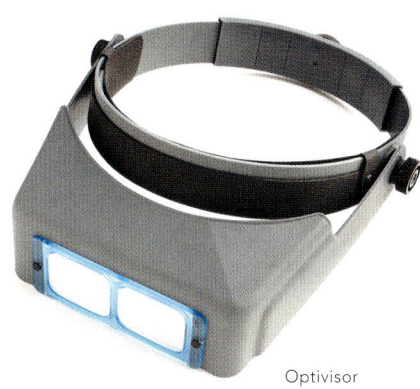
Optivisor

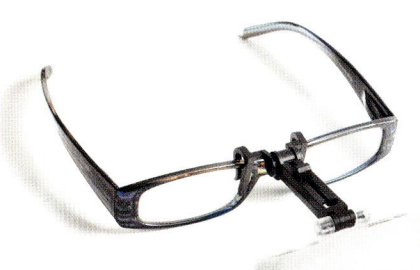
Clip-on magnifying lenses

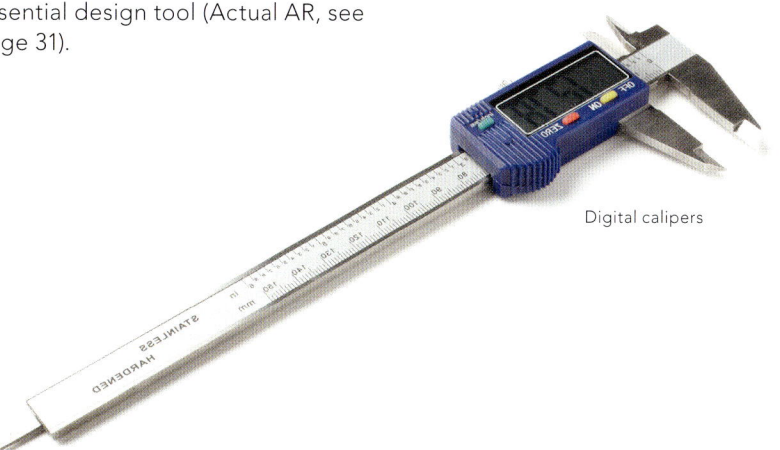
Digital calipers

Introduction

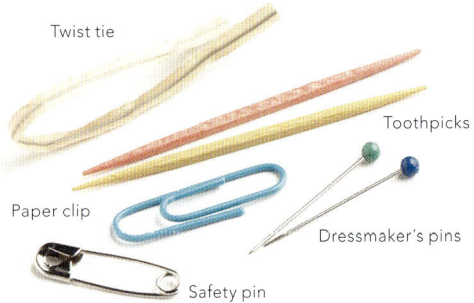

Twist tie
Toothpicks
Paper clip
Dressmaker's pins
Safety pin

Bracelet mandrel

Ring mandrel

Dapping punches and block

My other essential design tools are my ring and bracelet mandrels. I use them to help me get the proper fit on rings and bracelets.

▸ There are a few low-tech items I find handy to have around:

Tailor's tape measure—For measuring body parts to determine fit.

Toothpicks—Can be used much like an awl. They are handy for opening up a tight spot in your weave.

Dressmaker's pins or head pins—I use these as I would a toothpick, but for micro-weaves.

Paper clips—Great starting aids for weaves (my favorite!). I always have them on hand, and I pass out tons of them when teaching. A **safety pin**, **twist tie**, or a small length of wire can all be used as starting aids as well.

Tape—My second favorite starting aid. I often use masking tape or blue painter's tape to secure the start of flat weaves and to secure scales when weaving scale maille.

▸ If you plan to embellish your maille, there are lots of other jewelry-making tools you might want to have. The most common are:

Round-nose pliers for making loops and spirals.

Chain-nose pliers for general wire tasks.

Flush wire cutters for cutting wire.

Jewelry file for smoothing the ends of homemade ear wires.

▸ If you are thinking of incorporating some sheet metal, you might consider:

Hammer (ball-peen or chasing) for making hammer-textured embellishments.

Steel bench block to hammer on.

Saw frame and **saw blades** to cut wire or sheet metal.

Dapping punches and **dapping block** to shape metal.

Hole punch tool (screw punch or hole-punching pliers) allows you to pierce holes in sheet metal so you can connect it to your maille.

12   ADVANCED CHAIN MAILLE JEWELRY WORKSHOP

On the surface, jump rings seem simple. But every step of the manufacturing process affects the size of the finished ring which in turn affects your finished piece of jewelry.

Materials

To make chain maille, all you really need are jump rings and findings. In this book, I'm introducing some techniques that use metal scales as well. Findings are discussed in the Terminations, Attachments, and Finishing Touches chapter of the book (page 130).

JUMP RINGS

These come in a variety of metals and materials. No matter what metal you choose to work in, make sure the jump rings are of good quality with flush, saw-cut ends.

Sterling silver—This is my metal of choice. For chain maille, I prefer the traditional sterling alloy over the newer, tarnish-resistant alloys simply because there is a slight difference in jump ring size. However, I have "made the switch" to Argentium when it comes to making items from sheet metal because I like the way it solders and fuses, not to mention how it resists fire-scale!

Silver-filled—This is a relatively new addition to the market. It was introduced as a lower cost alternative when the silver market was very high. I find it works, feels, and looks like sterling. I have safely tumbled my silver-filled pieces and have not yet noticed any wear issues.

Gold-filled—Gold is very expensive, so gold-filled is my yellow metal of choice. It is more expensive than sterling, but nowhere near the cost of gold. I'm more of a silver girl than a gold girl, but I do like to use gold-filled jump rings as accents to enhance my designs.

note: *Gold-filled and silver-filled are not the same as gold- and silver-plated. Plated metals have only a very thin coating of the precious metal on the surface of the base metal. This thin layer can be scratched off easily. Gold-filled and silver-filled metals are more like thin-walled tubes of gold or sterling silver with a base metal core, resulting in a product with a thicker layer of precious metal on the outside.*

Bright aluminum—Bright aluminum is lightweight and very inexpensive. It is stiffer and more brittle than sterling. I buy a lot of bright aluminum jump rings to use for testing purposes—for example, when I'm trying to learn a new weave or I'm working out sizing issues.

Anodized aluminum—I buy a lot of anodized aluminum jump rings, too. I like to use them when I want to make something big, such as a collar or belt, which would be heavy to wear and expensive to make if made in a metal such as sterling silver. The colors are fun to play with, too.

Anodized niobium—For me, this metal is like the bridge between anodized aluminum and silver. The cost is closer to silver-filled. Its weight and working feel are much like sterling. It comes in fun colors, such as anodized aluminum. Bonus: it is hypoallergenic.

note: *Anodized colors can fade or darken with time, wear, or exposure. The colors are merely a surface treatment and can be scratched off. Keep pieces clean and handle them with care.*

Copper, brass, and bronze—Lately, these alternate metals have been gaining in popularity, due primarily to the rise in the price of silver. Lots of people love them, but they are just not my cup of tea. I feel that copper is too soft for chain maille. Chain maille is not soldered; metal

Gold-filled jump rings are accents.

Introduction 13

tension is the only thing that keeps the jump rings closed. Copper might be strong enough for making lightweight earrings, but I wouldn't feel comfortable using it for items that take more abuse when worn. Brass and bronze aren't as soft as copper but, like copper, these copper-based alloys tend to darken with wear. Some people have body chemistry that reacts to copper (or copper-based alloys). In such cases, green marks develop on their skin where the metal has touched it—not a great feature for jewelry, in my opinion.

Steel—I don't use it because it is a stiff metal and can be difficult to work with. If I want a white metal, I prefer the look of silver.

Rubber O-rings—These are great for fun, colorful projects or for when you want to add a little stretch to your weave. Different vendors offer different sizing and color options (including glow-in-the-dark and neon), so shop around to find exactly what you want.

SCALES

A popular trend in chain maille jewelry, metal scales are available in a variety of materials such as steel, brass, bronze, copper, silver, titanium, niobium, aluminum, and plastic. All of the projects in this book are made using anodized aluminum scales. I like anodized aluminum scales because they are lightweight, come in assorted fun colors, and are inexpensive—which allows for guilt-free experimentation.

The classic domed "leaf" shape is the shape I like to use, but some vendors offer other shapes as well (round and shield-shaped with two holes). Scales come in two basic sizes, large [⅞" × 1.41" (2.2 × 3.58 cm), hole size 0.35" (8.9 mm)] and small [⁹⁄₁₆" × ⅞" (1.4 × 2.2 cm), hole size 0.22" (5.59 mm)]. For jewelry applications, I prefer the small size. In fact, if any manufacturers are reading this, I would be very interested in purchasing "mini" size scales.

Different scale suppliers have different color offerings (even glow-in-the-dark!), so if one doesn't have what you want, check another. Some scale suppliers anodize the metal first and then punch out the scales, leaving the edges uncolored. Others anodize the actual scales, resulting in color on all surfaces. What is best is just a matter of preference. In fact, for a spiky, linear form, such as the Colorful Scale and Box Chain Necklace (see page 120), I prefer the scales with uncolored edges. I burnish along the edge of each scale to make them extra shiny and make the design pop.

Anodized aluminum scale bracelets

BUYING VS MAKING JUMP RINGS

I am often asked, "Why not just buy wire and make your own jump rings? It's cheaper." That's true. But there is more to it than that. When I was starting out in chain maille, I had visions of making all my own jump rings so that I'd have any size in any metal I desired at my disposal. There are advantages to making your own jump rings: **1** You are not limited by what is commercially available; **2** You can control every aspect of making them; and **3** You save money by purchasing wire instead of finished jump rings.

For me, handcutting proved to be very time-consuming. Therefore, I started to look at the motorized jump ring cutting sets. My jewelry-making friends will tell you that power tools make me break out in a cold sweat. It's a real phobia for me. In a class that I recently attended, I chose to bevel the edge of a steel blanking die I was working on with a hand file and sanding sticks, while all of my classmates were lined up to use the bench grinder (I hate it when those sparks start flying, and the noise . . . !).

The one exception to my power tool phobia is the flex shaft tool. Because motorized cutters are powered by a flex shaft, I decided to buy one. The game changer came when I installed the (very sharp) rotary blade. My paralyzing power tool anxiety was back. I forced myself to use it a few times, but I can't get over my feelings of anxiety. It is not safe to use tools that you are not comfortable handling.

Cutting jump rings is an entirely different skill from weaving jump rings. It is part art and part science, requiring many, many hours of practice to hone your technique to achieve consistent results. For your jewelry to have a professional look, you need to use well-crafted jump rings. If you don't have the time required to develop your cutting technique, buy your jump rings from a reliable vendor. Find a vendor that you can trust and rely on to deliver a quality and consistent product. If you can't get a consistent product, you will not get a consistent result. There are suppliers out there who have cut millions of jump rings and can therefore deliver a quality product that will elevate the look of your finished piece.

I feel that the cost saving is not that significant when other factors are considered, because cutting my own jump rings involves the expense of purchasing extra tools and materials:

Tool Purchases. You have to invest in one-time purchases such as a saw (motorized or hand tool), mandrels (many different sizes required), accessories such as a coil winder (hand winder or motorized drill), and a flex shaft (for motorized cutting). Plus, there is the ongoing expense of replacing saw blades (rotary blades for motorized cutting are fairly expensive), cutting lubricant, dowels, and tape (to stabilize coils for cutting).

Metal Waste. Some wire is wasted when cutting your own jump rings. When I purchase a troy ounce of jump rings, I get a full troy ounce of finished usable jump rings. If I buy a troy ounce of wire, I will lose some wire at each end of each coil I make. I will also lose a tiny bit of metal weight to the saw blade when the coil is cut. Occasionally, a whole coil gets destroyed—stuff happens! The discarded bits of wire and metal sweeps will be added to my refining scrap, but the end result of my labor is less than a full troy ounce of usable jump rings.

Labor Costs. The time required to make thousands of the jump rings I need takes time away from developing new designs, constructing new pieces, preparing samples and written material for classes, writing, taking photographs, updating my website, administrative paperwork, etc.

When pricing an item for sale, one must consider the cost of labor. If I cut my own jump rings, the materials cost would be less because I would purchase wire instead of finished jump rings. But the increased labor cost to cover my time cutting jump rings would offset at least some of those savings. In fact, my labor cost would likely be higher, because I cannot cut as efficiently as a reputable vendor who has cut millions of them.

I am not trying to discourage you from making your own jump rings. If you have a strong desire to do it, then go for it! It's nice to be able to tell customers that not only have you designed the piece and connected each individual jump ring, but that you have also made each individual jump ring. Quite an impressive accomplishment! Realize that it will take practice to produce jump rings of quality and consistency (straight cuts, burr-free, consistent in size, and sufficient in strength). I've simply decided I'm better off buying my jump rings—time saved and anxiety eliminated. Anyway, for me weaving is the fun part!

More Complex Techniques

The weaves in this book are definitely more complex than those in *Chain Maille Jewelry Workshop*. However, gaining the ability to construct more complex weaves is only one aspect of becoming an advanced maille weaver. There are other complex skills you can develop and techniques you can try that will greatly expand your design choices.

CLOSING A WEAVE FROM END TO END

This is always tricky but definitely worth learning. Forming closed circles is essential for creating rings, claspless bracelets, or long necklaces. These forms can also be used in unique ways, such as for bails, bezels, connectors, and design elements. How about nonjewelry applications, such as napkin rings or curtain ties? Specific instructions for closing several of the weaves are included in the weave chapters.

WEAVING MICRO-MAILLE

Using tiny-sized jump rings greatly elevates the difficulty level of even the most basic weave. The jump rings are difficult to see and handle. You need to have manual dexterity, steady hands, and proper tools. As I stated earlier, whether weaving regular size or micro, I prefer full-size flat-nose pliers. I find that the Tronex brand short-jawed flat-nose pliers have tips that are just slightly thinner than other pliers I've tried and fit into the tiny spaces better, making it easier to grasp the jump rings. Magnification is vital. Make sure you have proper eyewear and good lighting. Starting aids can be helpful. Try tape, tiny safety pins, or bits of thin wire. Also, lay off the caffeine to keep those hands steady.

WORKING LARGE

When I refer to working large, I don't mean using large jump rings. In fact, I start off my beginners with relatively large jump rings (16g) as they are easier to grasp and see—and they work up quickly. What I am referring to when I say "working large" is the ability to tackle projects that are large in size and scope, projects that involve many hours of labor and thousands of jump rings.

Mind and Body

Half the battle is psychological. It can be scary to attempt a large project. What if the project fails, after all of the time, energy, and money you've invested in it? Using an inexpensive material such as anodized aluminum can alleviate some of that pressure.

The other half of the battle is physical. When you're in it for the long haul, make sure you're physically comfortable: supportive chair, comfortable work surface height, good lighting, magnification tools, etc. Comfort also extends to using ergonomic handtools as you will be working with them for many hours at a time.

Best Practices

To make the most of the time you have available, employ some assembly-line technique efficiencies, like preopening and preclosing large quantities of jump rings. I've worked on projects where the first few days involved nothing but opening and closing jump rings. (Boring . . . z-z-z! I'm still waiting for someone to invent an automatic jump ring opening/closing machine!) Tasks like this are repetitive, so take frequent breaks to rest your eyes and stretch your back, neck, shoulders, and hands. Get up and move around periodically to keep your blood circulating. Make sure you drink water to stay hydrated as well.

Finally, create a soothing atmosphere in which to work. After all, you're going to be there a while. Listen to your favorite music or an interesting audio book (during baseball season, I like to weave while listening to the Red Sox broadcasts).

PLAY WITH ASPECT RATIO

Don't be afraid to use the AR calculation! It can help you make jewelry to proper scale, which looks better and will be more comfortable to wear. In the book, 16- and 18-gauge jump rings are recommended because they are the most common gauges used. But they may not be the best choice for your particular project. In general, I use 16g or 18g for most bracelets and necklaces and 20g or 22g for most rings and earrings, but not always. It really depends on the project. Playing with scale can result in some interesting forms.

Also, adjusting the AR can enable you to create forms for different purposes. For example, I often tighten up the AR of some chain weaves to create small, stiff bits of chain to use as toggle closures and also as beads.

FIXING MISTAKES

I often hear my less experienced students say, "Something in this weave is not right," but they cannot figure out what it is. As a seasoned chain maille artist, you have the ability to look at a weave and not only see where a mistake may have occurred, but also figure out how to remedy the situation. This means that you are able to read the cues from adjacent rows and pattern repeats to figure out where to place jump rings in a weave. This skill is essential when trying to keep the edges of complex sheet weaves uniform.

TAKE SPEED WEAVING OUTSIDE THE BOX

As they gain experience, many maille weavers begin to use speed weaving to improve efficiency by using preclosed jump rings when weaving. Speed weaving can also provide an opportunity for creativity. You can substitute other fun materials for those preclosed jump rings to add interest to your weaves. The size of the alternate material needs to be compatible with the size of the jump rings you are using in your weave, so you'll need to experiment. You can use any O-shaped item, such as rubber O-rings (which, if placed properly, can also add stretch to your weave), glass disk-shaped beads, washers, etc.

A Word on Safety

Chain maille construction is a serious endeavor, intended for adults. Small items, such jump rings, beads, and findings, can become choking hazards in the hands of a child. As well, the process involves working with metal and sharp tools (with or without power) that can cause injury. Plus, connecting jump ring after jump ring as you weave can cause repetitive stress injuries. It's worth taking precautions to stay safe and healthy in order to enjoy the fun and rewards of chain maille construction.

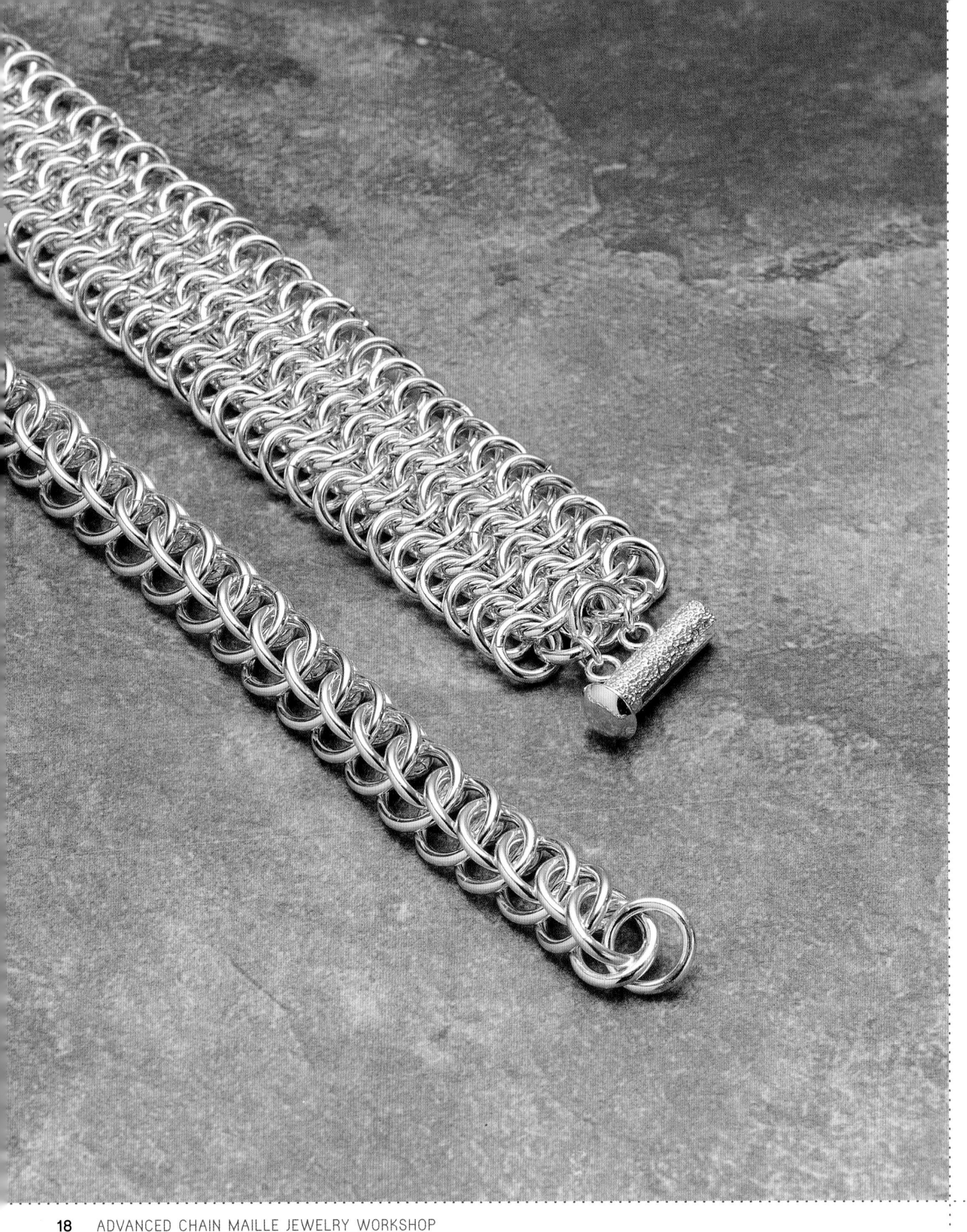

REVIEW MATERIAL

Many of the weaves presented in the following chapters use techniques learned in *Chain Maille Jewelry Workshop*—namely the European 4-in-1 weave and the Half Persian 3-in-1 weave. Both will be presented here so that all the information you need to complete the more complex weaves will be available to you in one volume.

Through-the-Eye (TE) vs. Around-the-Eye (AE) Connections

When 2 closely spaced adjacent jump rings overlap, resembling Venn diagrams (remember them from grade school math class?), the space formed by the overlap is referred to as the *eye*. The adjacent jump rings can be connected using a through-the-eye (TE) connection or an around-the-eye (AE) connection (**Figs. 1**–**3**). The type of connection determines the plane in which the connecting jump ring lies: vertical for TE and horizontal for AE.

Jump Ring Eye

Through the Eye Connection (TE)

Around the Eye Connection (AE)

Weaving a Strip of European 4-in-1

Instructions that follow describe the construction of a basic 3-row strip of European 4-in-1 (E41), which is used to start many E41-based designs. Depending on the project, you need to make your E41 strip with either 1 or 2 jump rings at the start and/or end. For example, to make a ring or a claspless bracelet, you will need to join the strip from end to end. Therefore, start and end with 1 jump ring: it is easier to join this way. Because this text is geared toward the advanced weaver, the E41 directions that follow are for the speed-weaving method.

SPEED WEAVE

Prepare Jump Rings

Open about one-third of your jump rings and close the remaining two-thirds.

Pattern Start

1. Thread 1 open (orange) jump ring through 4 closed (turquoise) jump rings and close the open jump ring (**Fig. 1**).

2. Arrange the jump rings in the same orientation (VERY important) as in **Fig. 2**. The front side is facing you, and the center (orange) jump ring passes over the front of the bottom pair of (turquoise) jump rings. In addition, the top pair of (turquoise) jump rings lies under the bottom pair of (turquoise) jump rings. The starting end of your weave has 2 (turquoise) jump rings. If that is the desired result, you can skip to the Pattern Repeat section.

3. If you wish your weave to have only 1 jump ring at the starting end, thread 1 open (gray) jump ring through the bottom pair of (turquoise) jump rings and close it (**Fig. 3**). Arrange the jump rings in the same orientation (VERY important) as in **Fig. 3**. The front side is facing you, a single (gray) jump ring is on the bottom, the center (orange) jump ring passes over the front of the bottom pair of (turquoise) jump rings, and the top pair of (turquoise) jump rings lies under the bottom pair of (turquoise) jump rings.

Pattern Repeat

1. Thread 1 open (orange) jump ring through 2 closed (turquoise) jump rings (**Fig. 4**).

2. Next, thread that open (orange, with the 2 closed jump rings on it) jump ring through the 2 (turquoise)

IMPORTANT

When speed weaving, the orientation of your piece is extremely important. Notice the different weaving paths in **Figs. 5** above and **8**. The path in **Fig. 5** is a very natural movement. If you accidentally flip the piece over so the back side is facing you and you try to weave as in **Fig. 5**, the jump rings will not lie properly. From the back side, you would need to weave following the path in **Fig. 8**, which is awkward. If you use tape to stabilize the start of the weave (which I highly recommend), mark the tape on the front side of the weave with a pen so you can always identify the correct side. In the absence of tape, remember that the front side is the "happy side" (**Figs. 5** and **9**)—the jump rings in the center row look like smiles. When speed weaving E41, always work on the "happy side," not the "sad side" (**Figs. 8** and **10**) (the jump rings in the center row look like frowns).

TIPS

When you pick up the piece to add the next set of jump ring(s), the jump rings in your piece will shift, making it difficult to determine how to proceed. Many of my students find it helpful to use tape (not shown in illustrations) to keep the start of the weave in the proper starting position (**Figs. 2** or **3**), which is very important in speed weaving. To easily identify the front of the weave at all times, mark the tape to indicate the position. You can remove the tape when you've woven enough length so that the weave stabilizes. Tape is especially helpful when weaving with tiny jump rings.

Make sure to reposition the jump rings after each step (to resemble the figures that follow). Repositioning enables you to see better where your next jump ring should be placed and will make any errors immediately apparent.

---

jump rings that are now at the top of your chain, following the path in **Fig. 5**. Then close the open jump ring (**Fig. 6**).

3. Reposition the jump rings so they resemble **Fig. 7**.

Repeat Steps 1 through 3 until you reach your desired length. If you want the end of your strip to have 2 jump rings, simply end on Step 3. If you want the end of your strip to have 1 jump ring, finish by weaving 1 open jump ring through the 2 jump rings that are at the top of your chain.

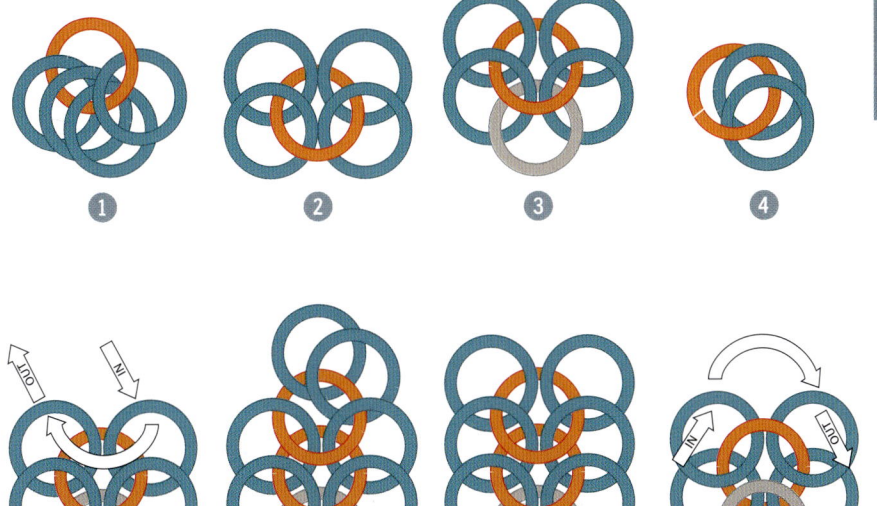

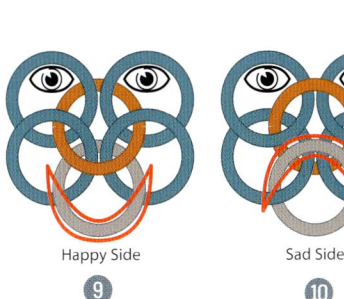

Review Material

Joining European 4-in-1 End to End

Your initial E41 strip should have 1 jump ring at the start and the end. If speed weaving with solid alternate materials (such as rubber O-rings), you must use the alternate joining method that follows.

JOINING

1. Bring both ends of the strip around to meet. BE SURE NOT TO TWIST the piece (**Fig. 1**).

2. Let the first and last (yellow/gray) jump rings at each end overlap, forming an "eye" (**Fig. 2**).

3. Thread 1 open (green) jump ring through the eye of the 2 (yellow/gray) jump rings at the ends of your chain. Make sure to follow the angle of the existing jump rings on the edge of the piece. Close this jump ring (**Fig. 3**).

4. Thread 1 open (purple) jump ring through the eye of the same 2 (yellow/gray) jump rings as in Step 3, except on the opposite edge of the piece. Make sure to follow the angle of the existing jump rings on the edge of the piece. Close this jump ring (**Fig. 4**).

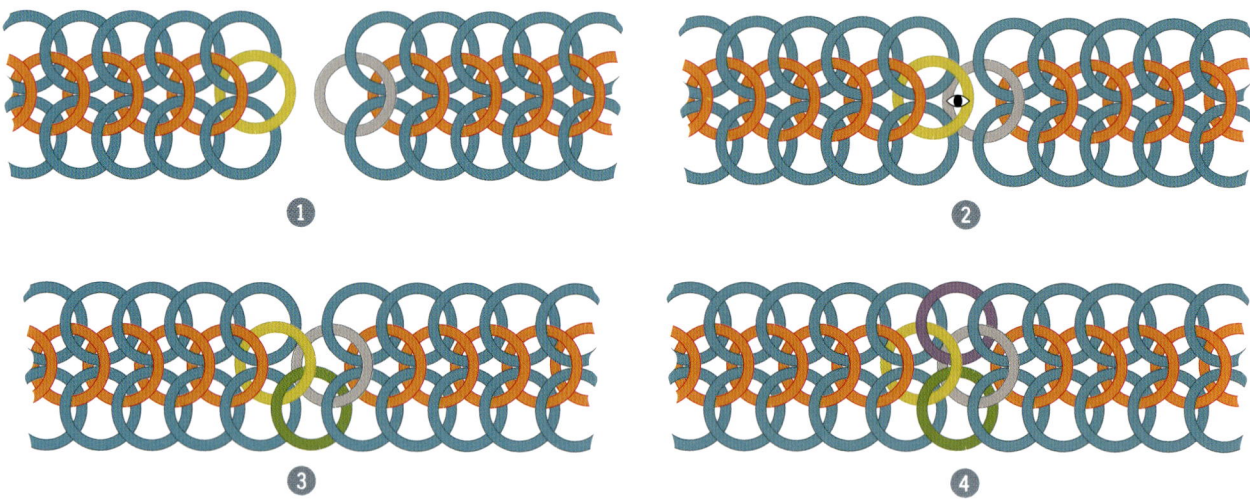

ALTERNATE JOINING METHOD

There are fewer steps involved in this alternate joining method, but it is a bit trickier to perform because the 1 jump ring you are adding has to pass through 4 jump rings, and it's situated in the middle of the weave. In the easier method described previously, you add 2 jump rings, but each only passes through 2 others and they are placed on the edge of the weave, which is easier to access.

1. Bring both ends around to meet (**Fig. 1**). BE SURE NOT TO TWIST the piece.

2. Thread 1 open (gray) jump ring through the 4 (turquoise, numbered) jump rings at the ends of your chain. Make sure to follow the angle of the existing (orange) jump rings in the center row of the piece (arrow in **Fig. 2** shows weaving path). Close this jump ring.

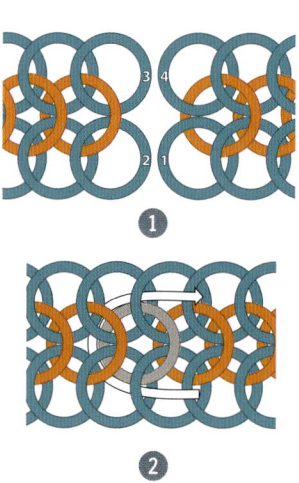

Starting Half Persian

SUPPLIES

- Tuff Brake, about 1½" × 3½" (3.8 × 9 cm) rectangle (or substitute with thin leather or other strong, thin, flexible material)
- 1/16" (2 mm) hole punch

The Half Persian weave is a very difficult weave to begin. Most people use some kind of aid or method, such as a starter patch. I created a tool to help me get the weave started that is very simple to make. I usually use this method with beginning students.

You can weave both Half Persian 3-in-1 and 4-in-1 with this tool. Just use 3 holes for 3-in-1 or all 4 holes for 4-in-1.

To make your own Starter Tool, follow these instructions:

In 3 corners, make 4 holes using the hole punch (**Fig. 1**). The holes spaced the widest are for larger-sized jump rings, the medium-spaced holes are for medium-sized jump rings, and the closely spaced holes are for smaller jump rings (**Fig. 2**).

If you are more advanced, just weave a small patch of European 4-in-1 to start your Half Persian weave (**Figs. 3** and **4**), then remove the extra jump rings from the starter patches (see arrows) when the weave is completed.

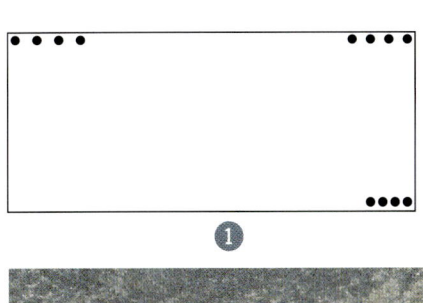

Half Persian 4-in-1

Half Persian 3-in-1

Review Material

USING A PATCH OF EUROPEAN 4-IN-1 FOR CLOSING HALF PERSIAN WEAVES

Closing Half Persian weaves can be very difficult. Using a small patch of E41 can make the closing procedure easier. Here's how it works:

1. To start your Half Persian weave, make a small patch of E41. Use a patch that has 4 jump rings along the edges for HP31 (**Fig. 1**) or a patch that has 5 jump rings along the edges for HP41 (**Fig. 2**). The top edge E41 jump rings are the base row jump rings (see HP Review section, page 26, for HP31 weaving directions. HP41 weaving directions can be found in *Chain Maille Jewelry Workshop*).

2. Use these patches as you would the Starter Tool to begin your Half Persian weaves. For HP31, thread 1 open (red) jump ring through the last 3 (base row) jump rings on the edge of the patch, in pattern, leaving the first (turquoise, base row) jump ring unwoven (**Fig. 3**). For HP41, thread 1 open (red) jump ring into the last 4 (base row) jump rings on the edge of the patch, in pattern, leaving the first (turquoise, base row) jump ring unwoven (**Fig. 4**).

3. Continue weaving your Half Persian chain as described on page 26 for HP31 or on page 107 in *Chain Maille Jewelry Workshop* for HP41, until it reaches the desired length (**Figs. 5** and **6**).

4. Bring both ends of your chain together, being careful not to twist the chain. Instead of picking up a new closed jump ring on the next open jump ring to continue the weave, "pick up" that first unwoven base row (turquoise) jump ring at the beginning of your patch, and thread the open (fuchsia) jump ring as usual (**Fig. 7** for HP31 or **Fig. 10** for HP41).

The chain ends are now connected, but there are gaps in the weave. You need to thread 2 more open (yellow and green) jump rings for HP31 (**Figs. 8** and **9**), or 3 more open (pale blue, orange, and blue) jump rings for HP41 (**Figs. 11–13**), in pattern (pick up the next base row jump ring to the right with a new open jump ring) and weave according to pattern to close the gaps and complete the weaves (**Figs. 14** and **15**). Remove the extra E41 jump rings from the starter patches to finish (see arrows on **Figs. 14** and **15**).

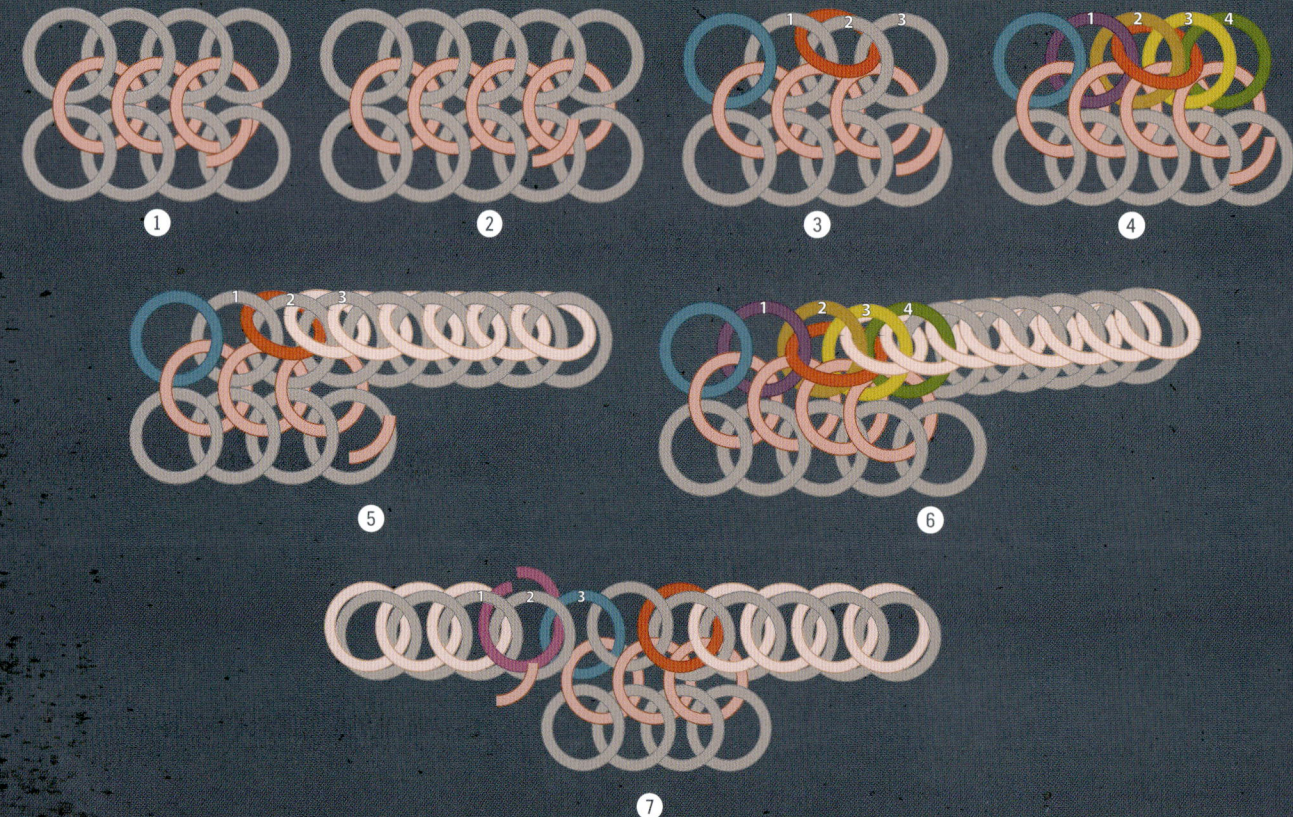

24 ADVANCED CHAIN MAILLE JEWELRY WORKSHOP

Review Material 25

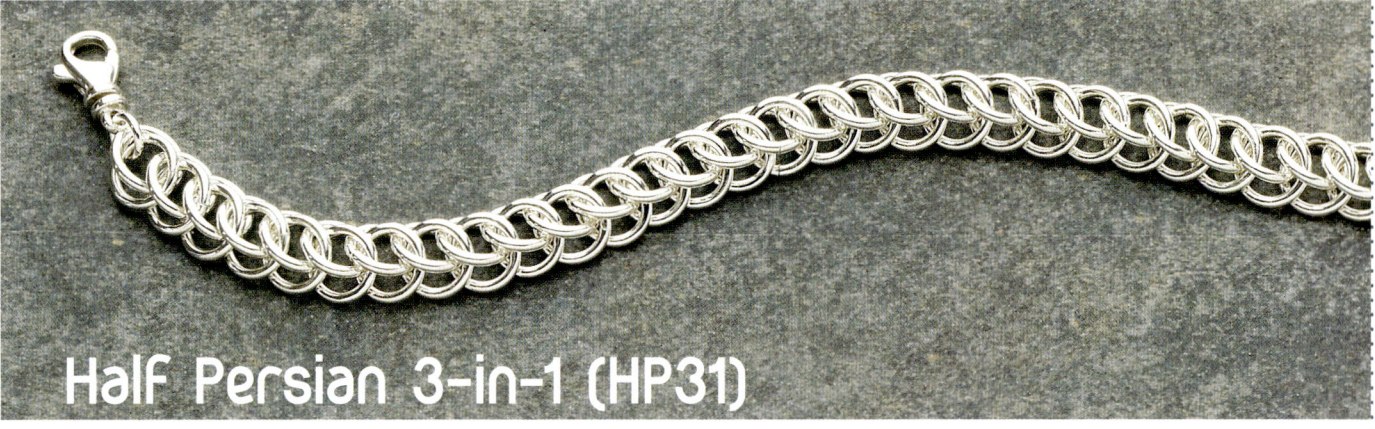

Half Persian 3-in-1 (HP31)

This weave produces a chain with a concave side and a convex side. The concave side provides a channel that makes the weave ideal as a bezel for a stone or other object.

In all figures, linking jump rings will be in color and base row jump rings will be silver.

> **NOTE**
>
> When weaving Half Persian 3-in-1 (HP31), the jump rings have one of two functions. They are either base row jump rings or linking jump rings. The preclosed jump rings make up the base row of the weave. Base row jump rings are passive: you thread into them, but you do not use them to thread into other jump rings. The open jump rings are the linking jump rings. They are the active jump rings. You thread the linking jump rings into the base row jump rings to construct the weave. Linking jump rings are only threaded into base row jump rings, not other linking jump rings. Each linking jump ring will pass through 3 base row jump rings: hence the name Half Persian 3-in-1.

Use the starting method you find most convenient. The figures show the use of the Half Persian Starter Tool to begin the weave.

Prepare Weave Starter and Jump Rings

Once you've decided how to start your weave (Starter Tool, E41 start, starter patch, etc.), prepare the remaining jump rings by opening half of them and closing the other half. The open jump rings are the linking jump rings, and the closed jump rings are the base row jump rings.

Start the Weave

Work from right to left.

1. Following the path in **Fig. 1**, thread 1 open (purple) jump ring through the eye between base row jump rings 3 and 2 by coming up from behind them and then around the eye between base row jump rings 2 and 1. This is the first linking jump ring.

2. Close the open jump ring (**Fig. 2**).

Weave the Pattern

3. Thread 1 open (green) jump ring through 1 closed jump ring (**Fig. 3**).

4. Thread that open (green, with the closed jump ring on it) jump ring through base row jump ring 3 by coming up from behind it and then around the eye between base row jump rings 3 and 2. Close the open jump ring. It should lie in front of the first linking (purple) jump ring. The closed (gray) jump ring just added becomes base row jump ring 4 (**Fig. 4**).

5. Thread 1 open (yellow) jump ring through 1 closed jump ring (**Fig. 5**).

6. Thread that open (yellow, with the closed jump ring on it) jump ring through the rightmost base row jump ring at the end of the chain (the new base row jump ring 4). To do this, come up from behind it and then around the eye between that base row jump ring and the base row jump ring immediately to its left (base row jump ring 3). Close the open jump ring. It should lie in front of the previous linking (green) jump ring. The closed (gray) jump ring just added becomes the next base row jump ring (base row jump ring 5) (**Fig. 6**).

7. Continue to weave in this manner until the chain reaches the desired length.

Finish the Chain

Finishing will differ slightly depending on the starting method chosen.

1. If using the Starter Tool, remove the chain from the tool as follows: One at a time, open each base row jump ring slightly and gently slip it off the tool only, preserving its position in the weave. Close it in place.

2. If using an E41 patch, remove the extra E41 jump rings from the chain.

3. Remove any single jump rings that may exist on either end of your chain (for example, jump rings 1 and 5 in **Fig. 6**), ensuring that your chain begins and ends with 2 jump rings (**Fig. 7**, top view, and **Fig. 8**, front view).

NOTE FOR LEFTIES

The instructions are written for right-handed people (I'm a righty!), so you will work in the opposite direction of the written instructions.

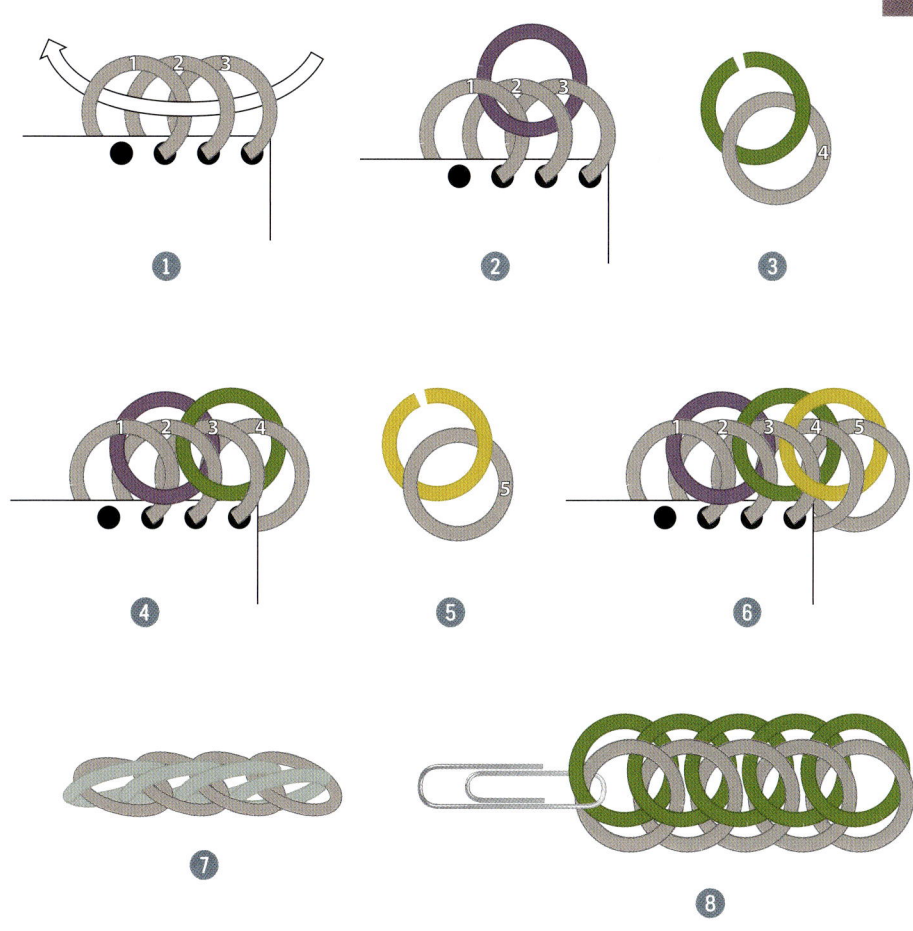

Review Material 27

Weaving Mirror-Image HP31 Chain

1. Use the opposite corner of the tool or orient your E41 starting patch in the opposite direction.

Work from right to left.

2. Follow the path in **Fig. 1** to add the first linking jump ring.

3. When adding additional linking jump rings, you can pick up a closed jump ring either before or after threading the open jump ring.

- If you choose not to pick up a closed jump ring first, thread a linking jump ring through the next base row jump ring to the left from behind and around the eye between that base row jump ring and the base row jump ring immediately to its left. Before closing the linking jump ring, thread a closed jump ring on it. This will be the next base row jump ring. Then, close the open jump ring.

- If you begin by picking up a closed jump ring on your open jump ring first, thread the open jump ring, in pattern, as described previously, and close it. Then position the closed jump ring in line with the other base row jump rings in the weave.

Left handers will perform Steps 1 through 3 working in the opposite direction as shown in **Fig. 2**.

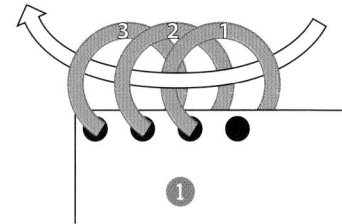

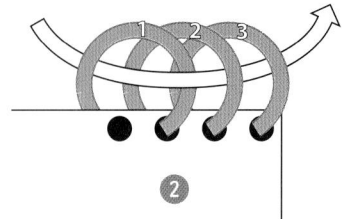

Weaving HP31 Edges

When weaving Half Persian 3-in-1 as an edging, you don't need to be concerned with adding base row jump rings. The base row jump rings *are* the edge jump rings of the piece. You simply thread open jump rings through the jump rings on the edge of the piece, just as you would thread the linking jump rings. Orient your piece properly (see figures that follow). If you are a righty, work from right to left as in **Fig. 1**. If you are a lefty, work from left to right as in **Fig. 2**.

1. Thread 1 open jump ring through the eye between edge jump rings 3 and 2 by coming up from behind them and then around the eye between edge jump rings 2 and 1. This is the first linking jump ring. Close the open jump ring.

2. Thread 1 open jump ring through the eye between edge jump rings 4 and 3 by coming up from behind them and then around the eye between edge jump rings 3 and 2. Close the open jump ring. It should lie in front of the first linking jump ring.

3. Continue in this manner until you've woven through all of the edge jump rings.

If you are weaving a mirror-image edge, follow the directions for HP31 mirror-image weaving, eliminating the addition of base row jump rings. If you are a righty, work from right to left as in **Fig. 3**. If you are a lefty, work from left to right as in **Fig. 4**.

4. Thread 1 open jump ring through edge jump ring 1 by coming up from behind it, then around the eye between edge jump rings 1 and 2 and finally through the eye between edge jump rings 2 and 3. This is the first linking jump ring. Close the open jump ring.

5. Thread 1 open jump ring through edge jump ring 2 by coming up from behind it, then around the eye between edge jump rings 2 and 3 and finally through the eye between edge jump rings 3 and 4. Close the open jump ring. It should lie in front of the first linking jump ring.

6. Continue in this manner until you've woven through all of the edge jump rings.

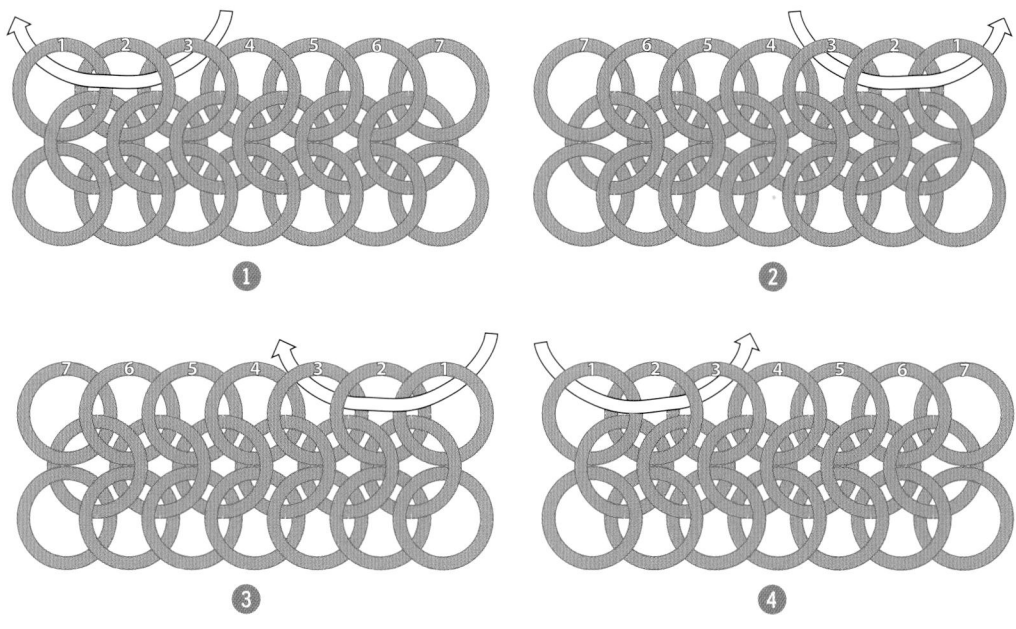

Review Material

Chain Maille Math

Wire Scale Comparison Chart

AWG Gauge	Diameter*	SWG Gauge	Diameter*
12g	2.05 mm	12g	2.64 mm
14g	1.63 mm	14g	2.03 mm
16g	1.29 mm	16g	1.63 mm
18g	1.02 mm	18g	1.22 mm
20g	0.81 mm	20g	0.91 mm
22g	0.64 mm	22g	0.71 mm

*Diameters are rounded

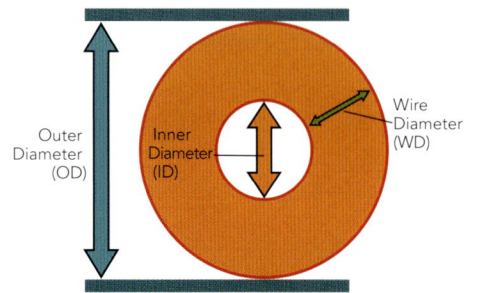

INNER DIAMETER (ID) AND OUTER DIAMETER (OD)

Some vendors use the outer diameter measurement of a jump ring to describe its size. To determine the inner diameter of a jump ring when you only know the wire gauge and outer diameter, perform the following calculation:

Inner Diameter (ID) =
Outer Diameter (OD) −
(2 × Wire Diameter (WD))

I recommend that you do not purchase jump rings from vendors who sell based on an OD measurement because when you do the math to determine the ID based on the OD, you'll get a strange fractional result. You are then forced to round the measurement and lose precision.

Vendors that specialize in chain maille supplies usually identify jump rings based on inner diameter (which represents the size of the mandrel used to make the wire coil).

If, for some reason, you do need to determine the outer diameter of your jump rings, use the following formula:

Outer Diameter (OD) =
Inner Diameter (ID) +
(2 × Wire Diameter (WD))

ASPECT RATIO (AR)

Aspect ratio is not a measurement. It is the ratio of the relationship between the thickness of the wire and the inner diameter of a jump ring, represented numerically. You can use the following aspect ratio formula to help you determine the jump ring size you need for almost any chain maille weave:

$$\text{Aspect Ratio (AR)} = \frac{\text{Inner Diameter (ID)}}{\text{Wire Diameter (WD)}}$$

Suppose you want to make an Interwoven 41 chain using 20g (AWG) jump rings. Here's how to do the math:

First, determine the aspect ratio for the Interwoven 41 weave by inserting the information you already know from the Interwoven 41 Jump Ring Sizing Chart (page 82) and the Wire Scale Comparison Chart (left) into the aspect ratio formula. We'll base our calculations on the sterling silver jump ring sizes, as the inner diameter measurements are shown in millimeters, which are compatible with the wire diameter measurements in the Wire Scale Comparison Chart (no imperial to metric conversions required):

$$AR\ (16g) = \frac{5.5\ mm}{1.29\ mm} = 4.3\ mm$$

- OR -

$$AR\ (18g) = \frac{4.5\ mm}{1.02\ mm} = 4.4\ mm$$

AR for Interwoven 41 = 4.3–4.4 mm

Now, you can use the calculation AR × WD = ID to determine the inner diameter size you will need to purchase to make the weave using 20g (AWG) jump rings:

AR (of Interwoven 41 Weave) ×
WD (of 20g AWG jump rings) =
ID (of 20g AWG jump rings)

AR (4.3–4.4 mm) × WD (0.81 mm) =
ID (3.48–3.56 mm)

The appropriate inner diameter for 20g (AWG) jump rings is in the 3.48 mm to 3.56 mm range. Therefore, I would select 20g, 3.5 mm ID jump rings.

Because AR is just a ratio, not a measurement, you can mix gauge scales. Let's say that you want to determine the size of jump rings you would need to make an Interwoven 41 chain using 20g (SWG) jump rings instead. The first

30 ADVANCED CHAIN MAILLE JEWELRY WORKSHOP

calculation to determine the aspect ratio remains exactly the same (figure the AR using what you know, the AWG silver sizes), so you will get the same result (AR of 4.3–4.4 mm). The difference is in the second calculation. You would insert the 20g SWG measurement (0.91 mm) in the WD portion of the calculation.

$$AR\ (4.3–4.4\ mm) \times WD\ (0.91\ mm) = ID\ (3.91–4.0\ mm)$$

The appropriate inner diameter for 20g (SWG) jump rings is between 3.91 mm and 4.0 mm. Therefore, I would select 20g (SWG), 4.0 mm ID jump rings.

Bear in mind that the calculations in the formulas provide guidelines only. Mathematical computations do not consider size variations in jump rings from different manufacturers (see Actual AR vs "Common" AR in the text that follows).

Also note that the AR calculation is not quite sufficient to determine jump ring sizes for weaves that incorporate jump rings of more than one size. The AR formula represents the relationship between the thickness of the wire and the inner diameter of a particular jump ring. It does not take into account the relationship between jump rings of various sizes that are contained in a single weave. You'll need to experiment to arrive at the right combination. In addition, the AR calculation is well suited to round wire. Wires of other shapes (half-round, square, twisted, etc.) complicate the issue.

USING THE ASPECT RATIO CHARTS

In the back of this book, you'll find charts for common gauges that include outer and inner diameters and aspect ratios. Use these Aspect Ratio Charts to determine alternate sizes needed for converting weaves to jump rings of different gauges—no math necessary!

We'll follow the same example as previously, converting an Interwoven 41 Weave to 20g (AWG) jump rings.

First, consult the Interwoven 41 Jump Ring Sizing Chart to determine the recommended inner diameter for this weave: a 16g (AWG) jump ring should have an inner diameter of 5.5 mm and an 18g (AWG) jump ring should have an inner diameter of 4.5 mm. Next, turn to the Aspect Ratio Charts (AWG) to find the aspect ratio for these jump rings. You'll see that the aspect ratio is 4.3 to 4.4 mm. Then, refer to the 20g Aspect Ratio Chart (AWG) to find the rounded aspect ratio within the 4.3 mm to 4.4 mm range—in this case, a 3.5 mm inner diameter jump ring has a 4.3 mm aspect ratio.

Again, because AR is a ratio, not a measurement, you can convert to a different gauge scale without having to do any additional conversion calculations. Let's determine what size of jump rings you would need to make an Interwoven 41 chain using 20g (SWG) jump rings instead. You would begin with what you know (AWG—16g, 5.5 mm ID and 18g, 4.5 mm ID). Look those up in the 16g and 18g AWG charts in the back of the book to find the ARs (4.3–4.4 mm) as previously. Now, turn to the 20g SWG chart at the back of the book and look down the AR column to find the rounded AR in the 4.3–4.4 mm range. In this case, a 4.0 mm inner diameter jump ring has a 4.4 mm aspect ratio.

ACTUAL AR VS "COMMON" AR

There are two methods to determine aspect ratio:

The first, called "actual" (or measured) AR, is based on measuring your jump rings with digital calipers to determine the true inner diameter and wire diameter measurements, then calculating your AR based on these measurements. *This is the most accurate way to determine AR.*

The second, I refer to as "common" AR. I call it common AR because it is based not on actual measurements but on standard sizes (mandrel size and standard wire diameter) commonly used to describe the size of a jump ring. It is alternatively referred to as "mandrel" AR, but I prefer to use the term "common" AR because the term "mandrel" addresses only half of the equation. Use this method when you do not have the actual jump rings available to measure. You base your calculation on mandrel size and the standard wire diameter measurement. This method does not consider slight differences that can occur in the manufacturing of wire, the springback* factor, or other variables involved in making jump rings. *This method is less exact.* The charts in the back of the book represent common AR.

After coiling wire around a mandrel, the wire "exhales" or "relaxes" when released. This action is referred to as "springback." Therefore, the actual inner diameter of the resulting jump rings will be slightly larger than the mandrel size. The type and temper of the metal used affect the amount of springback in the wire. Different metals produce differently sized jump rings.

PERSIAN WEAVES

The Persian weave family is one of my favorites. These intermediate/advanced-level weaves consist of intricate linkage patterns constructed with complex combinations of through-the-eye (TE) and around-the-eye (AE) connections. The weaves create beautiful chains that can be either tight and uniform in pattern and flat in profile or loopy and airy with elliptical profiles. I feel that these patterns are especially well suited to collars (my favorite necklace style) and cuffs (my favorite bracelet style).

I use tape as a starting aid when weaving these complex chains because it helps stabilize the first few jump rings of the weave, making the start easier. These weaves tend to twist slightly as you weave. To ensure that I can always identify the front side and the beginning end of the weave, I mark the front side of the tape with a pen. As each row of jump rings is added, the rows are positioned in alternating directions (forward or backward), creating a crosshatched pattern along the edge of the weave. An example of that crosshatched pattern is shown in the enlarged detail of the Great Southern Gathering (GSG) weave as shown on the top of the following page.

Great Southern Gathering (GSG) Weave

Jump Ring Chart

METAL	16 GAUGE ID	RPI	AR	18 GAUGE ID	RPI	AR
Sterling Silver (AWG)	6.0 mm	20	4.7	4.75 mm	24	4.6
Bright Aluminum (SWG)						
The Ring Lord	9/32"	16	4.7	7/32"	20	4.7
C&T Designs	9/32"	16	4.61	7/32"	24	4.65
Metal Designz	9/32"	18	4.5	7/32"	24	5.1

The GSG weave is essentially 2 rows of Half Persian 3-in-1 Sheet 6 woven on the bias. The GSG weave was named by Gary Dunham (aka Buddha) for the event where the weave made its debut. The event was the Great Southern Gathering of Chainmaillers in Dallas, Texas, hosted by Greg Grindstaff (aka Questor) in 2003. The weave produces a flat and somewhat tight chain that offers tons of design possibilities. This weaving method forms a thin, parallelogram-shaped piece (ends of the chain slant slightly like this / / or \ \).

Prepare Jump Rings
Close 2 jump rings and open the rest.

Start the Weave
1. Begin with 2 closed jump rings, overlapping them, left over right, so they form an eye (**Fig. 1**).

2. Secure the 2 jump rings with tape and mark the front with a pen (**Fig. 2**, first row of jump rings).

Weave the Pattern
Add 2 jump rings:

TIP
To create a mirror-image GSG chain, reverse the positioning of the first 2 overlapping jump rings contained in the tape (right over left), then position each jump ring that goes through the eye to the right instead of the left. The mirror-image weave differs in the direction of the grain and the slant of the ends. Combining original weaving and mirror-image weaving in the same piece can produce various shaping effects (see Lightning Bolt Earrings, page 37).

ADVANCED CHAIN MAILLE JEWELRY WORKSHOP

3. Thread 1 open (orange) jump ring through the eye formed by the 2 closed jump rings secured in the tape and then close it (**Fig. 3**).

4. Lay the (orange) jump ring just added to the left (**Fig. 4**).

5. Thread another open (fuchsia) jump ring around the eye formed by the 2 jump rings secured in the tape and then close it. It should sit above the (orange) jump ring just added (**Fig. 5**, second row of jump rings added).

6. Position the 2 (orange/fuchsia) jump rings just added as follows: Place your index finger on the back side of the weave under the 2 (orange/fuchsia) jump rings just added. Now, push them up and forward from the back of the weave* (**Fig. 6**).

Add the next 2 jump rings:

7. Thread 1 open (turquoise) jump ring through the eye formed by the 2 (orange/fuchsia) jump rings just added and then close it (**Fig. 7**).

QUICK FIX

If you start a piece but realize that you're weaving in the wrong orientation (this frequently happens to me when making the second earring), flip the piece over to its back side, ensuring that the tape (first row) is still on the bottom (south end) and remove the first row of jump rings along with the tape. Now the piece is in mirror-image orientation, and you can continue weaving at the finishing (north) end until you reach the desired length.

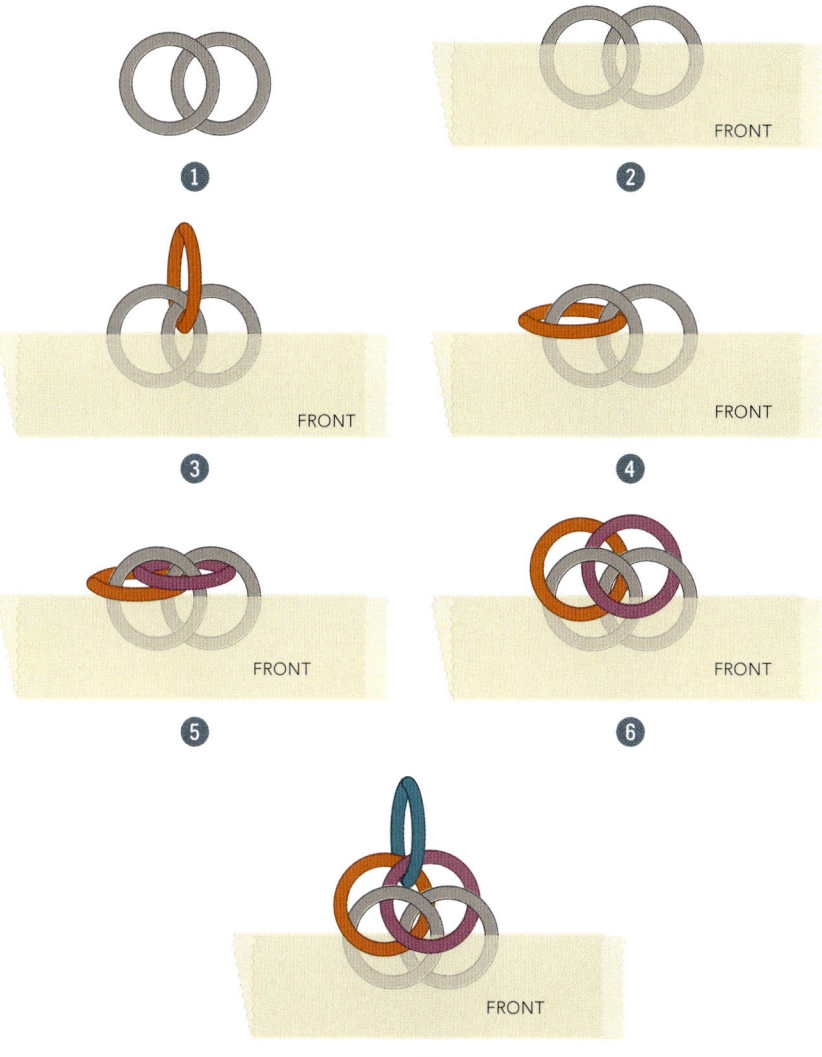

Persian Weaves 35

8. Lay the (turquoise) jump ring just added to the left (**Fig. 8**).

9. Thread another open (green) jump ring around the eye formed by the same 2 (orange/fuchsia) jump rings and then close it. It should sit above the (turquoise) jump ring just added (**Fig. 9**, third row of jump rings added).

10. Position the 2 (turquoise/green) jump rings just added as follows: Place your thumb on the front side of the weave under the 2 (turquoise/green) jump rings just added. Now push them up and back from the front of the weave* (**Fig. 10**).

*Alternating the positioning of each row of jump rings added by pushing one pair up and forward from the back and the next up and back from the front creates the crosshatch pattern on the edge of the weave as shown in the chapter's introduction. It is important to perform these positioning steps when beginning the weave. As the weave becomes longer and more stable, the jump rings will naturally begin to fall into the correct position.

Add the next 2 jump rings:

11. Thread 1 open jump ring through the eye formed by the 2 (turquoise/green) jump rings just added and then close it.

12. Lay the jump ring just added to the left.

13. Thread another open jump ring around the eye formed by the same 2 (turquoise/green) jump rings and then close it. It should sit above the jump ring just added (fourth row of jump rings added).

14. Position the 2 jump rings just added by pushing them up and forward from behind the weave.

Continue working in this manner, positioning each pair added in the opposite direction from the last pair added, until your piece is the desired length.

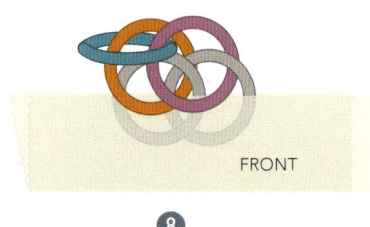

FRONT

8

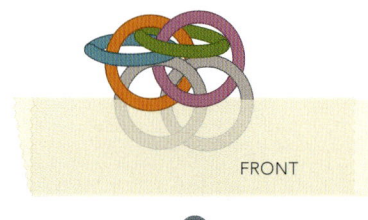

FRONT

9

FRONT

10

36 ADVANCED CHAIN MAILLE JEWELRY WORKSHOP

LIGHTNING BOLT EARRINGS

Take advantage of mirror-image weaving to create a pair of sterling silver lightning bolt–shaped earrings.

1. Beginning Section: Weave GSG with 24 jump rings. (Refer to the previous GSG weave instructions, weaving until the piece consists of 24 jump rings.)

note: *The last 2 jump rings added should be layered in the opposite direction from the first 2 jump rings in the tape (right over left).*

2. Center Section: Now weave GSG with 16 jump rings in mirror-image direction (first jump ring is threaded through the eye of the last 2 jump rings and positioned to the right).

note: *The last 2 jump rings added should be layered in the original direction (left over right).*

3. End Section: Weave GSG with 20 more jump rings in the original direction (first jump ring is threaded through the eye of the last 2 jump rings and positioned to the left).

4. Attach an ear wire to the jump ring at the end of the earring using 2 jump rings.

5. Repeat for second earring, this time beginning and ending with mirror-image weaving and original direction weaving in the center section.

SUPPLIES
- 124 sterling silver jump rings, 22g (AWG), 2.75 mm ID
- 1 pair sterling silver ear wires

GSG Sheet Weave

Jump Ring Chart

	16 GAUGE			18 GAUGE		
METAL	ID	RPI	AR	ID	RPI	AR
Sterling Silver (AWG)	6.5 mm	30	5.0	5.25 mm	30	5.1
Bright Aluminum (SWG)						
The Ring Lord	5/16"	27	5.2	1/4"	30	5.5
C&T Designs	5/16"	27	5.10	1/4"	33	5.29
Metal Designz	5/16"	24	5.4	15/64"	30	4.88

note: *Recommended jump ring sizes/counts for GSG Sheet weave listed in chart is based on a piece that is 3 jump rings wide.*

You can widen GSG into a sheet (technically this is Half Persian 3-in-1 Sheet 6, but I like to refer to this vertical method of construction as GSG Sheet). Simply increase the number of closed jump rings you tape together at the beginning of the weave. In the example that follows, I will show how to weave a sheet that is 3 jump rings wide. When widening to more than 3 jump rings wide, the weave begins to tighten vertically. Top-to-bottom movement becomes restricted, while horizontal side-to-side movement remains fairly flexible. To produce a wider vertical weave that is flexible, you will need to experiment. Try a larger aspect ratio to create the flexibility required for your particular project.

The traditional (horizontal) method to produce Half Persian 3-in-1 Sheet 6 (page 40) begins with a length of Half Persian 3-in-1 chain. This method produces a weave that is flexible along the horizontal length of the piece. It also has nice edge movement, which is great for collars.

These weaving methods form parallelogram-shaped pieces (ends of the chain slant slightly like this // or \\).

Prepare Jump Rings

Close 3 jump rings and open the rest.

Start the Weave

1. Begin with 3 closed jump rings and overlap them, left over right (**Fig. 1**).

2. Secure the 3 jump rings with tape and mark the front with a pen (**Fig. 2**, first row of jump rings).

Weave the Pattern

Add 3 jump rings:

3. Thread 1 open (orange) jump ring through the eye formed by jump rings 1 and 2. Close the open jump ring and lay it to the left (**Fig. 3**).

38 ADVANCED CHAIN MAILLE JEWELRY WORKSHOP

4. Thread another open (gold) jump ring through the eye formed by jump rings 2 and 3 and around the eye formed by jump rings 1 and 2 and then close it. It should sit above the (orange) jump ring just added (**Fig. 4**).

5. Thread a third open (yellow) jump ring around the eye formed by jump rings 2 and 3 and close it. It should sit above the (gold) jump ring just added (**Fig. 5**, second row of jump rings added).

6. Position the 3 (orange/gold/yellow) jump rings just added as follows: Place your index finger on the back side of the weave under the 3 (orange/gold/yellow) jump rings just added. Now, push them up and forward from the back of the weave* (**Fig. 6**).

Add 3 jump rings:

7. Thread 1 open (green) jump ring through the eye formed by (orange/gold) jump rings 1 and 2. Close the open jump ring and lay it to the left (**Fig. 7**).

8. Thread another open (turquoise) jump ring through the eye formed by (gold/yellow) jump rings 2 and 3 and around the eye formed by (orange/gold) jump rings 1 and 2 and then close it. It should sit above the (green) jump ring just added (**Fig. 8**).

9. Thread a third open (fuchsia) jump ring around the eye formed by (gold/yellow) jump rings 2 and 3 and then close it. It should sit above the (turquoise) jump ring just added (**Fig. 9**, third row of jump rings added).

10. Position the 3 (green/turquoise/fuchsia) jump rings just added as follows: Place your thumb on the front side of the weave under the 3 (green/turquoise/fuchsia) jump rings just added. Now, push them up and back from the front of the weave* (**Fig. 10**).

Alternating the positioning of each row of jump rings added by pushing one set of 3 up and forward from the back and the next set up and back from the front creates the crosshatch pattern on the edge of the weave as shown in the chapter's introduction.

TIP

To create a mirror-image GSG Sheet, start the weave by reversing the position of the first 3 overlapping jump rings contained in the tape (right over left). Next, the reference numbers on the 3 jump rings at the top of the weave must be reversed (leftmost jump ring is #3 and rightmost jump ring is #1). When weaving the jump rings that go through the eye only (first jump ring of each set of 3), position them in the opposite direction (to the right). The mirror-image weave differs in the direction of the grain and the slant of the ends. Combining original weaving and mirror-image weaving in the same piece can produce different shaping effects (see Two-Tone GSG Sheet Necklace project on page 56).

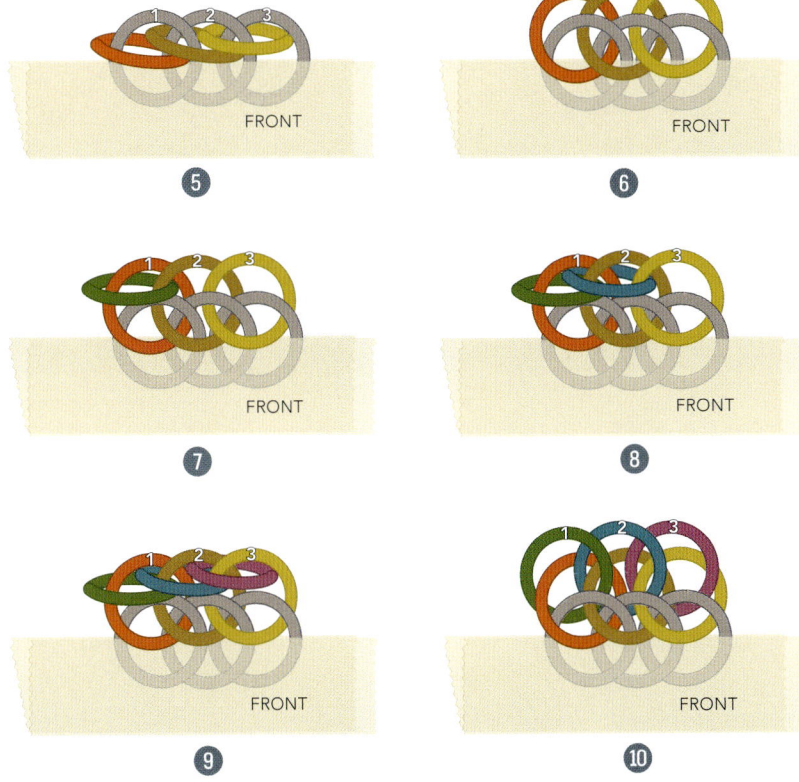

Persian Weaves **39**

It is important to perform these positioning steps when beginning the weave. As the weave becomes longer and more stable, the jump rings will naturally begin to fall into the correct position.

Add 3 jump rings:

11. Weave 1 open jump ring through the eye formed by jump rings 1 and 2. Close the open jump ring and lay it to the left.

12. Thread another open jump ring through the eye formed by jump rings 2 and 3 and around the eye formed by jump rings 1 and 2 and then close it. It should sit above the jump ring just added.

13. Thread a third open jump ring around the eye formed by jump rings 2 and 3 and then close it. It should sit above the jump ring just added (fourth row of jump rings added).

14. Position the 3 jump rings just added by pushing them up and forward from behind the weave.

Continue working in this manner, positioning each set of 3 jump rings added in the opposite direction from the last set added, until your piece reaches the desired length.

QUICK FIX

If you start a piece and realize that you're weaving in the wrong orientation (this frequently happens to me when making the second earring), flip the piece over to its back side, ensuring that the tape (first row) is still on the bottom (south end) and remove the first row of jump rings along with the tape. Now the piece is in mirror-image orientation and you can continue weaving at the finishing (north) end until you reach the desired length.

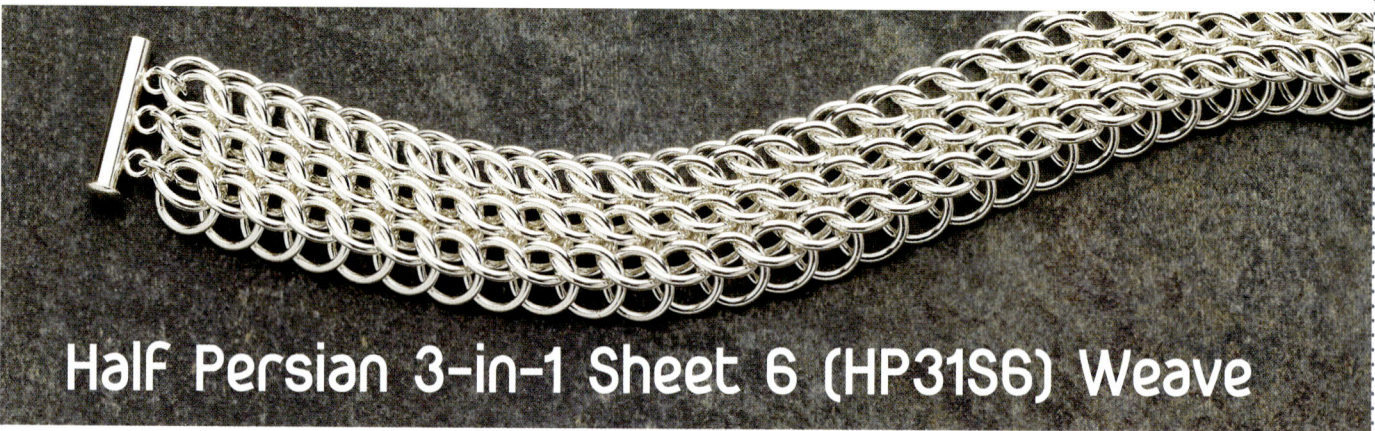

Half Persian 3-in-1 Sheet 6 (HP31S6) Weave

Jump Ring Chart

METAL	16 GAUGE ID	RPI	AR	18 GAUGE ID	RPI	AR
Sterling Silver (AWG)	6.5 mm	28	5.0	5.25 mm	36	5.1
Bright Aluminum (SWG)						
The Ring Lord	5/16"	24	5.2	1/4"	30	5.5
C&T Designs	5/16"	24	5.10	1/4"	30	5.29
Metal Designz	5/16"	24	5.4	15/64"	30	4.88

note: *Recommended jump ring sizes/counts for Half Persian 3-in-1 Sheet 6 weave listed in chart are based on a sheet that is 3 pattern repeats (original HP31 chain, plus 4 passes across).*

The name Half Persian 3-in-1 Sheet 6 (HP31S6) signifies that this is a sheet weave, based on the Half Persian 3-in-1 weave, where each jump ring in the weave (not including the jump rings along the edges) has 6 other jump rings passing through it. In my book *Chain Maille Jewelry Workshop*, an easier Half Persian Sheet version was presented (Half Persian 3-in-1 Sheet 5). That weave is less dense, as each jump ring in the weave (not including the jump rings along the edges) has only 5 other jump rings passing through it. It also tends to curl under at the transitions between each pattern repeat. HP31S6 is more closely packed and stays flat.

Weave a Length of Half Persian 3-in-1

1. Weave your HP31 base piece (see instructions in Review Material, page 26) a little bit longer than you think you need. As you weave into it to make HP31S6, it will reduce by about 5 percent of its original length. You'll need to experiment to arrive at the appropriate length.

2. Mark the starting end of the HP31 chain with a paper clip. Orange jump rings are linking jump rings, silver are base row jump rings (**Fig. 1**).

Prepare Jump Rings

Open remaining jump rings.

Weave the Pattern

Work in the back row of linking (orange) jump rings on the HP31 chain, weaving from left to right.

Add a row of jump rings along the horizontal length of the piece:

3. Thread 1 open (green) jump ring through the eye formed by linking jump rings 1 and 2. Close the open jump ring and lay it to the left (**Fig. 2**).

4. Thread another open (dark green) jump ring through the eye formed by linking jump rings 2 and 3 and around the eye formed by linking jump rings 1 and 2 and then close it. It should sit above the (green) jump ring just added (**Fig. 3**).

5. Thread another open (dark green) jump ring through the eye formed by linking jump rings 3 and 4 and around the eye formed by linking jump rings 2 and 3 and then close it. It should sit above the (green) jump ring just added (**Fig. 4**).

Continue along the horizontal length of the piece until you reach the last 2 linking jump rings (**Fig. 5**).

6. To end the row, thread 1 open (dark green) jump ring around the eye formed by the last 2 linking jump rings and then close it. It should sit above the last jump ring added (**Fig. 6**).

TIP

To create a mirror-image Half Persian 3-in-1 Sheet 6, start the weave by making a mirror-image length of Half Persian 3-in-1 chain (see Review Material, page 28). To weave, reverse the reference numbers on the figures (#1 will be the rightmost jump ring) and weave from right to left. The first jump ring placed (in the eye formed by jump rings 1 and 2) should be positioned in the opposite direction (to the right). Additional jump rings woven down the length will follow this orientation. The mirror-image weave differs in the direction of the grain and the slant of the ends.

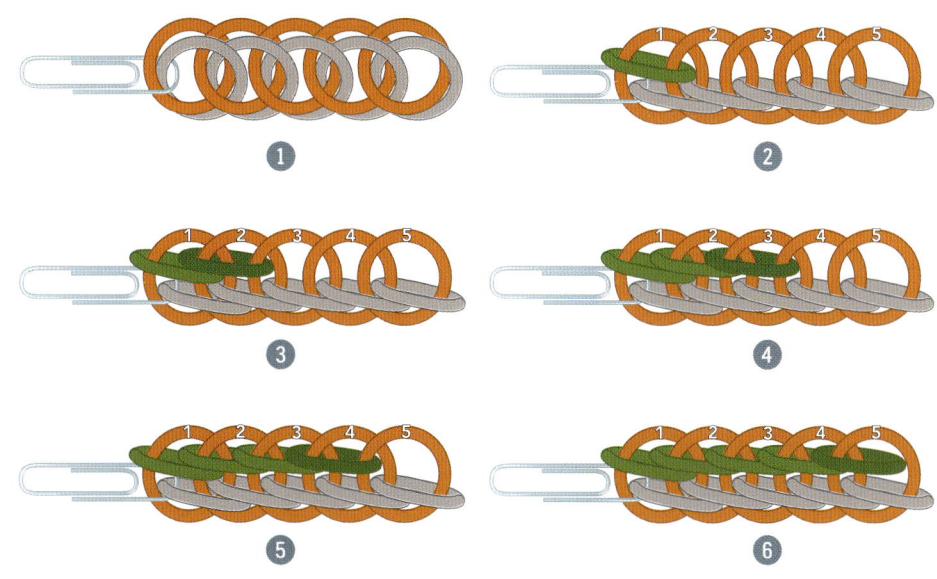

Persian Weaves

7. Position the row of (green) jump rings just added by pushing them up and back from the front of the weave (**Fig. 7**).

Add a row of jump rings along the horizontal length of the piece. Work in the last horizontal row of (green) jump rings added, weaving from left to right.

8. Thread 1 open (yellow) jump ring through the eye formed by jump rings 1 and 2. Close the open jump ring and lay it to the left (**Fig. 8**).

9. Thread another open (gold) jump ring through the eye formed by jump rings 2 and 3 and around the eye formed by jump rings 1 and 2 and then close it. It should sit above the (yellow) jump ring just added (**Fig. 9**).

10. Thread another open (gold) jump ring through the eye formed by jump rings 3 and 4 and around the eye formed by jump rings 2 and 3 and then close it. It should sit above the (yellow) jump ring just added (**Fig. 10**).

Continue along the horizontal length of the piece until you reach the last pair of jump rings along the top edge of the piece (**Fig. 11**).

11. To end the row, thread 1 open (gold) jump ring around the eye formed by the last 2 jump rings in the row and then close it. It should sit above the (yellow) jump ring just added (**Fig. 12**).

12. Position the row of (yellow) jump rings just added by pushing them up and forward from behind the weave (**Fig. 13**).

Working in the last horizontal row of jump rings added, repeat Steps 3–12 until your piece reaches the desired width.

QUICK FIX

If you're working on a piece and realize that you've woven in the wrong orientation, flip the piece over to its back side, ensuring that the first row (silver base row jump rings from the starting HP31 chain) is on the bottom (south) edge, and remove the first row of jump rings along the length of the piece. Now the piece is in mirror-image orientation, and you can continue weaving at the finishing (north) edge until you reach the desired width.

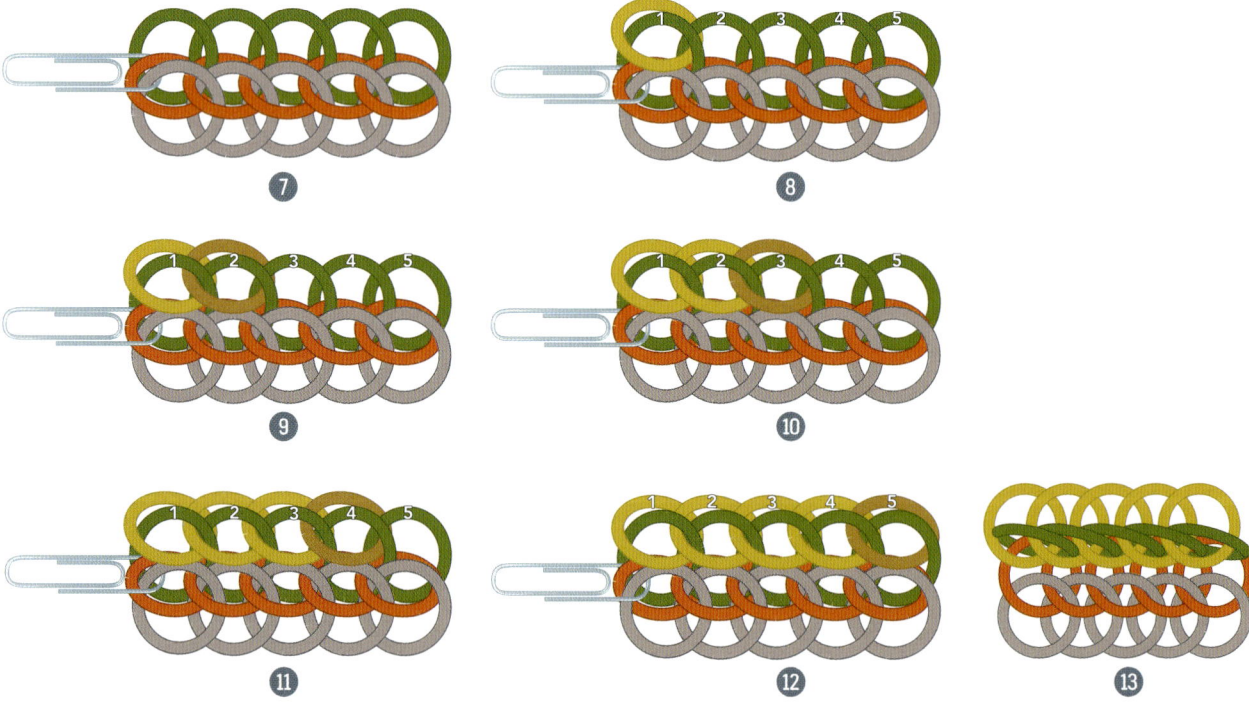

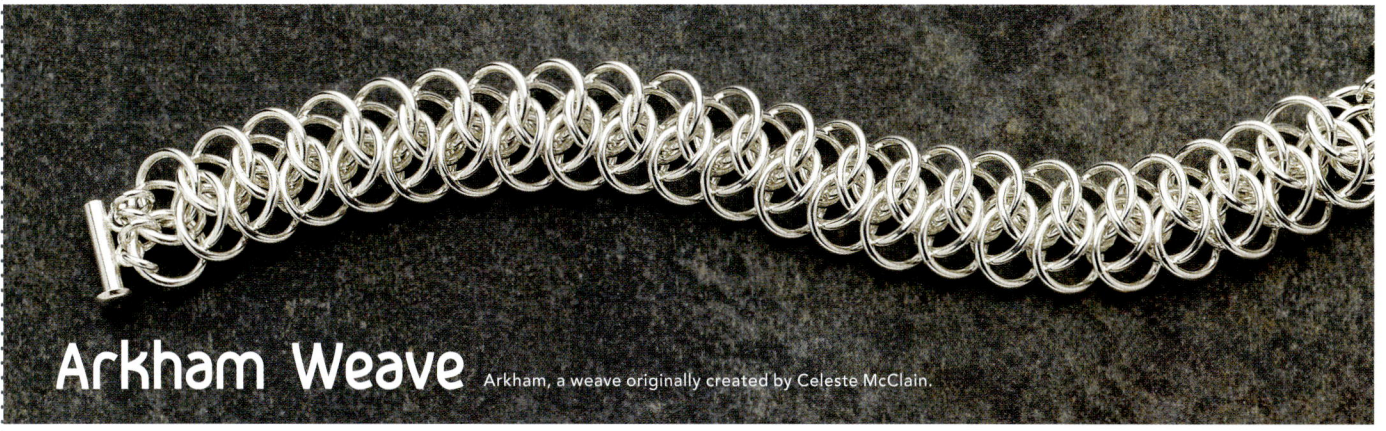

Arkham Weave
Arkham, a weave originally created by Celeste McClain.

Jump Ring Chart

	16 GAUGE			18 GAUGE		
METAL	ID	RPI	AR	ID	RPI	AR
Sterling Silver (AWG)	7.0 mm	16	5.4	5.5 mm	20	5.4
Bright Aluminum (SWG)						
The Ring Lord	3/8"	12	6.3	1/4"	18	5.5
C&T Designs	11/32"	16	5.6	17/64"	20	5.63
Metal Designz	11/32"	16	5.9	1/4"	20	5.7

The Arkham weave is very similar to the GSG weave. The difference occurs when weaving the jump rings that go through the eye. For GSG, each jump ring that goes through the eye lies in the same direction. For Arkham, each jump ring that goes through the eye alternates positions, first lying to one side, then lying to the other. This difference gives Arkham a look that is more open and airy than that of GSG. This weave looks wonderful in 18g and curves beautifully, perfect for necklaces.

Prepare Jump Rings
Close 2 jump rings and open the rest.

Start the Weave
1. Begin with 2 closed jump rings and overlap them, left over right until they form an eye (**Fig. 1**).

2. Secure the 2 jump rings with tape and mark the front with a pen (**Fig. 2**, first row of jump rings).

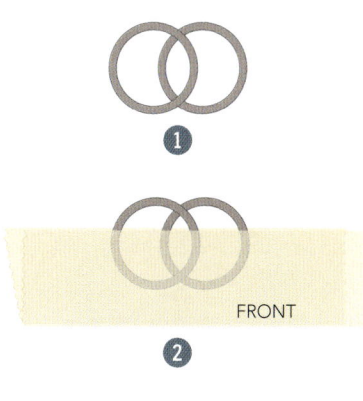

TIP
To create a mirror-image Arkham chain, start the weave by reversing the position of the first 2 overlapping jump rings contained in the tape (right over left). Then, when weaving the jump rings that go through the eye, position them in the opposite direction (lay the first jump ring that goes through the eye to the left, the second to the right, the third to the left, and so on). The mirror-image weave differs in the direction of the grain. The difference is very subtle.

Persian Weaves

Weave the Pattern

Add 2 jump rings:

3. Thread 1 open (yellow) jump ring through the eye formed by the 2 jump rings secured in the tape. Close the open jump ring and lay it to the right (**Fig. 3**).

4. Thread another open (orange) jump ring around the eye formed by the 2 jump rings secured in the tape and then close it. It should sit above the (yellow) jump ring just added (**Fig. 4**, second row of jump rings added).

5. Position the 2 (yellow/orange) jump rings just added as follows: Place your index finger on the back side of the weave under the 2 (yellow/orange) jump rings just added. Now push them up and forward from the back of the weave* (**Fig. 5**).

Add the next 2 jump rings:

6. Thread 1 open (gold) jump ring through the eye formed by the last 2 (yellow/orange) jump rings added. Close the open jump ring and lay it to the left (**Fig. 6**).

7. Thread another open jump ring (turquoise) around the eye formed by the last 2 (yellow/orange) jump rings added and then close it. It should sit above the (gold) jump ring just added (**Fig. 7**, third row of jump rings added).

8. Position the 2 (gold/turquoise) jump rings just added as follows: Place your thumb on the front side of the weave under the 2 (gold/turquoise) jump rings just added. Now push them up and back from the front of the weave* (**Fig. 8**).

Alternating the positioning of each row of jump rings added by pushing one pair up and forward from the back and the next up and back from the front creates the crosshatch pattern on the edge of the weave as shown in the chapter's introduction. It is important to perform these positioning steps when beginning the weave. As the weave becomes longer and more stable, the jump rings will naturally begin to fall into the correct position.

Add the next 2 jump rings:

9. Thread 1 open (green) jump ring through the eye formed by the last 2 (gold/turquoise) jump rings added. Close the open jump ring and lay it to the right (**Fig. 9**).

10. Thread another open (fuchsia) jump ring around the eye formed by the last 2 (gold/turquoise) jump rings added and then close it. It should sit above the (green) jump ring just added (**Fig. 10**, fourth row of jump rings added).

11. Position the 2 (green/fuchsia) jump rings just added by pushing them up and forward from behind the weave (**Fig. 11**).

Repeat Steps 6–11 until your piece reaches the desired length.

44 ADVANCED CHAIN MAILLE JEWELRY WORKSHOP

Arkham Sheet

You can expand the Arkham weave into a sheet. You can make it wider by increasing the number of closed jump rings you tape together at the start. The length grows vertically. In Method 1, I will show how to weave a sheet that is 3 jump rings wide. When expanding to a width of more than 3 jump rings, the weave begins to tighten vertically. Top-to-bottom movement becomes restricted, while horizontal side-to-side movement remains fairly flexible. To produce a wider vertical weave that is flexible, try using a larger aspect ratio.

You'll also notice that Arkham Sheet, constructed vertically, tends to twist. The jump ring sizes I recommend for vertical construction achieve a nice balance between the tightness of the weave and the amount of twist for a piece that is 3 jump rings wide. Feel free to experiment to achieve the balance that you find most pleasing and appropriate for your project.

If you want to make a very wide Arkham Sheet, it will be difficult to begin the weave by taping jump rings together. An option is to use a length of Half Persian 3-in-1 chain (page 26) to begin Arkham Sheet as in Method 2. The length grows horizontally and the weave doesn't twist. This method produces a piece that is flexible along its horizontal length. One edge will flex more than the other. The linkage pattern reminds me of rows of knitted stitches. The weave's horizontal orientation is great for collars.

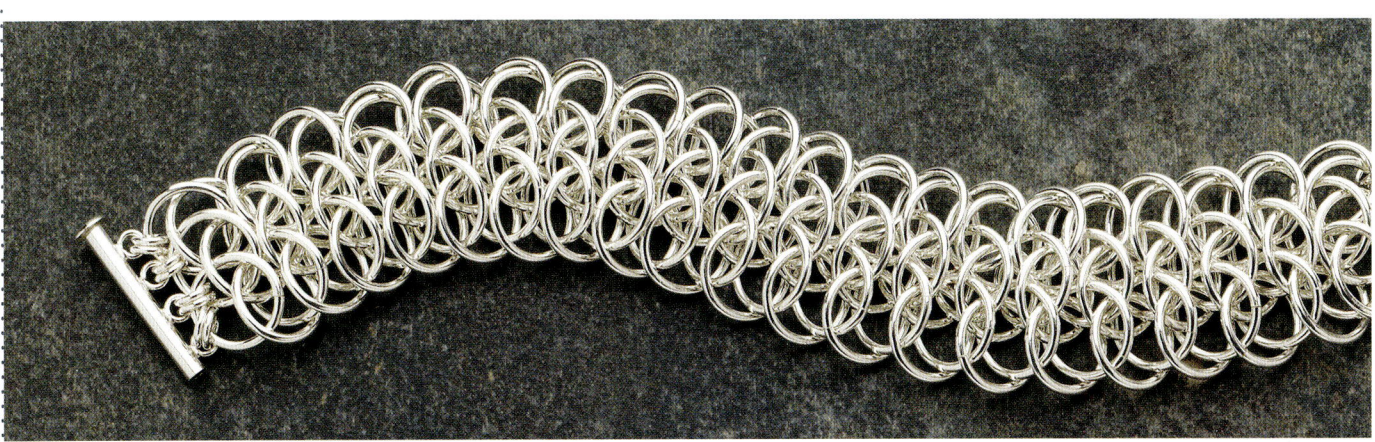

METHOD 1—ARKHAM SHEET, VERTICAL CONSTRUCTION

Jump Ring Chart

	16 GAUGE			18 GAUGE		
METAL	ID	RPI	AR	ID	RPI	AR
Sterling Silver (AWG)	9.0 mm	21	7.0	7.0 mm	27	6.8
Bright Aluminum (SWGv)						
The Ring Lord	7/16"	18	7.4	5/16"	24	6.8
C&T Designs	7/16"	21	7.05	*	*	*
Metal Designz	7/16"	18	7.3	5/16"	30	7.1

note: *Recommended jump ring sizes/counts for vertical Arkham Sheet weave listed in chart above are based on a piece that is 3 jump rings wide.*

*18g, 5/16" C&T Designs Bright Aluminum jump rings have an AR of 6.56 and produce a weave that is a bit too tight and has a pronounced twist. This is the largest size they currently offer in 18g bright aluminum.

Persian Weaves

Prepare Jump Rings

Close 3 jump rings and open the rest.

Start the Weave

1. Begin with 3 closed jump rings and overlap them, left over right (**Fig. 1**).

2. Secure the 3 jump rings with tape and use a pen to mark the front (**Fig. 2**, first row of jump rings).

Weave the Pattern

Add 3 jump rings:

3. Thread 1 open (yellow) jump ring through the eye formed by jump rings 1 and 2. Close the open jump ring and lay it to the right (**Fig. 3**).

4. Thread another open (orange) jump ring through the eye formed by jump rings 2 and 3 and around the eye formed by jump rings 1 and 2 and then close it. It should sit above the (yellow) jump ring just added (**Fig. 4**).

5. Thread a third open (green) jump ring around the eye formed by jump rings 2 and 3 and then close it. It should sit above the (orange) jump ring just added (**Fig. 5**, second row of jump rings added).

6. Position the 3 (yellow/orange/green) jump rings just added as follows: Place your index finger on the back side of the weave under the 3 (yellow/orange/green) jump rings just added. Now push them up and forward from the back of the weave* (**Fig. 6**).

Add 3 jump rings:

7. Thread 1 open (fuchsia) jump ring through the eye formed by (orange/green) jump rings 2 and 3. Close the open jump ring and lay it to the left (**Fig. 7**).

8. Thread another open (turquoise) jump ring around the eye formed by (orange/green) jump rings 2 and 3 and through the eye formed by (yellow/orange) jump rings 1 and 2 and then close it. It should sit above the (fuchsia) jump ring just added (**Fig. 8**).

9. Thread a third open (pale blue) jump ring around the eye formed by (yellow/orange) jump rings 1 and 2 and then close it. It should sit above the (turquoise) jump ring just added (**Fig. 9**, third row of jump rings added).

10. Position the 3 (fuchsia/turquoise/pale blue) jump rings just added as follows: Place your thumb on the front side of the weave under the 3 (fuchsia/turquoise/pale blue) jump rings just added. Now, push them up and back from the front of the weave* (**Fig. 10**).

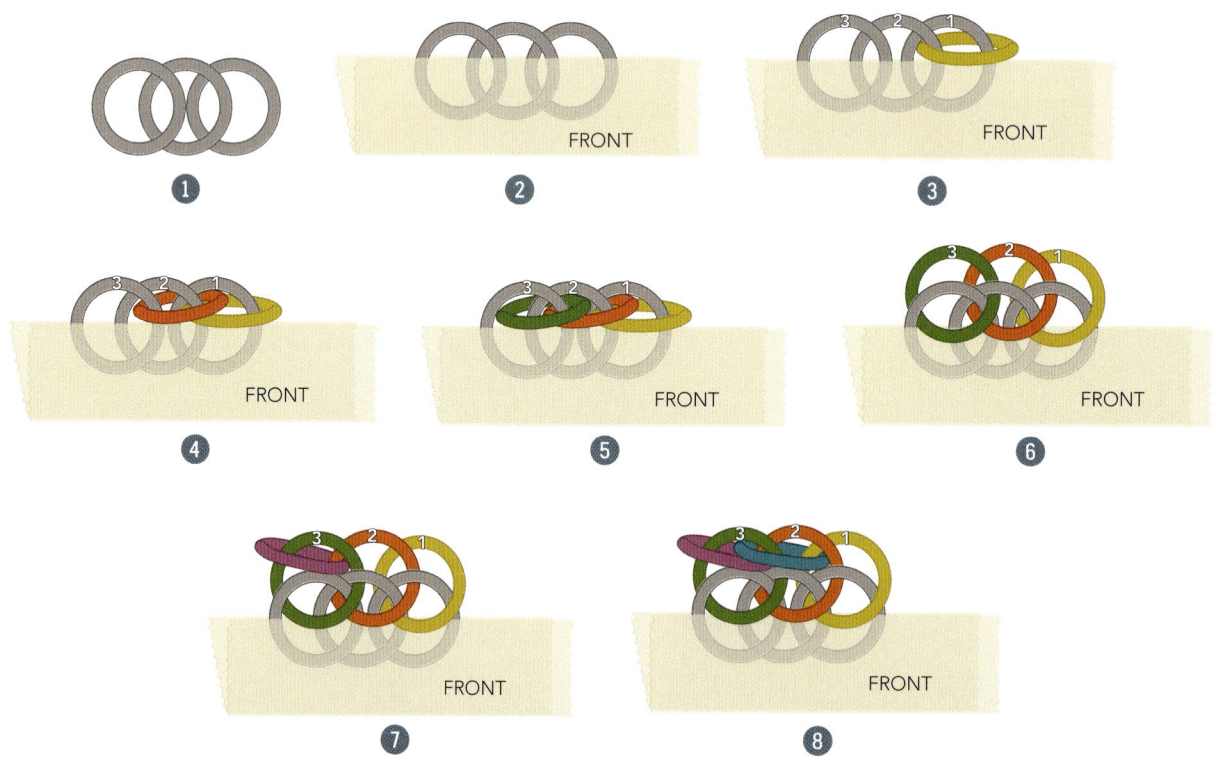

46 ADVANCED CHAIN MAILLE JEWELRY WORKSHOP

*Alternating the positioning of each row of jump rings added by pushing one set of 3 up and forward from the back and the next set up and back from the front creates the crosshatch pattern on the edge of the weave as shown in the chapter's introduction. It is important to perform these positioning steps when beginning the weave. As the weave becomes longer and more stable, the jump rings will naturally begin to fall into the correct position.

Add 3 jump rings:

11. Thread 1 open (purple) jump ring through the eye formed by (pale blue/turquoise) jump rings 1 and 2. Close the open jump ring and lay it to the right (**Fig. 11**).

12. Thread another open (gold) jump ring through the eye formed by (turquoise/fuchsia) jump rings 2 and 3 and around the eye formed by (pale blue/turquoise) jump rings 1 and 2 and then close it. It should sit above the (purple) jump ring just added (**Fig. 12**).

13. Thread a third open (red) jump ring around the eye formed by (turquoise/fuchsia) jump rings 2 and 3. Close the open jump ring. It should sit above the (gold) jump ring just added (**Fig. 13**, fourth row of jump rings added).

14. Position the 3 (purple/gold/red) jump rings just added by pushing them up and forward from behind the weave.

Repeat Steps 7–14 until your piece reaches the desired length.

TIP

To create a mirror-image Arkham Sheet, start the weave by reversing the position of the first 3 overlapping jump rings contained in the tape (right over left). Next, the reference numbers on the 3 jump rings at the top of the weave must be reversed (rightmost jump ring is #3 and leftmost jump ring is #1). When weaving the jump rings that go through the eye only (first jump ring of each set of 3), lay that first jump ring in the opposite direction of the instructions (beginning with the left), and so on. The mirror-image weave differs in the direction of the grain. The difference is very subtle.

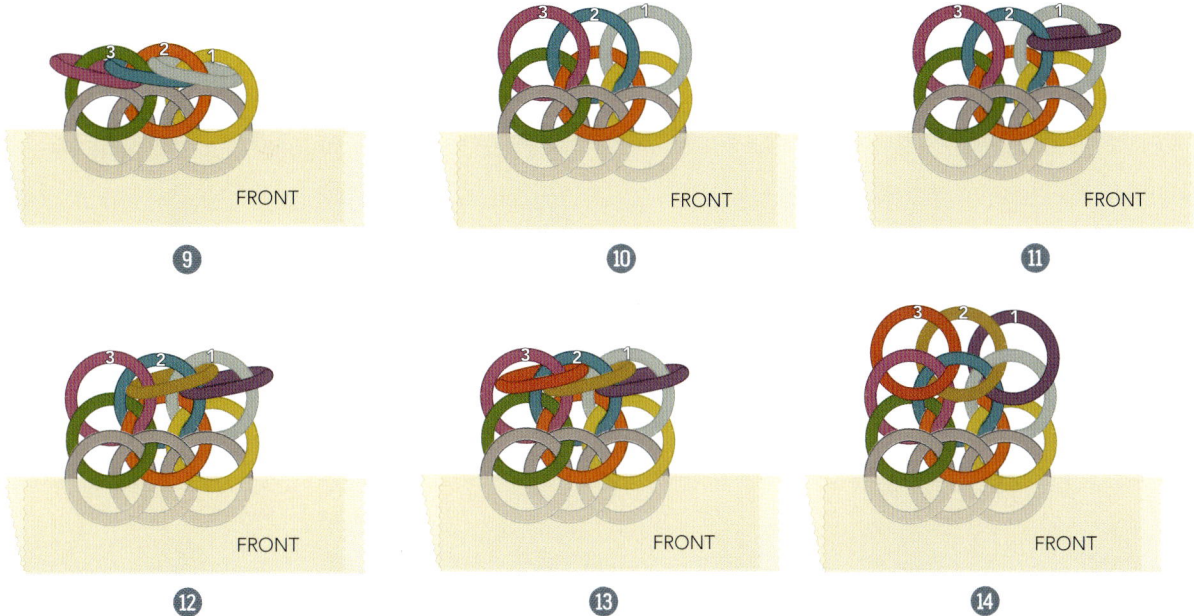

Persian Weaves 47

METHOD 2—ARKHAM SHEET, HORIZONTAL CONSTRUCTION

Jump Ring Chart

| | 16 GAUGE ||| 18 GAUGE |||
METAL	ID	RPI	AR	ID	RPI	AR
Sterling Silver (AWG)	8.5/9 mm*	24/25	6.6/7.0	7 mm	30	6.8
Bright Aluminum (SWG)						
The Ring Lord	7/16"	18	7.4	5/16"	24	6.8
C&T Designs	7/16"	24	7.05	5/16"	30	6.56
Metal Designz	7/16"	18	7.3	5/16"	30	7.1

note: *Recommended jump ring sizes/counts for horizontal Arkham Sheet weave listed in chart are based on a sheet that is 3 pattern repeats (original HP31 chain, plus 4 passes back and forth).*

16g (AWG) 8.5 mm produces a weave with a tighter appearance than 9 mm. The 8.5 mm weave flexes well in length and on one edge. The 9 mm weave flexes well in length and on both edges.

TIP

Adding this first row of jump rings is really tricky! The jump rings in the HP31 chain shift as you weave. Make sure to grasp the weave tightly in your nondominant hand and hold the jump rings in the HP31 chain in the proper position for weaving. You will need to do this along the entire length of the HP31 chain.

Make a Length of Half Persian 3-in-1

1. Make your HP31 base piece (see instructions in Review Material, page 26) longer than you think you will need. As you weave into it to make Arkham Sheet, it will reduce by about 25 percent of the original length. Some experimentation will be required to arrive at the appropriate length.

2. Mark the starting end of the chain with a paper clip. Orange jump rings are linking jump rings, silver are base row jump rings (**Fig. 1**).

Prepare Jump Rings

Open remaining jump rings.

Start the Weave

3. Turn the HP31 chain over to the concave side—this is now the front (**Fig. 2**).

4. Fold down the jump rings that lean toward the front (silver base row jump rings) until they are upside down and now lean toward the back—now the back loops (**Fig. 3**).

Weave the Pattern

Add a row of jump rings along the horizontal length, working from left to right and in the back loops (**Fig. 4**):

5. Thread 1 open (green) jump ring through the eye formed by back loops 1 and 2. Close the open jump ring and lay it to the left (**Fig. 5**).

6. Thread another open (dark green) jump ring through the eye formed by back loops 2 and 3 and around the eye formed by back loops 1 and 2 and then close it. It should sit above the (green) jump ring just added (**Fig. 6**).

48 ADVANCED CHAIN MAILLE JEWELRY WORKSHOP

7. Thread another open (dark green) jump ring through the eye formed by back loops 3 and 4 and around the eye formed by back loops 2 and 3 and then close it. It should sit above the (green) jump ring just added (**Fig. 7**).

Continue along the horizontal length of the piece until you reach the last pair of back loops along the top edge of the piece (**Fig. 8**).

8. To end the row, thread 1 open (dark green) jump ring around the eye formed by the last pair of back loops and then close it. It should sit above the last (green) jump ring added (**Fig. 9**).

9. Position the row of jump rings just added by pushing them up and back from the front of the weave (**Fig. 10**).

Add a row of jump rings along the horizontal length of the piece, working in the last horizontal row of (green) jump rings added, weaving from right to left:

TIP

To weave Arkham Sheet in mirror-image, start the weave by making a mirror-image length of Half Persian 3-in-1 chain (see Review Material, page 28). To weave, reverse the reference numbers on the illustrations. The first jump ring placed (in the eye formed by jump rings 1 and 2) should be positioned in the opposite direction. Additional jump rings woven down the length will follow this orientation. The mirror-image weave differs in the direction of the grain. The difference is very subtle.

Persian Weaves 49

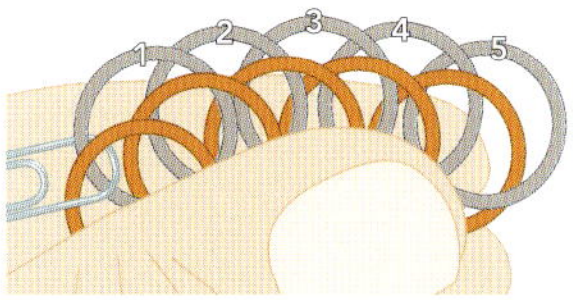

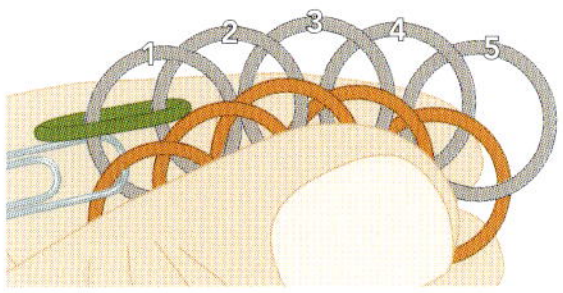

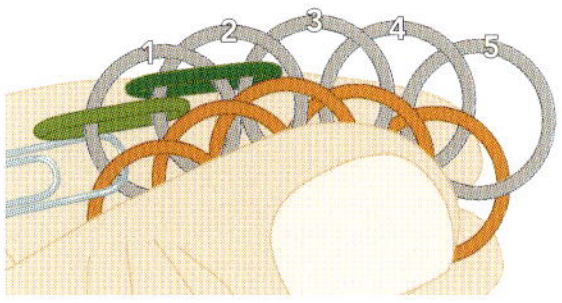

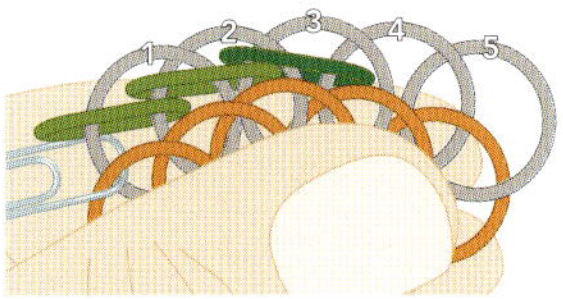

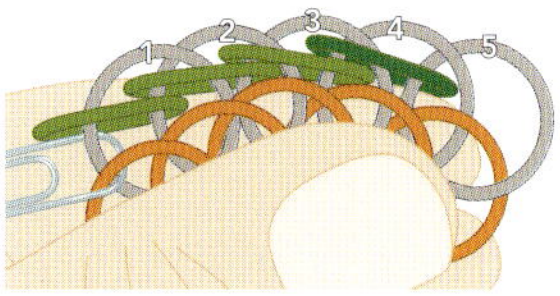

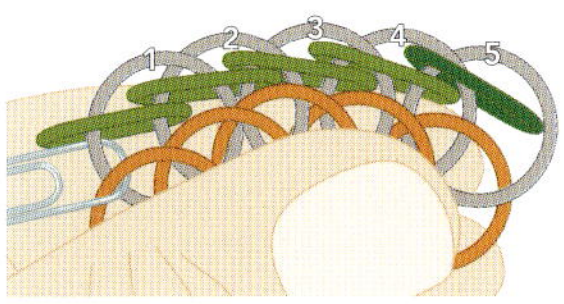

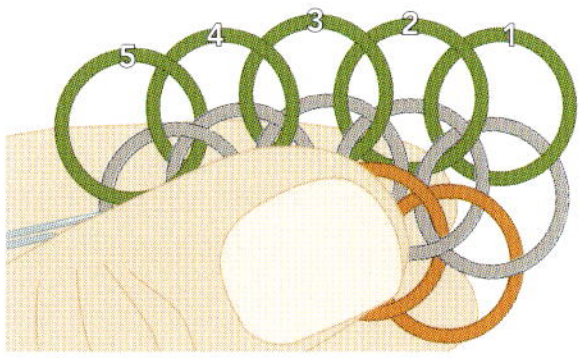

10. Thread 1 open (yellow) jump ring through the eye formed by jump rings 1 and 2. Close the open jump ring and lay it to the right (**Fig. 11**).

11. Thread another open (gold) jump ring around the eye formed by jump rings 1 and 2 and through the eye formed by jump rings 2 and 3 and then close it. It should sit above the (yellow) jump ring just added (**Fig. 12**).

12. Thread another open (gold) jump ring around the eye formed by jump rings 2 and 3 and through the eye formed by jump rings 3 and 4 and then close it. It should sit above the (yellow) jump ring just added (**Fig. 13**).

Continue along the horizontal length of the piece until you reach the last 2 jump rings (**Fig. 14**).

13. To end the row, thread 1 open (gold) jump ring around the eye formed by the last 2 jump rings in the row and then close it. It should sit above the (yellow) jump ring just added (**Fig. 15**).

14. Position the row of jump rings just added by pushing them up and forward from behind the weave (**Fig. 16**).

Working in the last horizontal row of jump rings added, repeat Steps 5–14 until your piece reaches the desired length.

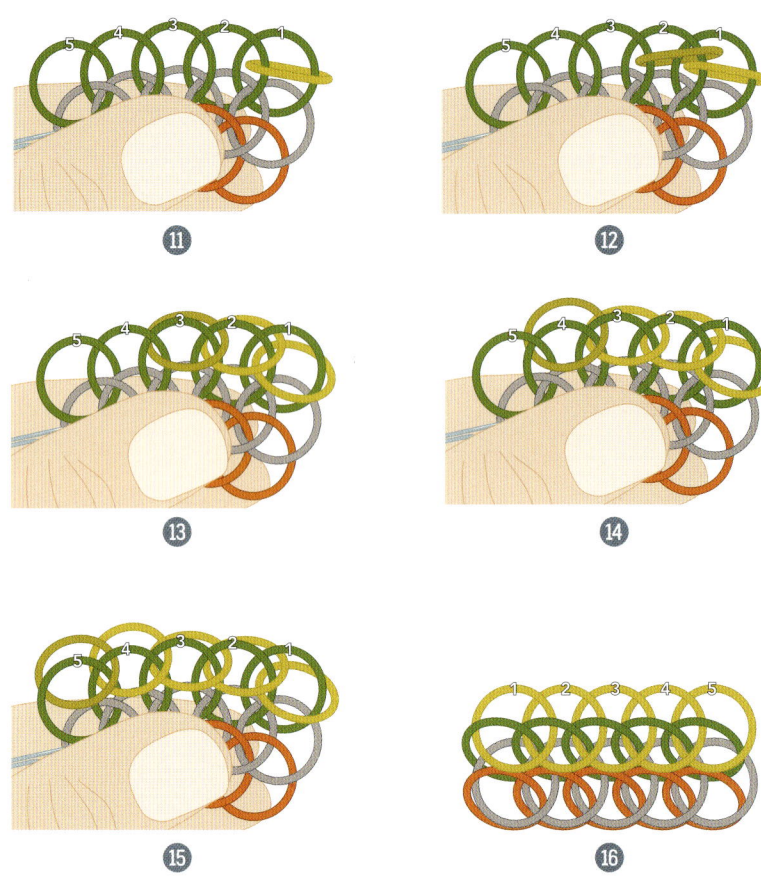

50   ADVANCED CHAIN MAILLE JEWELRY WORKSHOP

Crotalus Weave

Originally created by Laura Hepworth of Handmaden Designs LLC.

Jump Ring Chart

METAL	16 GAUGE ID	16 GAUGE RPI	16 GAUGE AR	18 GAUGE ID	18 GAUGE RPI	18 GAUGE AR
Sterling Silver (AWG)	6 mm	25	4.7	4.75 mm	30	4.6
Bright Aluminum (SWG)						
The Ring Lord	9/32"	20	4.7	7/32"	25	4.7
C&T Designs	9/32"	20	4.61	7/32"	25	4.65
Metal Designz	9/32"	20	4.5	13/64"	30	4.6

Crotalus is another cool Persian weave, similar to GSG and Arkham. When weaving GSG and Arkham, rows of jump rings are added in pairs. When weaving Crotalus, rows of jump rings are added in alternating sets of 2 jump rings and 3 jump rings. This weave is thicker in the middle and flat on the edges; therefore, the crosshatch pattern is not as pronounced. One edge flexes more than the other. You can use color to accentuate the thick center and thin edges of the weave.

Prepare Jump Rings

Open the jump rings.

Start the Weave

1. Make a 1-1-1-chain.

2. Arrange the jump rings as in **Fig. 1**.

3. Secure the 3 jump rings with tape and mark the front with a pen (**Fig. 2**, first row of jump rings).

Weave the Pattern

Add 2 jump rings:

4. Thread 1 open (orange) jump ring around the eye formed by jump rings 1 and 2 and then close it (**Fig. 3**).

5. Thread another open (gold) jump ring around the eye formed by jump rings 2 and 3, and through the last (orange) jump ring added. Close the open jump ring (**Fig. 4**, second row of jump rings added).

6. Position the 2 (orange/gold) jump rings just added as follows: Place your thumb on the front side of the weave under the 2 (orange/gold) jump rings just added. Now, push them up and back from the front of the weave*.

*Alternating the positioning of each row of jump rings added by pushing one row up and back from the front and the next up and forward from the back creates a subtle crosshatch pattern on the edge of the weave similar to that shown in the chapter's

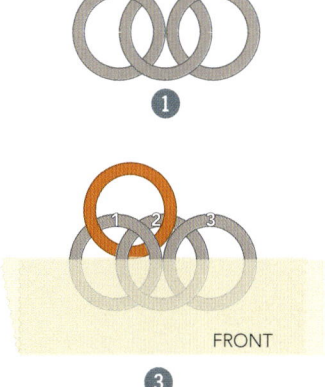

Persian Weaves 51

introduction. It is important to perform these positioning steps when beginning the weave. As the weave becomes longer and more stable, the jump rings will naturally begin to fall into the correct position.

Add 3 jump rings:

7. Thread 1 open (yellow) jump ring around the eye formed by 2 (orange/gold) jump rings just added and then close it (**Fig. 5**).

8. Thread another open (green) jump ring around the eye formed by the left (orange) jump ring of the 2 jump rings added previously and the center (yellow) jump ring just added and then close it. It should lie to the left (**Fig. 6**).

9. Thread a third open (turquoise) jump ring around the eye formed by the right (gold) jump ring of the 2 jump rings added previously and the center (yellow) jump ring just added and then close it. It should lie to the right (**Fig. 7**, third row of jump rings added).

10. Position the 3 (yellow/green/turquoise) jump rings just added as follows: Place your index finger on the back side of the weave under the 3 (yellow/green/turquoise) jump rings just added. Now push them up and forward from the back of the weave*.

Add 2 jump rings:

11. Weave 1 open (purple) jump ring around the eye formed by the left (green) jump ring previously added and the center (yellow) jump ring previously added. Close the open jump ring (**Fig. 8**).

12. Thread another open (fuchsia) jump ring around the eye formed by the right (turquoise) jump ring previously added and the center (yellow) jump ring previously added and through the last (purple) jump ring added. Close the open jump ring (**Fig. 9**, fourth row of jump rings added).

13. Position the 2 (purple/fuchsia) jump rings just added by pushing them up and back from in front of the weave.

Add 3 jump rings:

14. Thread 1 open (pale blue) jump ring around the eye formed by 2 (purple/fuchsia) jump rings just added and then close it (**Fig. 10**).

15. Thread another open (blue) jump ring around the eye formed by the left (purple) jump ring of the 2 jump rings added previously and the center (pale blue) jump ring just added and then close it. It should lie to the left (**Fig. 11**).

16. Thread a third open (red) jump ring around the eye formed by the right (fuchsia) jump ring of the 2 jump rings added previously and the center (pale blue) jump ring just added and then close it. It should lie to the right (**Fig. 12**, fifth row of jump rings added).

17. Position the 3 (pale blue/blue/red) jump rings just added by pushing them up and forward from behind the weave.

Continue working in this manner, adding 2 jump rings and then 3 jump rings, until your piece reaches the desired length.

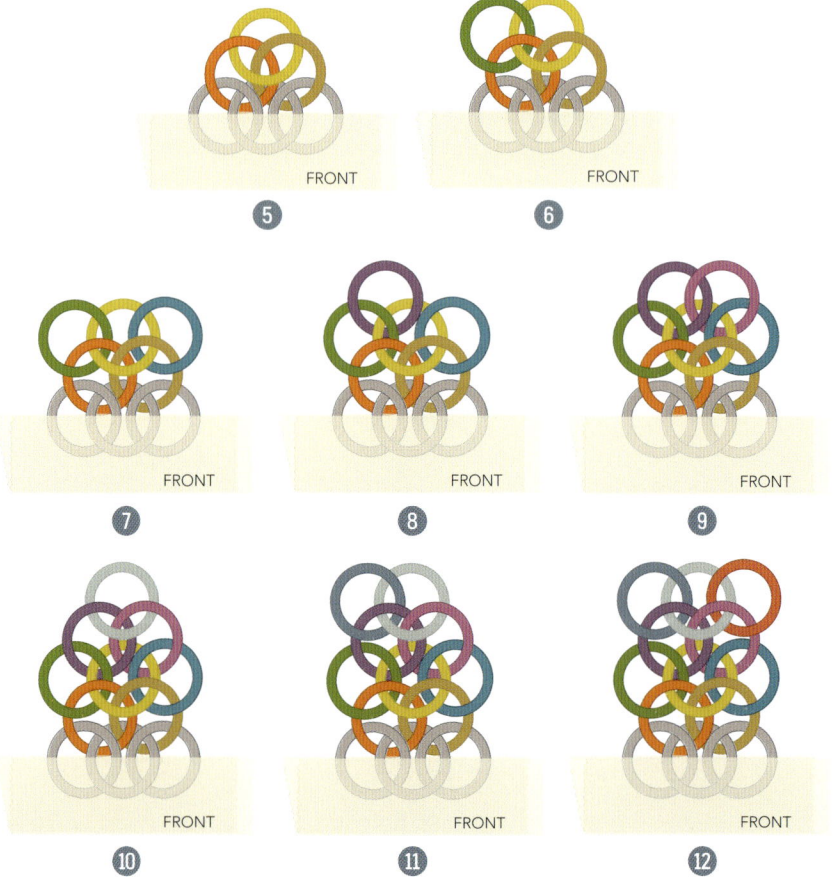

52   ADVANCED CHAIN MAILLE JEWELRY WORKSHOP

Viperscale Weave

Originally created by Jessica Gump (Lady Lockeout)

Jump Ring Chart

	16 GAUGE			18 GAUGE		
METAL	ID	RPI	AR	ID	RPI	AR
Sterling Silver (AWG)	8 mm	25	6.2	6 mm	30	5.9
Bright Aluminum (SWG)						
The Ring Lord	3/8"	15	6.3	9/32"	20	6.2
C&T Designs	3/8"	20	6.11	9/32"	25	5.96
Metal Designz	3/8"	15	6.5	9/32"	20	5.85

Viperscale is a Persian weave, similar in construction to Crotalus, that produces an open and airy chain with an elliptical profile. Just as in weaving Crotalus, you add rows of jump rings in alternating sets of 2 jump rings and 3 jump rings. With Viperscale, however, some jump rings are woven from the front of the weave, while others are woven from the back, complicating the weaving. Therefore, it is very important to mark the tape with a pen to designate the front side of the weave. Viperscale weave has a wonderful drape, making it perfect for neckpieces. Its openness also provides lots of opportunities for embellishment. It looks especially cool when woven in micro-scale.

Prepare Jump Rings

Open your jump rings.

Start the Weave

1. Make a 1-1-1-chain.

2. Arrange the jump rings as in **Fig. 1**.

3. Secure the 3 jump rings with tape and mark the front with a pen (**Fig. 2**, first row of jump rings).

Weave the Pattern

Add 2 jump rings:

4. Thread 1 open (gold) jump ring through the eye formed by jump rings 3 and 2, and around the eye of jump rings 2 and 1 and then close it (**Fig. 3**).

❶

❷

❸

Persian Weaves 53

5. Thread another open (orange) jump ring around the eye formed by jump rings 3 and 2, and through the eye of jump rings 2 and 1 and then close it. This (orange) jump ring should sit above the previous (gold) jump ring added (**Fig. 4**, second row of jump rings added).

6. Position the 2 (gold/orange) jump rings just added as follows: Place your index finger on the back side of the weave under the 2 (gold/orange) jump rings just added. Now push them up and forward from the back of the weave* (**Fig. 5**).

Add 3 jump rings:

7. Thread 1 open (yellow) jump ring around the eye formed by the 2 (gold/orange) jump rings just added and then close it (**Fig. 6**).

8. Position the (yellow) jump ring just added as follows: Place your thumb on the front side of the weave under the (yellow) jump ring just added. Now, push it up and back from the front of the weave* and then flip the weave over like you would a pancake (**Fig. 7**, back).

*Alternating the positioning of each row of 2 jump rings added and the center jump ring of each row of 3 jump rings added by pushing the pair up and forward from the back and the center jump ring up and back from the front creates the crosshatch pattern on the edge of the weave as shown in the chapter's introduction. It is important to perform these positioning steps when beginning the weave. As the weave becomes longer and more stable, the jump rings will naturally begin to fall into the correct position.

9. Thread another open (turquoise) jump ring through the last 3 (yellow/gold/orange) jump rings added by weaving under the center (yellow) jump ring and up through the eye of the horizontal (orange/gold) jump rings (**Fig. 8**). Close the open jump ring and position it to the right side of the weave.

10. Thread 1 open (green) jump ring through the same 3 (yellow/orange/gold) jump rings by weaving under the center (yellow) jump ring and up through the eye of the horizontal (orange/gold) jump rings (**Fig. 9**). Close the open jump ring and position it to the left side of the weave (third row of jump rings added).

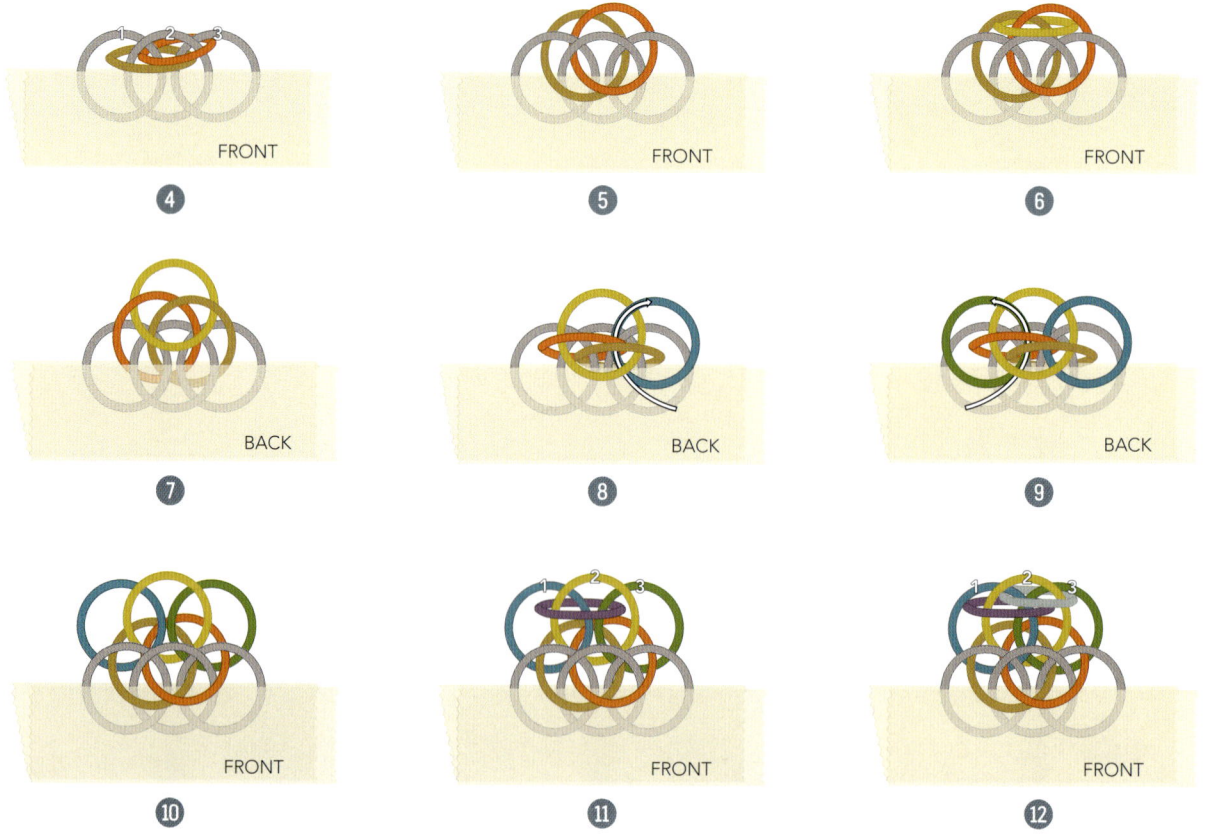

54 ADVANCED CHAIN MAILLE JEWELRY WORKSHOP

11. Flip the piece over like you would a pancake (**Fig. 10**, front).

Add 2 jump rings:

12. Thread 1 open (purple) jump ring through the eye formed by (green/yellow) jump rings 3 and 2, and around the eye of (yellow/turquoise) jump rings 2 and 1. Close the open jump ring (**Fig. 11**).

13. Thread another open (pale blue) jump ring around the eye formed by (green/yellow) jump rings 3 and 2, and through the eye of (yellow/turquoise) jump rings 2 and 1. Close the open jump ring. This (pale blue) jump ring should sit above the previous (purple) jump ring added (**Fig. 12**, fourth row of jump rings added).

14. Position the 2 (purple/pale blue) jump rings just added by pushing them up and forward from behind the weave (**Fig. 13**).

Add 3 jump rings:

15. Thread 1 open (red) jump ring around the eye formed by the 2 (purple/pale blue) jump rings just added and then close it (**Fig. 14**).

16. Position the (red) jump ring just added by pushing it up and back from the front of the weave and flip the weave over as you would a pancake (**Fig. 15**, back).

17. Thread another open (fuchsia) jump ring through the last 3 (red/purple/pale blue) jump rings added by weaving under the center (red) jump ring and up through the eye of the horizontal (purple/pale blue) jump rings (**Fig. 16**). Close the open jump ring and position it to the right side of the weave.

18. Thread 1 open (blue) jump ring through the same 3 (red/purple/pale blue) jump rings by weaving under the center (red) jump ring and up through the eye of the horizontal (purple/pale blue) jump rings (**Fig. 17**). Close the open jump ring and position it to the left side of the weave (fifth row of jump rings added).

19. Flip the piece over as you would a pancake (**Fig. 18**, front).

Continue working in this manner, adding 2 jump rings and then 3 jump rings, until your piece reaches the desired length.

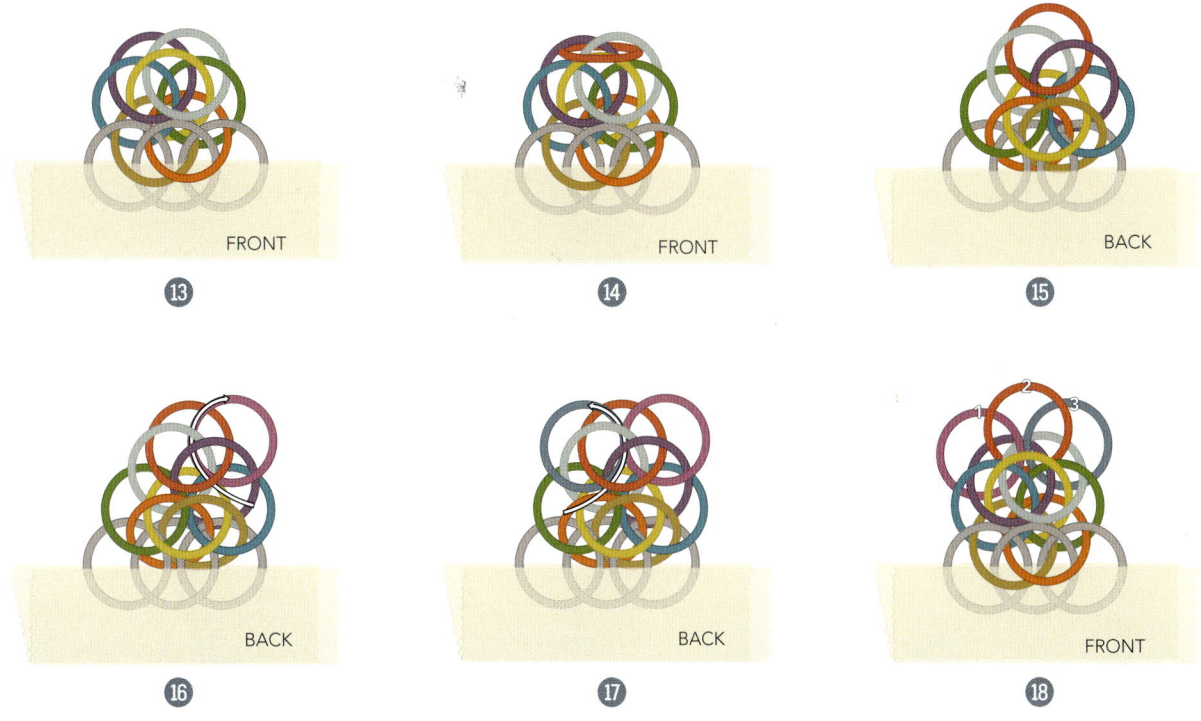

Persian Weaves 55

SUPPLIES

- 358 cobalt blue niobium jump rings, saw-cut, 20g (AWG), 5/32" ID
- 352 teal niobium jump rings, saw-cut, 20g (AWG), 5/32" ID
- 1 silver-plated brass 2-strand slide clasp

FINISHED LENGTH

- 17" (43 cm) not including clasp

TWO-TONE GSG SHEET NECKLACE

This anodized niobium necklace project in cool blue tones illustrates shaping by incorporating mirror-image weaving. Using two colors highlights the change in weaving direction, and the cool blue tones project a casual vibe, perfect to pair with your favorite jeans. Of course, you can change the color scheme to match any outfit or suit any mood. For example, you could combine orange and red jump rings to heat things up or make a bold statement by pairing complementary colors such as turquoise and copper. You could also make a more traditional, subtler version using classic sterling silver jump rings.

Weave the Pattern

1. Weave one side of the GSG sheet (vertical, 3 jump rings across) necklace using 354 cobalt blue jump rings as shown on page 38. The final 3 jump rings added should be layered in the opposite direction from the first 3 jump rings in the tape (right over left): 4 cobalt blue jump rings will remain.

2. Begin the other side of the necklace by adding the next row of 3 jump rings. Work in the opposite direction (mirror image) using the teal jump rings. Thread the first teal jump ring through the eye on the right side of the weave and position it to the right. The weave will be tight at the corner just formed.

3. Continue weaving the teal jump rings in the new direction until the necklace is complete: 4 teal jump rings will remain.

Finish

4. Attach one half of the 2-strand clasp by threading 4 cobalt blue jump rings (2 in each loop of the clasp) through the 2 eyes at the end of the cobalt blue side of the chain.

5. Attach the other half of the 2-strand clasp by threading 4 teal jump rings (2 in each loop of the clasp) through the 2 eyes at the end of the teal side of the chain.

MIXED-METAL CLASPLESS VIPERSCALE BRACELET

Weave the Pattern

This project will teach you how to connect the ends of the Viperscale weave to create a closed circle that can be used for claspless bracelets, rings, and more. Create a classic piece in precious metal or mix up some colorful anodized aluminum jump rings for a fun, more playful look.

1. Weave a Viperscale chain that consists of 54 gold-filled jump rings and 81 sterling silver jump rings (see page 53). Begin with 3 sterling silver jump rings in the tape. The next 2 jump rings threaded should be gold-filled, and the next 3 jump rings sterling silver.

2. Continue alternating 2 gold-filled jump rings, then 3 sterling silver jump rings until your chain is complete. You should end the chain with 2 gold-filled jump rings.

Close the chain:

3. Remove the tape from the beginning end of the weave and bring together the beginning and finishing ends. (Don't twist the band!)

4. On the beginning end, open the center jump ring, retaining its place in the weave **(Fig. 1)**.

Thread that open jump ring around the eye formed by the 2 jump rings at the finishing end of the weave. Close the open jump ring **(Fig. 2)**.

SUPPLIES

- 81 sterling silver jump rings, 16g (AWG), 8 mm ID
- 54 gold-filled jump rings, 16g (AWG), 8 mm ID

FINISHED LENGTH

- About 7¾" (19.5 cm) open flat (length before closing)

5. Open the right jump ring at the beginning end of the chain, retaining its place in the weave.

Thread the open jump ring through the eye formed by the 2 jump rings at the finishing end of the weave. Close the open jump ring (**Fig. 3**).

6. Open the left jump ring at the beginning end of the chain, retaining its place in the weave.

Thread the open jump ring through the eye formed by the 2 jump rings at the finishing end of the weave. Close the open jump ring (**Fig. 4**).

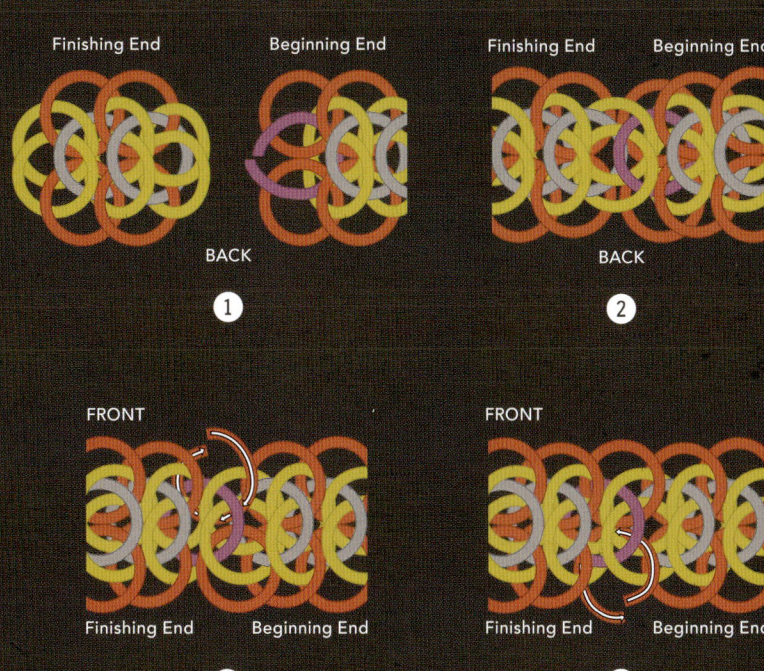

VIPERSCALE CUFF DESIGN OPTION

To create a fun, more casual look for this Viperscale cuff, I wove it with 46 royal blue, 46 sky blue, and 23 seafoam anodized aluminum jump rings from The Ring Lord [16 g (SWG), ⅜" (1 cm) ID, saw-cut]. In place of sterling silver jump rings, use royal blue and seafoam (royal blue on the left and right and seafoam in the middle). In place of gold-filled jump rings, use sky blue. The finished bracelet is equivalent in size to the precious metal version—and every bit as beautiful.

ELF WEAVES

Elfweave is in the European family of weaves. It is a 4-in-1 variation. The ideal form is flat, but the weave can be unstable, compressing to form a chain with a square profile. The sheet forms of the weave presented in this chapter are stable weaves. They possess lovely, intricate linkage patterns that are ideal for statement jewelry pieces.

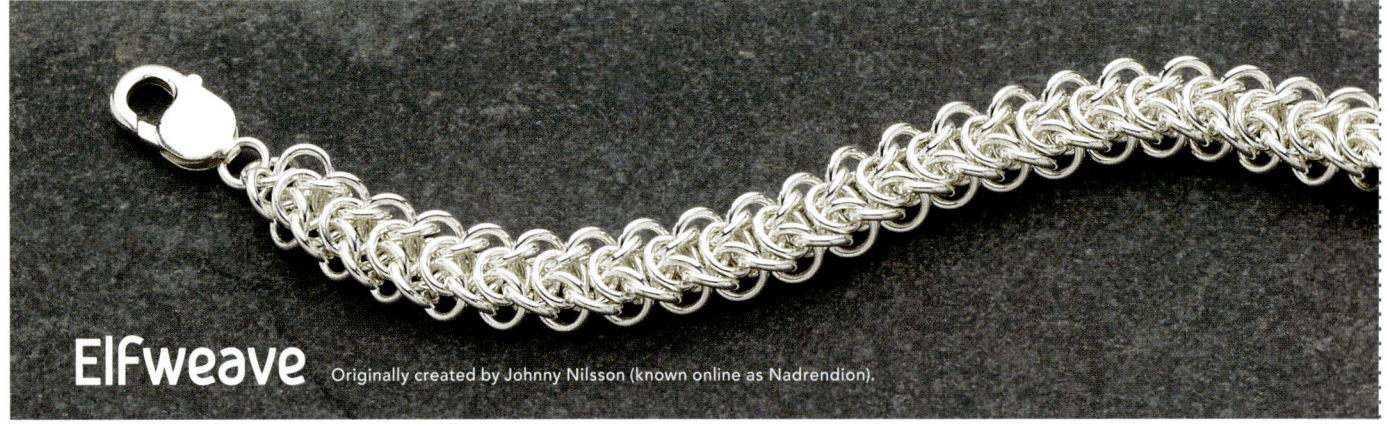

Elfweave
Originally created by Johnny Nilsson (known online as Nadrendion).

Jump Ring Chart

	16 GAUGE			18 GAUGE		
METAL	ID	RPI	AR	ID	RPI	AR
Sterling Silver (AWG)	4.75 mm	26	3.7	3.75 mm	30	3.7
Bright Aluminum (SWG)						
The Ring Lord	¼"	18	4.1	³⁄₁₆"	24	4.1
C&T Designs	¹⁵⁄₆₄"	24	3.82	¹¹⁄₆₄"	30	3.69
Metal Designz	¹⁵⁄₆₄"	24	4.0	¹¹⁄₆₄"	30	4.0

Elfweave is a flat chain weave that can be unstable. However, I've found that using the right size of jump rings can produce a chain with stability. The sterling silver sizes listed in the chart make a nice stable weave. Even after tumbling them for 3 hours, the jump rings stayed put. If you use jump rings with a slightly larger aspect ratio, the jump rings in the chain may shift, forming a chain with a square profile (which is not the desired form, but I think it is also kind of cool—see Square Elfweave sidebar, page 66). The aluminum jump rings are not offered in the same wide range of inner diameter sizes as the silver jump rings, so the sizes recommended in the chart above may not be as stable, but they are what I consider to be the best options. Experiment with the jump rings you plan to use to find the size that is right for your project.

I'm presenting two methods to construct Elfweave. Method 1, which uses a 1-by-1 chain as a base, is a very popular method. I like it best because I find it easy to start, quicker to weave, and an easy way to join the weave end to end. However, many beginners do not like this method. The long 1-by-1 chain can be difficult to control, making it easy to lose your place when weaving. It is also difficult to determine the proper length for the starting chain. Unfortunately, simply weaving 1 jump ring at a time presents its own challenges. It is an extremely difficult weave to start because the jump rings are very unstable at this stage. Therefore, Method 2 demonstrates the method I often use with beginners—the starter patch method. Try both and see which you prefer.

METHOD 1: 1-BY-1 CHAIN START

Prepare Jump Rings
This method of construction is a two-step process. First, you need to make a long 1-by-1 base chain. You will then weave additional jump rings into that base chain to form the Elfweave pattern. To prepare the jump rings for the base chain, open half and close half, then speed-weave the 1-by-1 chain. Open the rest of the jump rings (for completing Elfweave).

Start the Pattern
1. Make a 1-by-1 base chain with an odd number of jump rings (**Fig. 1**). Make your 1-by-1 chain much longer than you think you need. To work the pattern, you will begin by folding it in half. Then, as you weave into the folded chain to make Elfweave, it will reduce. The final result will be much shorter. As you weave, check the length of your chain periodically. If needed, add jump rings to the base 1-by-1 chain. After all, it is easier to remove the extra jump rings at the end of the chain than it is to determine where in the pattern to add additional jump rings.

62 ADVANCED CHAIN MAILLE JEWELRY WORKSHOP

2. Fold your 1-by-1 base chain in half. Mark the center jump ring of your base chain with a starting aid (for example, a paper clip). The orange jump ring in **Fig. 1** is the center jump ring.

3. Orient the jump rings emanating from the center jump ring as follows: The 2 (turquoise) jump rings connected to the center (orange) jump ring should make an inverted V (a mountain). The next pair of (gray) jump rings should make a V (a valley). Continue this pattern of orientation down the length of the chain as you work (**Fig. 2**).

4. Thread 1 open (pale blue) jump ring straight through the eyes formed between the 2 (turquoise) jump rings of the first mountain and the 2 (gray) jump rings of the first valley (**Fig. 3**, side view; **Fig. 4**, front view). Close the open (pale blue) jump ring (**Fig. 5**). You can recognize the front of the weave by looking just below the center jump ring. You should see the "peak of the first mountain" (turquoise jump rings).

> Based on tests I performed, about two-thirds of the length of the original 1-by-1 chain will be lost. I started with two 12" (30.5 cm) 1-by-1 chains in 16g and 18g aluminum jump rings. The chains were then folded in half, resulting in 2 doubled chains that were each 6" (15 cm) in length. As I wove into each 6" (15 cm) doubled chain, they reduced in length by about one-third, leaving me with two Elfweave chains, about 4" (10 cm) in length each. Your results may vary. You'll need to experiment some to arrive at the appropriate length for your project.

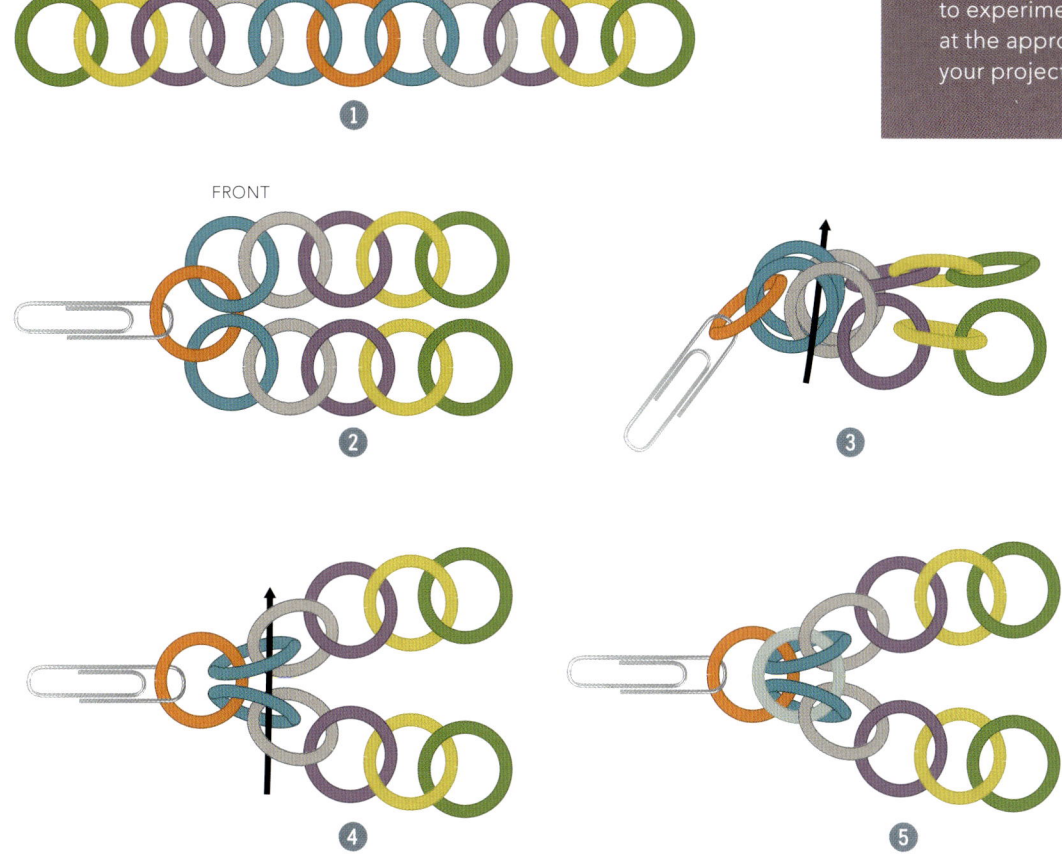

Elf Weaves

Weave the Pattern

5. Flip the weave over as you would a pancake (**Fig. 6**, back view).

6. Arrange the next 2 pairs of (gray/purple) jump rings in the proper mountain/valley orientation. (Notice that on the back side, the gray jump rings form a mountain—they formed a valley on the front side.)

7. Thread 1 open (red) jump ring straight through the eyes between the pairs of jump rings that form the next (gray) mountain and the next (purple) valley (**Fig. 7**, side view; **Fig. 8**, back view). Close the open (red) jump ring (**Fig. 9**).

8. Repeat Steps 5–7 (**Fig. 10**, front, blue added; **Fig. 11**, back, fuchsia added) until you reach the desired length.

METHOD 2: USE A STARTER PATCH

Prepare Jump Rings

Open your jump rings for weaving.

Make the Starter Patch

1. Make a 1-by-1 chain that is 13 links long. I find this length makes a nice stable starter. Attach a paper clip to the center link and fold the chain in half.

2. Orient the jump rings emanating from the center jump ring to form mountain/valley pairs as described in Method 1.

3. As described in Method 1, thread 1 open jump ring straight through the eyes between the pairs of jump rings that form the first mountain and the first valley—1 open jump ring added.

4. Flip the weave over to the back side and thread 1 open jump ring straight through the eyes between the pairs of jump rings that form the next mountain and the next valley—2 open jump rings added.

5. Flip the weave over to the front side and thread 1 open jump ring straight through the eyes between the pairs of jump rings that form the next mountain and the next valley—3 open jump rings added.

6. Flip the weave over to the back side and thread 1 open jump ring straight through the eyes between the pairs of jump rings that form the next mountain and the next valley—4 open jump rings added.

7. Flip the weave over to the front side and thread 1 open jump ring straight through the eyes between the pairs of jump rings that form the next mountain and the next valley—5 open jump rings added.

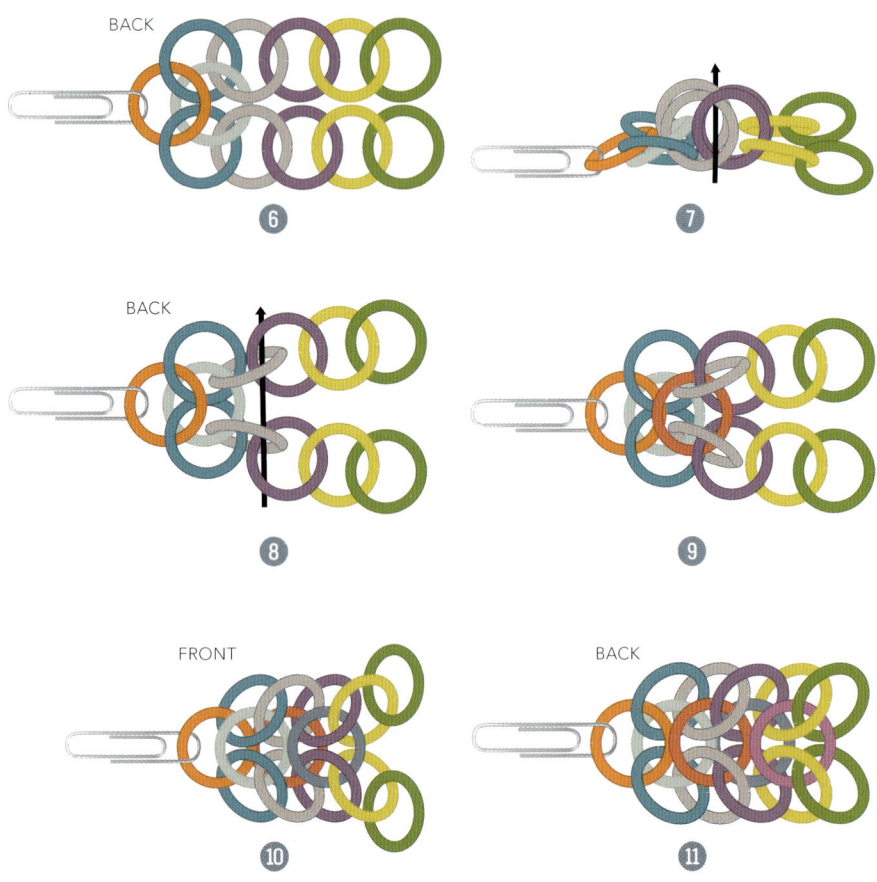

64 ADVANCED CHAIN MAILLE JEWELRY WORKSHOP

8. Flip the weave over.

We are now on the back side of the weave. You will notice that there is not a mountain/valley pair at the end of the weave. There is just a mountain (**Fig. 1**, orange jump rings).

Weave the Pattern

We will now begin to weave 1 jump ring at a time.

9. Thread 1 open (yellow) jump ring through the (orange) "mountain jump rings" at the end of the weave (**Fig. 2**).

10. Position the (yellow) jump ring just added so that it leans toward the beginning end of the chain (**Fig. 3**).

note: *The 3 (orange/yellow) jump rings now at the end of the weave form 2 eyes (see arrows in* **Fig. 3**).

11. Thread 1 open (green) jump ring through the eye formed by the center (yellow) jump ring and the left (orange) jump ring (**Fig. 4**).

12. Thread 1 open (blue) jump ring through the eye formed by the center (yellow) jump ring and the right (orange) jump ring (**Fig. 5**).

13. Flip the weave over.

Notice that there is now a mountain (formed by the green and blue jump rings just added) at the end of the chain (**Fig. 6**), just as in **Fig. 1**, only now on the front of the chain. Repeat Steps 9–13 until your weave reaches the desired length.

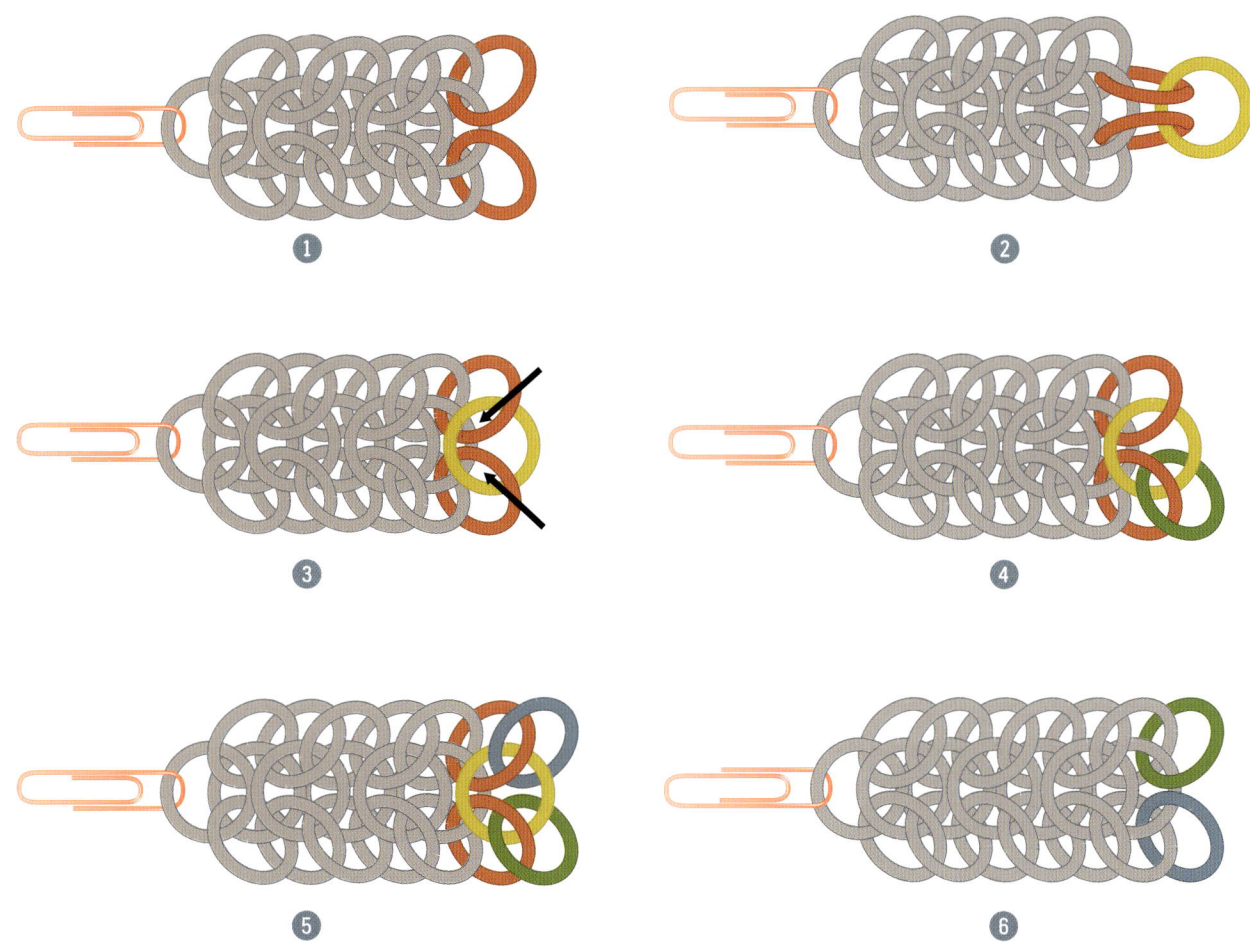

Elf Weaves 65

SQUARE ELFWEAVE

To make typical Elfweave, you need to choose the jump ring size that is just right for it to be stable. For a square Elfweave, you will need to make a flat Elfweave chain with jump rings that have a slightly larger aspect ratio allowing the jump rings in the weave to shift a bit (see chart that follows for recommended sizes). Then, to manipulate that flat Elfweave chain to form a square profile, just squeeze in on its edges. I have made bracelets using jump rings in the sizes recommended in the chart. The square profile held, even after tumbling!

Jump Ring Chart

METAL	16 GAUGE ID	16 GAUGE RPI	16 GAUGE AR	18 GAUGE ID	18 GAUGE RPI	18 GAUGE AR
Sterling Silver (AWG)	5.25 mm	26	4.1	4.0 mm	30	3.9

To Finish Square Elfweave

1. Remove any extra (turquoise) jump rings that might exist at the end of your chain (**Fig. 1**).

2. Insert a second (red) jump ring into the first/last mountain/valley pair at each end of the chain, on the opposite side (**Fig. 2**).

3. Push the 2 (red) jump rings in the end mountain/valley pairs toward the ends of the chain (**Figs. 3** and **4**).

4. On the starting end of the chain, reopen the center (turquoise) jump ring and add a clasp to it (**Fig. 3**).

5. On the finishing end of the chain, add a center (turquoise) jump ring [thread between the 2 (red) jump rings pushed up in Step 3 and through the 2 jump rings at the end of the chain] to act as a catch for the clasp (**Fig. 4**).

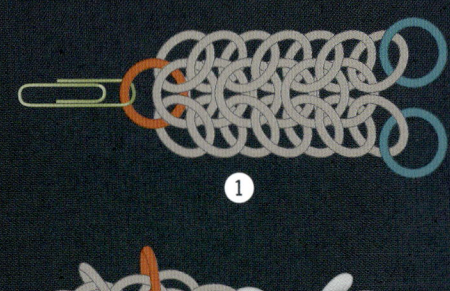
❶

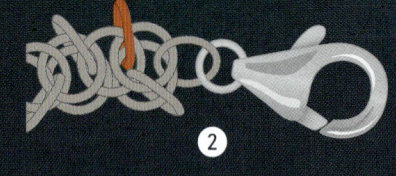
❷

❸ ❹

Elfsheet

Originally created by Johnny Nilsson (known online as Nadrendion).

Jump Ring Chart

METAL	16 GAUGE ID	RPI	AR	18 GAUGE ID	RPI	AR
Sterling Silver (AWG)	5.25 mm	49	4.1	4.0 mm	68	3.9
Bright Aluminum (SWG)						
The Ring Lord	¼"	56	4.1	³⁄₁₆"	70	4.1
C&T Designs	¼"	56	4.11	¹³⁄₆₄"	64	4.25
Metal Designz	¼"	56	4.2	³⁄₁₆"	68	4.1

Elfsheet and Tiffany are sheet forms of Elfweave. Each begins with an Elfweave chain. These sheet weaves can be a bit tricky to comprehend. You always need to be aware of which is the front side and which is the back side, as well as where the starting and finishing ends are. It helps if you learn to recognize the important "Elf landmarks" in the weaves.

Using a starting aid (such as a paper clip) is the easiest and most obvious way to distinguish the starting end from the finishing end. Another way to distinguish the ends is to notice that there is a single jump ring at the starting end. This becomes less obvious as you widen the Elfweave to a sheet form, which is why using a starting aid is a good idea.

To distinguish the front of the weave from the back is a bit trickier. First, find the starting end. There should be a mountain peak just below the starting aid (if you see a valley, you are looking at the back side). To make the front side easily identifiable, you can attach some type of marker (purple jump ring in **Fig. 1**) to your weave.

The colors in **Fig. 2** help to illustrate some of the landmarks. Note that there is a row of horizontal (silver) jump rings that runs down the center of the chain. These were the jump rings that were woven through the eyes of the mountain/valley pairs of the starting Elfweave chain. (If using starter patch method, these are the center jump rings that are woven through each mountain.)

Four side-leaning (green/blue) jump rings pass through each of these horizontal jump rings: 1 green and blue pair passes out to the left and the other to the right. These were the 1-by-1 base chain jump rings for the starting Elfweave chain. (If using starter patch method, these are the 2 jump rings woven through the eyes of the 3 jump rings at the end of the chain.)

1

2 — Horizontal jump rings / Side-leaning jump ring pairs

Elf Weaves 67

There is more than one way to make Elfsheet and Tiffany. I have provided instructions for three methods of construction for each of these sheet weaves. Method 1, for both sheet weaves, shows how to construct the sheets by joining Elfweave chains. Method 2, for both sheet weaves, shows how to symmetrically expand an Elfweave chain into each sheet variation. Method 2 is my favorite method for both Elfsheet and Tiffany. Method 3, for both sheet weaves, shows how to expand an Elfweave chain asymmetrically.

METHOD 1

Method 1 involves making 2 Elfweave chains and connecting them. This is the least complicated method. However, the weaving becomes very tight when trying to connect the 2 Elfweave chains. There is little room for your pliers to grasp the connecting jump rings, often causing the pliers to slip. This results in nicks and scratches on your jump rings, or worse, cuts and scratches on your hands and is, therefore, not the method I prefer.

Make 2 Equal-Length Elfweave Chains

Follow the Elfweave instructions (page 62) to make 2 chains of equal length.

Prepare Jump Rings

Open your jump rings for weaving.

Connect 2 Elfweave Chains

1. Line up your 2 Elfweave chains, side by side, with front sides facing you and beginning ends pointing south.

2. Working from the beginning ends of the Elfweave chains, thread 1 open (fuchsia) jump ring through the first 2 side-leaning (green/blue) jump rings of 1 Elfweave chain and the corresponding pair of side-leaning jump rings of the other Elfweave chain (see weaving path in **Fig. 3**). Continue along the entire length of the chain. Close each open jump ring before weaving the next.

3. Flip the weave over and connect all of the corresponding pairs of side-leaning jump rings on the back side in the same manner.

To make your sheet even wider, you can continue to attach additional Elfweave chains.

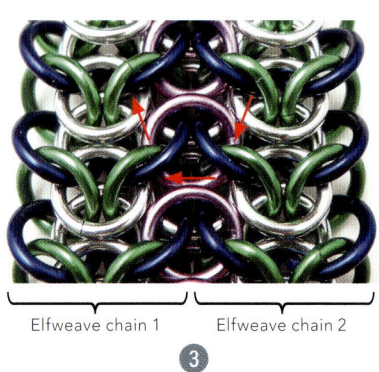

Elfweave chain 1   Elfweave chain 2

3

METHOD 2

Method 2 is a bit more difficult to understand than Method 1, but the actual weaving process is much easier, making it my method of choice. For this method, we will be working symmetrically, first on the left edge and then on the right edge of the weave.

note: *References to the left and right edges of the weave are based on the perspective of holding the weave front side up and beginning end (where the paper clip is) pointing north.*

Make an Elfweave Chain

Follow the instructions on page 62 to make an Elfweave chain.

Prepare Jump Rings

Open your jump rings for weaving.

Add Edge Jump Rings to the Front and Back Sides of the Weave

Position your Elfweave chain so that the beginning end points north and the front side is up. Work from the beginning end of the chain (where the paper clip is) to the finishing end of the chain on both the left and right edges of the weave, front and back.

1. One at a time, thread 1 open (gold) jump ring through each pair of side-leaning (green/blue) jump rings along the left and right edges of the Elfweave chain. Close each open jump ring before proceeding to weave the next. When finished, your piece should resemble **Fig. 1**.

2. Flip the weave over as you would a pancake. You are now working on the back side.

3. One at a time, thread 1 open (orange) jump ring through each pair of side-leaning (green/blue) jump rings along the left and right edges of the Elfweave chain. Close each open jump ring before proceeding to weave the next. When finished, your piece should resemble **Fig. 2**.

4. Flip the weave back over so the front side is facing up.

You have now added all of the edge jump rings to the Elfweave chain.

68   ADVANCED CHAIN MAILLE JEWELRY WORKSHOP

Connect Front and Back Edge Jump Rings on Both Sides of the Weave

Work with front side facing up, from the finishing end of the chain to the beginning end of the chain (where the paper clip is) on both the left and right sides of the weave. When working on the left side, you will work in a right-to-left direction; when working on the right side, you will work in a left-to-right direction. The working direction is very important, because if you work from the beginning end to the finishing end instead, you will not get the correct linkage pattern. The grain of the edges will run in the wrong direction and the weave will be less flexible. (In the right circumstances, however, this could work to your advantage. Don't be afraid to play. That's how new weaves are invented!)

Except for the first open jump ring, each open jump ring you add will pass through 3 jump rings (the previous edge jump ring, the previously added open jump ring, and the next edge jump ring on the opposite side of the weave). You will weave in a zigzag pattern (see arrows in **Fig. 3**, left side).

Begin with the edge jump ring that is the farthest edge jump ring from the beginning end (see yellow jump ring 1 in **Fig. 3**). Depending on the length of your Elfweave chain, the jump ring on the farthest edge may be either on the front or the back edge of your piece. Either is acceptable. In our example, it is on the front edge.

Connect front and back edge jump rings on the left side of the weave.

5. Thread 1 open (pink) jump ring through the farthest edge (gold #1) jump ring and across to the farthest edge (orange #1) jump ring on the opposite side of the weave. Close the open jump ring (**Fig. 4**).

TIP

You can make your Elfsheet even wider by repeating Steps 1–10 above. Note that each time you repeat these steps you must work in the opposite direction from the previous pass. Also, as you continue to widen your sheet, the steps for keeping the edges even may differ slightly from the previous pass. There may be different configurations of jump rings at the ends of rows. Therefore, remember to take cues from pattern repeats in adjacent rows to determine when to add or omit a connection on the edges of sheet weaves to keep them uniform. As you widen, the weave tightens a bit, so you may need to adjust the aspect ratio, depending on the desired result.

FRONT

1

BACK

2

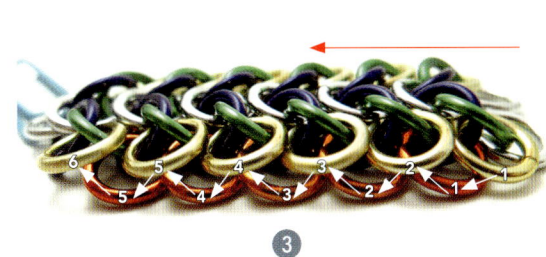

3

4

ELF Weaves 69

6. Thread 1 open (purple) jump ring through the (pink) jump ring just added and the last edge (orange #1) jump ring using a TE connection, and across to the next edge (gold #2) jump ring on the opposite side of the weave. Close the open jump ring (**Fig. 5**).

7. Thread 1 open (turquoise) jump ring through the (purple) jump ring just added and the last edge (gold #2) jump ring using a TE connection, and across to the next edge (orange #2) jump ring on the opposite side of the weave. Close the open jump ring (**Fig. 6**).

note: *Sample weaving paths are shown in the figures. Experiment to find the weaving path that is most comfortable for you.*

8. Continue weaving through the previously added jump ring, the last edge jump ring, and the next edge jump ring on the opposite edge of the weave in a zigzag pattern, until you have connected all of the edge jump rings.

Connect front and back edge jump rings on the right side of the weave.

9. Rotate the weave 180° to the right (do not flip over). Now, connect the edge jump rings in the same manner used on the left side, but in the opposite direction (**Figs. 7–9**).

Even the ends of your weave.

When widening a chain to make a sheet, you'll need to add or omit extra jump rings at the beginning or end of your piece to keep the ends even. The exact steps required will vary depending on the finished length of your base chain and the method of construction chosen. The directions that follow show one example of this and provide the basic idea behind the concept.

Take cues from adjacent rows on your base piece to determine when to add or omit a connection at the ends of your weave to keep them even.

10. At both the starting and finishing ends (left edge/back side of weave pictured—**Fig. 10**, starting end, and **Fig. 11**, finishing end, shown from the back side), thread 1 extra (orange) jump ring through the last 2 (gold/blue) jump rings on the edge to mirror the adjacent (green) jump ring, making the edge symmetrical.

Repeat on the right edge of the weave.

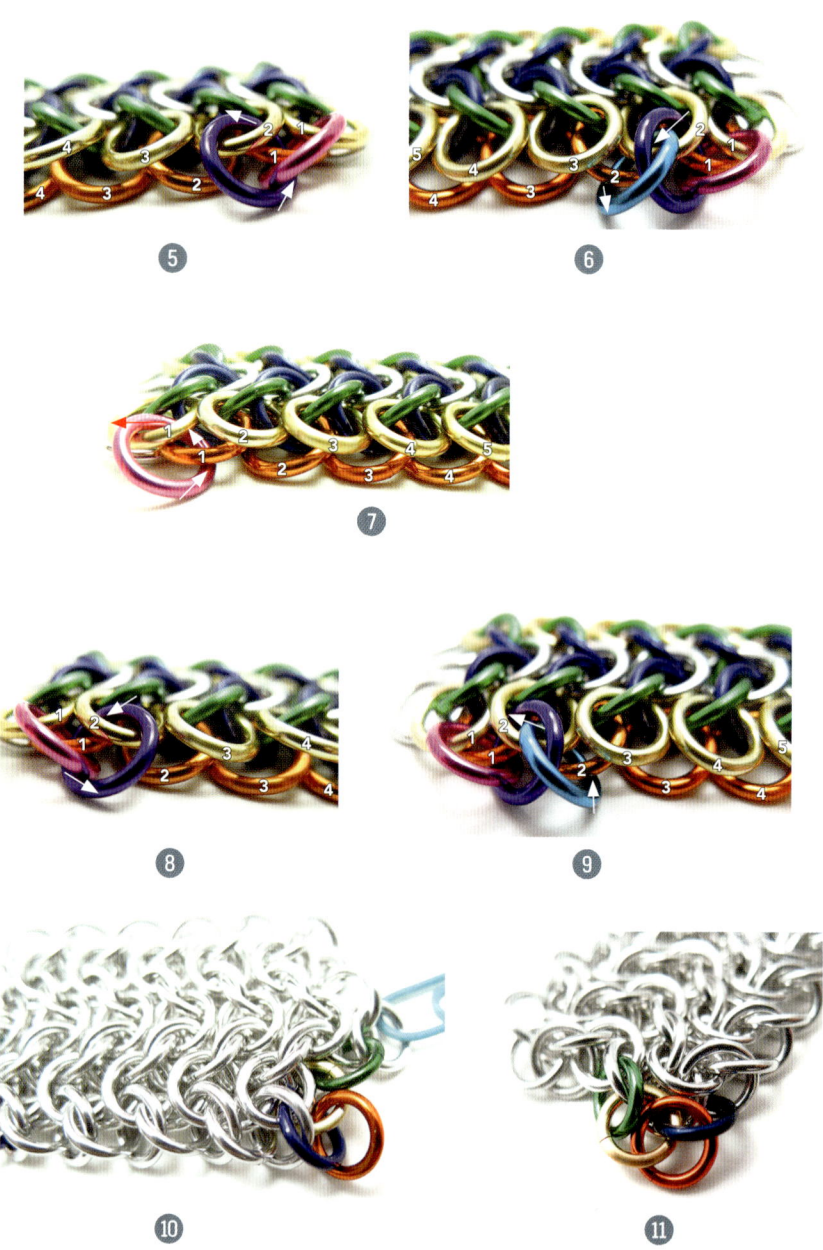

70   ADVANCED CHAIN MAILLE JEWELRY WORKSHOP

METHOD 3

In Method 2, you work on both edges of the weave to produce a sheet that is equal to 2 connected Elfweave chains (same result as Method 1). You work Method 3 almost exactly the same way as you would work Method 2. The difference between the two methods is that in Method 3, you work asymmetrically, on only one edge of the weave (either the right or the left, your choice). Therefore, you need to make two passes on that one edge (instead of one pass on two edges as in Method 2) to get the same result. If you made only one pass on one edge, it would be like connecting one and a half Elfweave chains. A pass consists of adding the edge jump rings (both front and back), then connecting those edge jump rings and ensuring even ends (see Method 2, Steps 1–10).

The important part for either method is that you change your working direction after each pass.

Therefore, when working Method 2, weaving on two edges with each edge requiring only one pass, we work each edge in the same direction. With Method 3, we are making two passes on one edge, so the second pass has to be worked in the opposite direction from the first pass.

If you wish to widen your sheet using either method, you need to change your working direction on each additional pass.

Make an Elfweave Chain

Follow the instructions to make an Elfweave chain (page 62).

Prepare Jump Rings

Open your jump rings for weaving.

1. Add edge jump rings to one edge (left or right) of the weave on both the front and back sides. Work *from the beginning end* of the chain (where the paper clip is) *to the finishing end* of the chain. For details, refer to Method 2, Steps 1–4.

2. Connect the front and back edge jump rings just added. Work *from the finishing end* of the chain *to the beginning end* of the chain (where the paper clip is). For details, refer to Method 2, Steps 5–9.

3. Even the ends if necessary, referring to Method 2, Step 10.

4. Repeat Step 1 on the same edge of the weave. This time, work *from the finishing end* of the chain *to the beginning end* of the chain (where the paper clip is).

5. Repeat Step 2 on the same edge of the weave. This time, work *from the beginning end* of the chain (where the paper clip is) *to the finishing end* of the chain.

6. Repeat Step 3 if necessary.

Continue in this manner until your weave reaches the desired width.

Tiffany Weave

Originally created by Louis K. Gorczyca, aka "chaine_maile" 2005–2013.

Jump Ring Chart

METAL	16 GAUGE ID	RPI	AR	18 GAUGE ID	RPI	AR
Sterling Silver (AWG)	5.5 mm	58	4.3	4.5 mm	68	4.4
Bright Aluminum (SWG)						
The Ring Lord	9/32"	42	4.7	7/32"	56	4.7
C&T Designs	9/32"	46	4.61	7/32"	56	4.65
Metal Designz	9/32"	42	4.5	13/64"	56	4.6

Tiffany, named after the woman who inspired the weave, is a variation of Elfsheet. The difference occurs when adding the horizontal/edge jump rings to the weave. These jump rings are woven through a side-leaning pair and the horizontal jump ring just below that pair. The rest of the construction is the same as Elfsheet. Tiffany uses all of the same "Elf landmarks" discussed in the Elfsheet section.

The weave itself is tighter than Elfsheet: therefore, a slightly larger aspect ratio is needed. The resulting piece is slightly thinner in width. The linkage pattern is quite intricate and beautiful. Use this weave when you want to make a real statement piece.

METHOD 1

Just as with Elfsheet, you can make Tiffany by connecting 2 Elfweave chains. As with Elfsheet, this method is the easiest to understand in terms of construction, but is the hardest to weave due to the tight space remaining for the joining row. There is little room for your pliers to grasp the connecting jump rings. Thus, your pliers may slip, which results in nicks and scratches on your jump rings or, worse, cuts and scratches on your hands! Therefore, I recommend using Method 2 or 3 instead.

Make 2 Equal-Length Elfweave Chains

Make 2 chains of equal length following the Elfweave instructions (page 62).

Prepare Jump Rings

Open your jump rings for weaving.

Connect 2 Elfweave Chains

1. Line up your 2 Elfweave chains side by side, same sides facing you.

note: *I find it easier to weave with the beginning ends of the chains facing south. In this orientation, the "lower" horizontal jump rings will actually be above their corresponding side-leaning jump ring pairs. Fig. 1 is positioned with the beginning ends facing north (to make it easy to identify the lower horizontal jump rings). You may find it helpful to turn your book or e-reader upside down to view the illustration in the orientation preferred for weaving. See weaving path (white arrow) in Fig. 1.*

2. Working from the beginning ends of the Elfweave chains, thread 1 open jump ring through the first pair of side-leaning jump rings and the horizontal jump ring just below the horizontal jump ring that the pair passes through (now called lower horizontal jump ring) on one Elfweave chain (see yellow dots in **Fig. 1**), and the corresponding pair of side-leaning jump rings and lower horizontal jump ring on the other Elfweave chain (see red dots in **Fig. 1**). Continue along the entire length of the chain. Close each open jump ring before weaving the next (fuchsia jump rings in **Fig. 1**).

3. Flip the weave over as you would a pancake and connect all of the corresponding pairs of side-leaning jump rings and lower horizontal jump rings on the back side.

To make your sheet even wider, you can continue to attach additional Elfweave chains as described above.

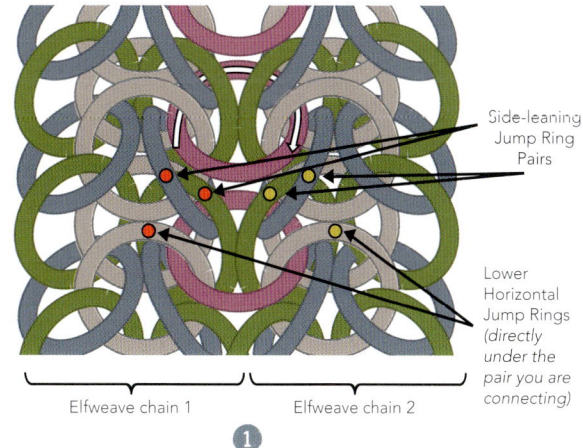

METHOD 2

Method 2 is a bit more difficult to understand than Method 1, but the actual weaving is much easier, making it my method of choice. For this method, we will be working symmetrically, first on the left edge and then on the right edge of the weave.

note: *References to the left and right edges of the weave are based on the perspective of holding the weave front side up and beginning end (where the paper clip is) pointing north.*

Make an Elfweave Chain

Follow the instructions to make an Elfweave chain (page 62).

Prepare Jump Rings

Open your jump rings for weaving.

Add Edge Jump Rings to the Front and Back Sides of the Weave

As with Elfsheet, position your Elfweave chain so that the beginning end points north and the front side is facing up. Work from the beginning end of the chain (where the paper clip is) to the finishing end of the chain on both the left and right edges of the weave, front and back.

This time, you will add the edge jump rings to the front and back sides of the weave by weaving through each pair of side-leaning (green/blue) jump rings *and* the pair's nearest lower horizontal (silver) jump ring. This is the only difference between Tiffany and Elfsheet.

1. One at a time, thread 1 open (yellow) jump ring through each pair of side-leaning (green/blue) jump rings and the pair's nearest lower horizontal (gray, marked with star) jump ring along the left and right edges of the Elfweave chain (see **Fig. 1**: arrow shows weaving path).

Close each open jump ring before proceeding to weave the next.

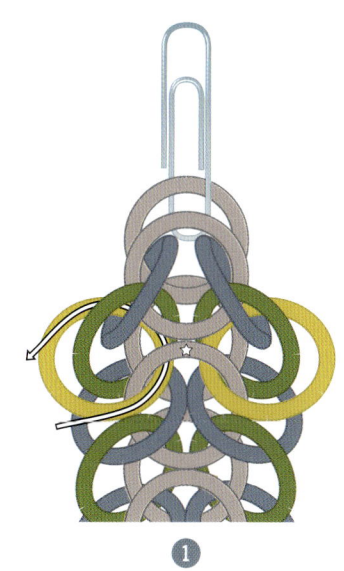

NOTE

When adding the edge jump rings, sometimes you may encounter unusual configurations of jump rings at the beginning or end of your piece depending on the finished length of your base chain and the method of construction you choose. Steps 2 and 4 show examples of this and illustrate some techniques used to keep the pattern even. Take cues from adjacent rows on your base piece to determine how to proceed.

Elf Weaves 73

2. At the finishing end of the chain, there is an extra pair of side-leaning (green/blue) jump rings on each edge of the weave. To make the pattern even, one at a time, thread 1 open (yellow) jump ring through each pair of side-leaning (green/blue) jump rings at the finishing end of the weave (**Fig. 2**). Close the first open jump ring before proceeding to weave the next. When finished, your piece should resemble **Fig. 3**.

3. Flip the weave over as you would a pancake. You are now working on the back side of the weave.

4. At the beginning end of the chain, there is an "incomplete pair" of side-leaning (blue only) jump rings on each edge of the weave. To make the pattern even, one at a time, thread an open (orange) jump ring through each "incomplete pair" of side-leaning (blue) jump rings at the beginning end of the weave and each incomplete pair's nearest lower horizontal (gray, marked with star) jump ring (see **Fig. 4**: arrow shows weaving path). Close the first open jump ring before proceeding to weave the next.

TIP

You can make Tiffany even wider by repeating Steps 1–7. Note that each time you repeat these steps, you must work in the opposite direction from the previous pass. Also, as you continue to widen your sheet, the steps for keeping the edges even may differ slightly from the previous pass. The exact steps required will vary depending on the finished length of your base chain and the method of construction chosen. There may be different configurations of jump rings at the ends of rows. Therefore, remember to take cues from pattern repeats in adjacent rows to determine when to add or omit a connection on the edges of sheet weaves to keep them uniform, similar to Step 10, Method 2, Elfsheet. As you widen, the weave tightens a bit, so you may need to adjust the aspect ratio, depending on the desired result.

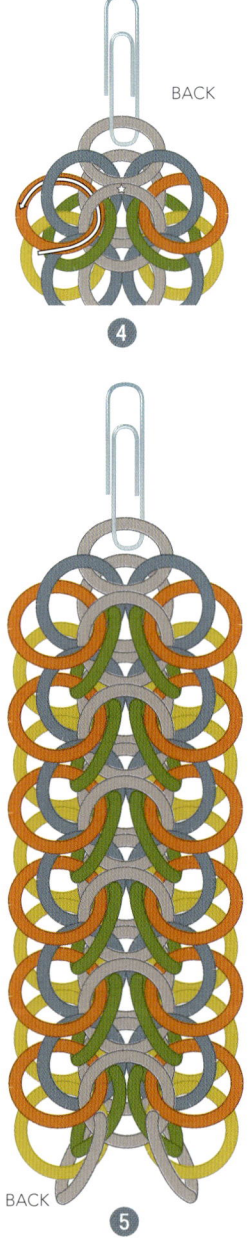

74 ADVANCED CHAIN MAILLE JEWELRY WORKSHOP

5. One at a time, thread an open (orange) jump ring through each pair of side-leaning (green/blue) jump rings and the pair's nearest lower horizontal (gray) jump ring along the left and right edges of the Elfweave chain. Close each open jump ring before proceeding to weave the next. When finished your piece should resemble **Fig. 5**.

6. Flip the weave back over so the front side is facing up.

You have now added all of the edge jump rings to the Elfweave chain.

Connect Front and Back Edge Jump Rings on Both Sides of the Weave

7. Work, as for Elfsheet, Method 2, Steps 5–9, from the finishing end of the chain to the beginning end of the chain (where the paper clip is) on both the left and right edges of the weave. When working on the left edge, you will work in a right-to-left direction and when working on the right edge, you will work in a left-to-right direction.

Except for the first open jump ring, each open jump ring you add will pass through 3 jump rings (the previous edge jump ring, the previously added open jump ring, and the next edge jump ring on the opposite side of the weave). You will begin with the edge jump ring that is the farthest edge jump ring from the beginning end and weave in a zigzag pattern.

METHOD 3

The difference between Tiffany Method 2 and Tiffany Method 3 is basically the same as the difference between Elfsheet Method 2 and Elfsheet Method 3. In Method 2, you are working symmetrically (on both the right and left edges of the weave). In Method 3, you are working asymmetrically (on only one edge of the weave). You may work on either the right or left edge— the choice is yours.

You will need to make two passes on that one edge (instead of one pass on two edges as in Method 2) to get the same result produced using Method 1. A pass consists of adding the edge jump rings (both front and back), and then connecting those edge jump rings and ensuring even ends.

The important part for either method is that you change your working direction after each pass. Therefore, when working Method 2, weaving on two edges with each edge requiring only one pass, we work each edge in the same direction. With Method 3, we are making two passes on one edge, so the second pass has to be worked in the opposite direction from the first pass.

If you wish to widen your sheet using either method, you need to change your working direction on each additional pass.

Make an Elfweave Chain

Follow the instructions to make an Elfweave chain (page 62).

Prepare Jump Rings

Open your jump rings for weaving.

1. Add edge jump rings to one edge (left or right) of the weave on both the front and back sides. Work *from the beginning end* of the chain (where the paper clip is) *to the finishing end* of the chain. For details, refer to Tiffany Method 2, Steps 1–6.

2. Connect the front and back edge jump rings just added. Work *from the finishing end* of the chain *to the beginning end* of the chain (where the paper clip is). For details, refer to Elfsheet Method 2, Steps 5–8.

3. Even the ends if necessary, similar to Elfsheet Method 2, Step 10.

4. Repeat Step 1 on the same edge of the weave. This time work *from the finishing end* of the chain *to the beginning end* of the chain (where the paper clip is).

5. Repeat Step 2 on the same edge of the weave. This time work *from the beginning end* of the chain (where the paper clip is) *to the finishing end* of the chain.

6. Repeat Step 3 if necessary.

Continue in this manner until your weave reaches the desired width.

Elf Weaves

SUPPLIES

- 2 sterling silver jump rings, 20g (AWG), 6 mm ID
- 2 sterling silver jump rings, 20g (AWG), 2.75 mm ID
- 2 sterling silver jump rings, 22g (AWG), 3.25 mm ID
- 206 sterling silver jump rings, 22g (AWG), 2.5 mm ID
- 1 pair of sterling silver ear wires
- 2 teal pressed-glass dagger beads, 5 × 16 mm

FINISHED LENGTH

- 1¼" (3.2 cm) not including ear wire

76 ADVANCED CHAIN MAILLE JEWELRY WORKSHOP

ELFWEAVE LOOP EARRINGS

Elfweave chain creates a lacy oval loop to make a perfect frame for a dagger bead in these dramatic drop earrings. The dagger beads add lively color and movement.

1. Create 2 Elfweave chains of equal length (make each 1-by-1 base chain 67 jump rings long). When weaving into the 1-by-1 chain to form Elfweave, be sure to thread an open jump ring through all complete mountain/valley pairs. Set aside when finished. (See Method 1 instructions, page 62.)

2. Create spacers by closing six 2.5 mm jump rings and set aside.

3. Thread 1 open 3.25 mm jump ring through each dagger bead and close.

4. Thread 1 open 2.75 mm jump ring through each of the closed jump rings just added to each bead in Step 3. Close the open jump rings and set beads aside.

5. To assemble 1 earring:

- Open a 6 mm jump ring and set aside.

- Remove the center jump ring at the beginning end of 1 Elfweave chain (the jump ring with the starting aid attached) and replace it with the 6 mm open jump ring. Do not close the large jump ring. Set piece aside.

- Close the jump ring that was removed from the Elfweave chain and place it on the 6 mm jump ring (this is the first spacer ring).

- Place 1 of the 2.5 mm spacer rings set aside in Step 2 on the 6 mm jump ring.

- Connect the dagger bead to the 6 mm jump ring by threading the 6 mm jump ring through the top jump ring connected to the bead.

- Add 2 more spacer rings onto the 6 mm jump ring.

- Thread the 6 mm jump ring through the 2 jump rings at the end of the Elfweave chain. (Be careful not to twist the chain.)

- Connect 1 ear wire to the 6 mm jump ring.

- Close the 6 mm jump ring.

6. Repeat Step 5 to assemble second earring.

OMBRE ELFSHEET RING

This intricate ring band has a metallic color fade that is on trend. To make it, you simply close an Elfweave chain from end to end, then expand it into Elfsheet. The asymmetrical weaving method was chosen for this project to make it easy to develop the color fade. You can also choose to weave this ring symmetrically if you prefer, but you'll have to make adjustments to the colors used to get the correct color fade.

1. Make two 1-by-1 chains using 33 silver jump rings each.

2. Thread 1 silver jump ring through the ends of one chain creating a closed circle. Repeat with the other chain. Each closed chain consists of 34* jump rings.

3. Holding the 2 closed 1-by-1 chains next to each other, position each to make mountain and valley pairs, as for Elfweave (see Elfweave Method 1, page 62).

4. Thread 34 open silver jump rings through these mountain/valley pairs, in pattern, around the length of the chains to create a closed silver Elfweave chain. The final jump ring can be very tricky to weave in!

*If you want to adjust the size, make sure that your two 1-by-1 chains each contain an odd number of jump rings. When closed to form a circle, each chain will contain an even number of jump rings.

5. Now, follow the instructions for asymmetrical Elfsheet, Method 3 (page 71). Alternate weaving open silver and gold-filled jump rings (17 total) through each pair of side-leaning jump rings along your chosen edge of the Elfweave chain on the outside of the closed band. Close each open jump ring before proceeding to thread the next.

6. Repeat Step 5 along the same edge of the Elfweave chain on the inside of the closed band.

SUPPLIES
- 119 sterling silver jump rings, 22g (AWG), 2.625 mm ID
- 119 gold-filled jump rings, 22g (AWG), 2.625 mm ID

FINISHED SIZE
- Approximate Woman's U.S. Ring Size = a tight 7

TIP
If you're having trouble threading that last jump ring, try this: Thread through only the first 3 jump rings of the last mountain/valley pairs. Then, open the threading jump ring in the opposite direction and pick up the fourth jump ring. Once the open jump ring has passed through all four mountain/valley pair jump rings, close it and you're done!

7. Now, you will connect the jump rings added in Steps 5 and 6 in a manner similar to the instructions for asymmetrical Elfsheet, Method 3 (page 71), using 34 gold-filled jump rings. Except for the first and last open jump rings, each open jump ring you add will pass through 3 jump rings (the previous edge jump ring, the previously added open jump ring, and the next edge jump ring on the opposite side of the band). You will weave in a zigzag pattern as shown in Elfsheet instructions. Begin anywhere on the edge of the band. Notice the grain of the weave and work in the direction from the finishing point to the starting point.

Connect front and back edge jump rings to the edge of the band.

- Thread 1 open jump ring through 2 edge jump rings that are across from each other on the inside and outside of the band and then close it.

- Thread 1 open jump ring through the jump ring just added and the last edge jump ring using a TE connection, and across to the next edge jump ring on the opposite side of the band. Close the open jump ring.

Continue weaving through the previously added jump ring, the last edge jump ring, and the next edge jump ring on the opposite side of the band in a zigzag pattern, until you have used 33 gold-filled jump rings.

Thread the last open gold-filled jump rings through the last 4 jump rings on the closed band (the jump ring just added, the last edge jump ring using a TE connection, and across to the next edge jump ring and the first open jump ring added). This can be a bit tricky.

8. Repeat Step 5 with 17 gold-filled jump rings.

9. Repeat Step 6 with 17 gold-filled jump rings.

10. Repeat Step 7 with 34 gold-filled jump rings. Notice the grain of the weave and work in the direction from the starting point to the finishing point (opposite working direction from Step 7).

DESIGN NOTE

When working Steps 5 and 6, you will alternate silver and gold-filled jump rings to create a color blend, producing the ombre fade. When the number of jump rings in your initial 1-by-1 chain divides by 2 to result in an odd number (as in this project: 34 ÷ 2 = 17), you will end up having 2 same-color jump rings side by side at the beginning/ending point. If you find this bothersome, make sure the number of jump rings in your initial 1-by-1 chain divides by 2 to produce an even result. This will, however, change the ring size, so you may need to choose between perfectly alternating colors or a ring that fits.

HYBRID WEAVES

Hybrid weaves combine features from more than one weave group or family. The four weaves introduced in this chapter combine characteristics from the European and Persian weave families. Each of the weaves presented begins with a base piece of the European 4-in-1 weave. Additional jump rings are added to the edges of the base using Persian around-the-eye (AE) connections. The edges are then closed in the same manner used to close a sheet of European 4-in-1 into round maille to complete the weaves (a technique introduced in *Chain Maille Jewelry Workshop*).

Interwoven 4-1
Originally created by Jeffrey W. Olin (known online as Phong).

Jump Ring Chart

METAL	16 GAUGE ID	RPI	AR	18 GAUGE ID	RPI	AR
Sterling Silver (AWG)	5.5 mm	27	4.3	4.5 mm	36	4.4
Bright Aluminum (SWG)						
The Ring Lord	9/32"	24	4.7	7/32"	33	4.7
C&T Designs	9/32"	27	4.61	13/64"	36	4.25
Metal Designz	9/32"	27	4.5	7/32"	33	5.1

The name Interwoven 4-1 is derived from the fact that this weave is a 4-in-1 weave that is essentially 2 strips of European 4-in-1 (E41) woven together, one on top of the other. I will present two methods below: the simple weaving method, where the weaving is done one jump ring at a time, and the speed weaving method, using some preclosed jump rings. When I construct this weave, I like to speed-weave the E41 base piece and then complete the weave using the simple method, if possible. The Interwoven Stretch Cuff project (page 100) requires speed weaving, as the rubber O-rings cannot be opened.

METHOD 1: SIMPLE WEAVE (one jump ring at a time)

Prepare Jump Rings
For the European 4-in-1 base piece, prepare jump rings as directed in the Review Material section (page 20). Open the remaining jump rings for weaving Interwoven 4-1.

Build the E41 Base
Make your E41 base piece (see instructions in Review Material, page 20) longer than you think you need it. As you weave into the base piece to make Interwoven 4-1, it will reduce by about 10 percent of the original length. Your results may vary slightly: therefore, some experimentation will be required to arrive at the appropriate length. Orient your E41 base piece as in **Fig. 1**.

Weave into E41 Base to Make Interwoven 4-1
Do not accidentally flip the weave over while working on it. Although at first glance the back looks very much like the front, the orientation of the grain is different.

Start Interwoven.

1. Thread 1 open (fuchsia) jump ring through edge jump rings 1 and 2 on the bottom edge of the E41 base piece using an around-the-eye (AE) connection (**Fig. 2**). Close the open jump ring.

2. Thread 1 open (green) jump ring through edge jump rings 2 and 3 on the bottom edge of the E41 base piece using an AE connection (**Fig. 3**). Close the open jump ring. The (green) jump ring just added overlaps in front of the last (fuchsia) jump ring added.

82 ADVANCED CHAIN MAILLE JEWELRY WORKSHOP

3. Thread 1 open (turquoise) jump ring through edge jump rings 1 and 2, on the top edge of the E41 base piece using an AE connection (**Fig. 4**). Close the open jump ring.

4. Thread 1 open (orange) jump ring through edge jump rings 2 and 3 on the top edge of the E41 base piece using an AE connection (**Fig. 5**). Close the open jump ring. The (orange) jump ring just added sits above the last (turquoise) jump ring added.

5. Thread 1 open (yellow) jump ring through the 4 AE (fuchsia/green/turquoise/orange) jump rings just added. Thread down into the 2 bottom-edge AE (fuchsia/green) jump rings from above using a TE connection, then thread up through the 2 top-edge AE (turquoise/orange) jump rings from below using a TE connection (see weaving path, **Fig. 6**). Close the open jump ring.

Weave Interwoven pattern.

> **NOTE**
>
> You can also construct Interwoven 4-1 by first weaving in all of the top- and bottom-edge jump rings on the E41 strip using AE connections and then connecting them all up the middle with open jump rings. I find that adding all the edge jump rings first can cause the weave to look a bit jumbled, which can make weaving the connecting center rings more difficult. Try both methods to see which you prefer.

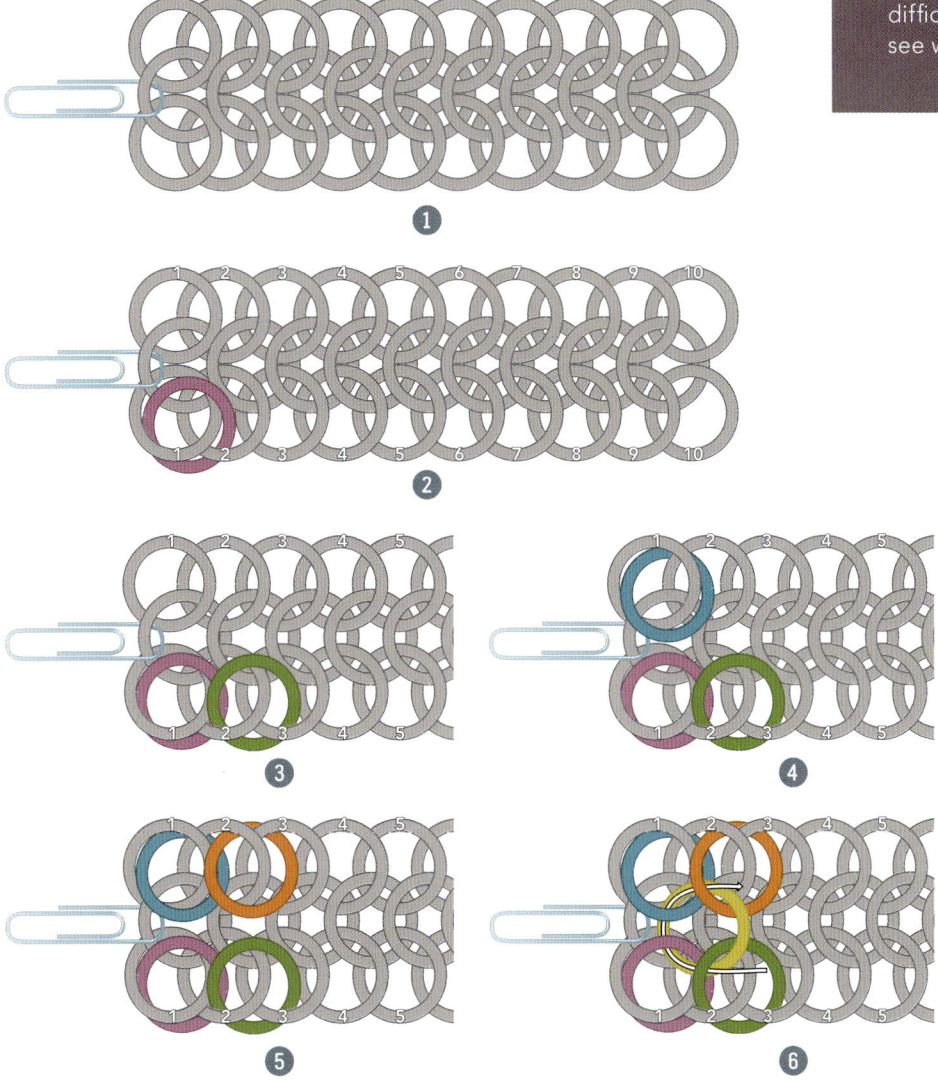

Hybrid Weaves

6. Working on the bottom edge of the weave, thread 1 open (blue) jump ring through edge jump rings 3 and 4 on the E41 base piece using an AE connection (**Fig. 7**). Close the open jump ring. The (blue) jump ring just added overlaps in front of the previous edge (green) jump ring added on the bottom edge.

7. Working on the top edge of the weave, thread 1 open (purple) jump ring through edge jump rings 3 and 4 on the E41 base piece using an AE connection (**Fig. 8**). Close the open jump ring. The (purple) jump ring just added sits above the previous edge (orange) jump ring added on the top edge.

8. Thread 1 open (red) jump ring through the last 4 AE (blue/green/orange/purple) jump rings added. Thread down into the last 2 bottom-edge AE (green/blue) jump rings added from above using a TE connection, then thread up through the last 2 top-edge AE (orange/purple) jump rings added from below using a TE connection (see weaving path, **Fig. 9**). Close the open jump ring.

Continue in this manner until you reach the end of your piece (**Fig. 10**).

TIP

In **Fig. 10**, you'll notice that I added a small colored jump ring to the final piece to indicate the front side. This small jump ring, together with the paper clip, helps me to keep my piece in proper orientation while I work. It will be removed when my work is done. Other items such as a small piece of wire, a safety pin, a twist tie, or some string can be used as an indicator as well.

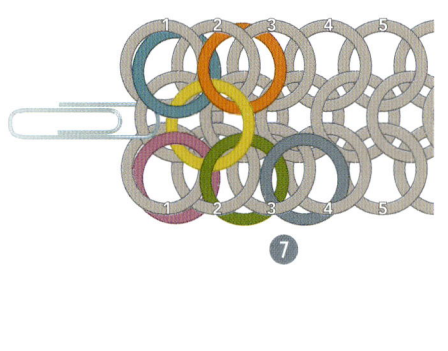

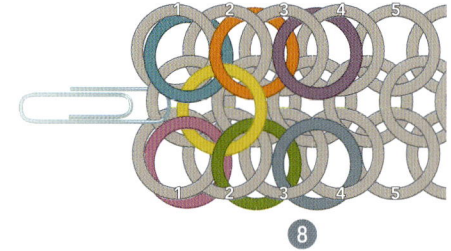

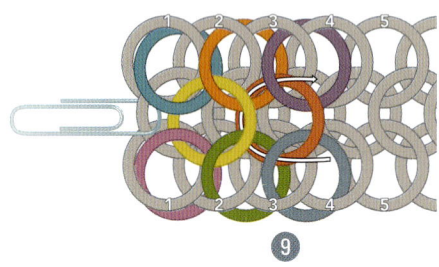

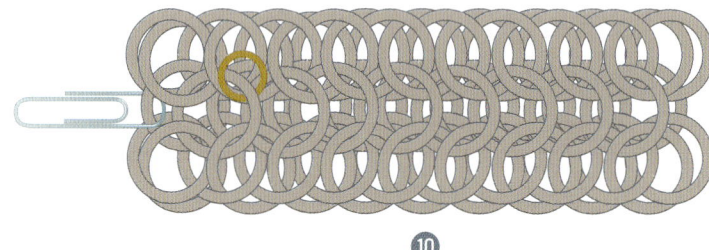

METHOD 2: SPEED WEAVE

Prepare Jump Rings

E41 Jump Rings: Close two-thirds of your jump rings and open the remaining third of your jump rings.

Remaining Jump Rings for Interwoven: Close one-third of your jump rings and open the remaining two-thirds of your jump rings.

Build the E41 Base

Make your E41 base piece (see instructions in Review Material, page 20) longer than you think you need it. As you weave into the base piece to make Interwoven 4-1, it will reduce by about 10 percent of its original length. Your results may vary slightly: therefore, some experimentation will be required to arrive at the appropriate length.

Weave into E41 Base to Make Interwoven 4-1

Do not accidentally flip the weave over while working on it. Although at first glance the back looks very much like the front, the orientation of the grain is different.

Start Interwoven.

1. Thread 1 open (fuchsia) jump ring through 1 closed (yellow) jump ring. Do not close the open jump ring (**Fig. 1**).

2. Now, thread that open (fuchsia) jump ring through edge jump rings 2 and then 1 on the bottom edge of the E41 base piece using an AE connection. Close the open (fuchsia) jump ring and arrange both jump rings as in **Fig. 2**.

3. Working on the top edge of the weave, thread 1 open (turquoise) jump ring up through edge jump ring 2 from underneath, then up through the last closed (yellow) jump ring added from underneath, and finally down through edge jump ring 1 on the E41 base piece (**Fig. 3**). Close the open jump ring.

Weave Interwoven pattern.

4. Thread 1 open (green) jump ring through 1 closed (orange) jump ring. Do not close the open jump ring (**Fig 4**).

5. Now, working on the bottom edge of the weave, thread the open (green) jump ring through edge jump rings 3 and then 2 on the E41 base piece using an AE connection and down through the closed (yellow) jump ring previously added from above. Close the open (green) jump ring and arrange the jump rings just added as in **Fig. 5**.

6. Working on the top edge of the weave, thread 1 open (pale blue) jump ring up through edge jump ring 3 from underneath then up through the last 2 closed (yellow/orange) jump rings added from underneath and finally down through edge jump ring 2 on the E41 base piece. Close the open jump ring (**Fig. 6**).

Continue in this manner (repeating Steps 4–6) until you reach the end of your piece.

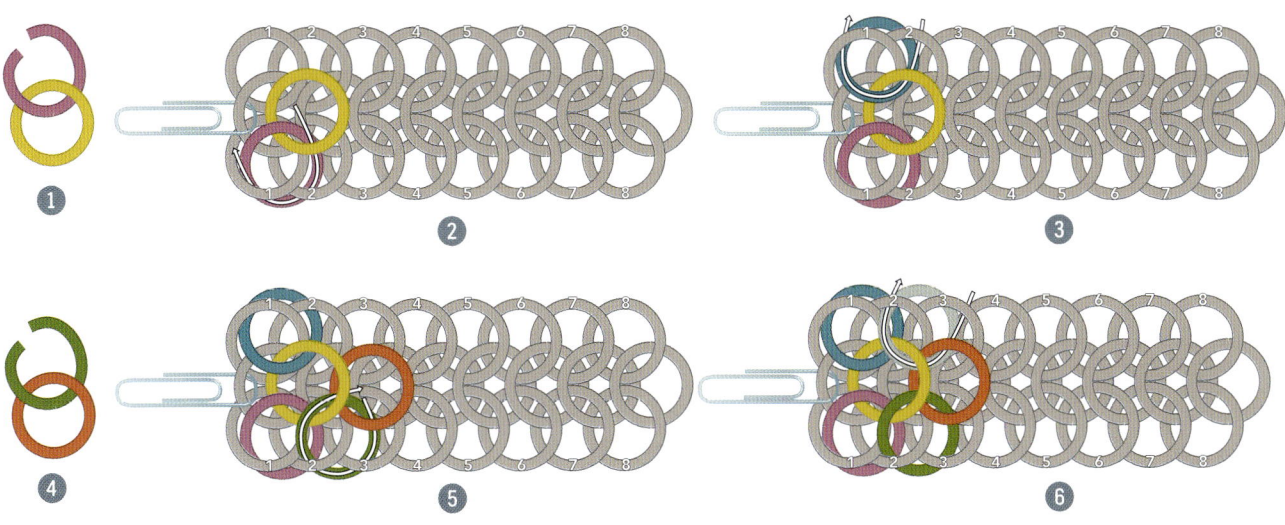

Hybrid Weaves

Interwoven Sheet

Originally created by Jeffrey W. Olin (known online as Phong).

Jump Ring Chart

METAL	16 GAUGE ID	16 GAUGE RPI	16 GAUGE AR	18 GAUGE ID	18 GAUGE RPI	18 GAUGE AR
Sterling Silver (AWG)	6 mm	58	4.7	4.75 mm	68	4.6
Bright Aluminum (SWG)						
The Ring Lord	5/32"	59	4.7	7/32"	73	4.7
C&T Designs	5/32"	62	4.61	7/32"	76	4.65
Metal Designz	5/32"	62	4.5	7/32"	76	5.1

Interwoven Sheet is a dense and flexible sheet weave. Because there is more than one way to make Interwoven Sheet, I will provide instructions for three methods of construction. Method 1 shows how to construct the sheet by joining 2 Interwoven 4-1 chains. Method 2 shows how to symmetrically expand an Interwoven 4-1 chain into Interwoven Sheet. And finally, Method 3 shows how to expand an Interwoven 4-1 chain asymmetrically.

METHOD 1

In Method 1, you will make 2 Interwoven 4-1 chains and connect them. This is the simplest method to use, especially if your Interwoven 4-1 chain is a bit on the loose side. The slack in the chain will allow your pliers to fit into the weave in order to add the connecting jump rings. However, if your Interwoven 4-1 chain is a bit tight, you may find Method 2 or 3 easier, even though the actual weaving pattern is more complex.

Make 2 Equal-Length Interwoven 4-1 Chains

Make 2 chains of equal length following the Interwoven 4-1 instructions (page 82). Your chains should resemble the chain in **Fig. 1**.

Prepare Jump Rings

Open your jump rings for weaving.

Connect 2 Interwoven 4-1 Chains

To join the 2 chains, you will use open jump rings to connect pairs of side (orange) jump rings (see **Fig. 1**) on one chain with the corresponding 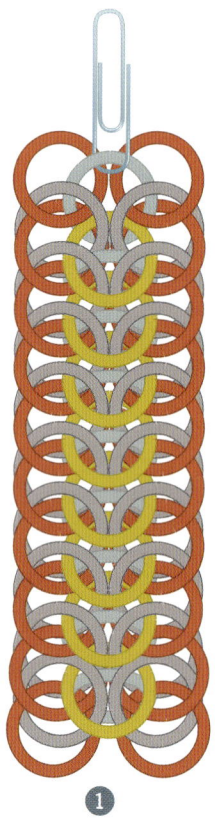 pair of side jump rings on the other chain—each open jump ring will pass through 4 side jump rings (2 on each chain).

1. Line up your 2 Interwoven 4-1 chains side by side, front sides facing you, beginning end pointing north.

86 ADVANCED CHAIN MAILLE JEWELRY WORKSHOP

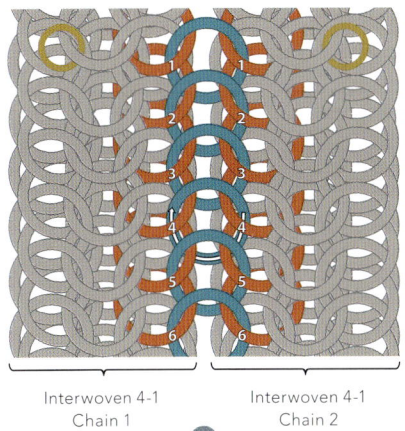

Interwoven 4-1 Chain 1   Interwoven 4-1 Chain 2

2

2. Working from the beginning ends of the Interwoven 4-1 chains, thread 1 open (turquoise) jump ring through side (orange) jump rings 1 and 2 on one Interwoven 4-1 chain (TE connection) and the corresponding pair of side jump rings on the other Interwoven 4-1 chain (TE connection). Close the open jump ring (see sample weaving path in **Fig. 2**).

3. Thread 1 open (turquoise) jump ring through side (orange) jump rings 2 and 3 on one Interwoven 4-1 chain (TE connection) and the corresponding pair of side jump rings on the other Interwoven 4-1 chain (TE connection). Close the open jump ring.

Continue adding jump rings in this manner until you reach the end of your chains.

Flip the weave over as you would a pancake and connect all of the corresponding pairs of side jump rings on the back side in the same manner.

To make a wide piece, you can connect several Interwoven 4-1 chains.

METHOD 2

Method 2 is more difficult to understand than Method 1, but it is worth your effort because it can be very helpful when weaving in micro-scale. For this method we will work symmetrically, first on the left edge*, then on the right edge* of the weave.

*References to the left and right edges of the weave are based on the perspective of holding the weave front side facing up and beginning end (where the paper clip is) pointing north.

Make an Interwoven 4-1 Chain

Follow the instructions to make an Interwoven 4-1 chain (page 82).

Prepare Jump Rings

Open your jump rings for weaving.

Add 3 Rows of Edge Jump Rings to the Front and Back Sides of the Weave

Position your Interwoven 4-1 chain so that the front side is facing up. Work from the beginning end of the chain (where the paper clip is) to the finishing end of the chain on both the left and right edges of the weave, front and back.

When adding each row of edge jump rings to keep the ends even, it will sometimes be necessary to add or omit jump rings at the beginning or end of your Interwoven 4-1 chain. The exact steps required will vary depending on the finished length of your Interwoven 4-1 chain. The following directions show one example of this and illustrate the basic idea behind the concept. To determine when to add or omit a connection at the ends of your weave to keep your ends even, take cues from adjacent rows on your base piece.

First Row of Edge Jump Rings on Front of Weave (**Fig. 1**).

1. Thread 1 open (yellow) jump ring through side (orange) jump rings 1 and 2 on one edge of the Interwoven 4-1 chain (TE connection). Close the open jump ring.

2. Thread 1 open (yellow) jump ring through side (red) jump rings 2 and 3 on the same edge of the Interwoven 4-1 chain (TE connection). Close the open jump ring.

3. Continue in this manner until you've added edge jump rings through all the pairs of side jump rings on one edge on the front side of the chain.

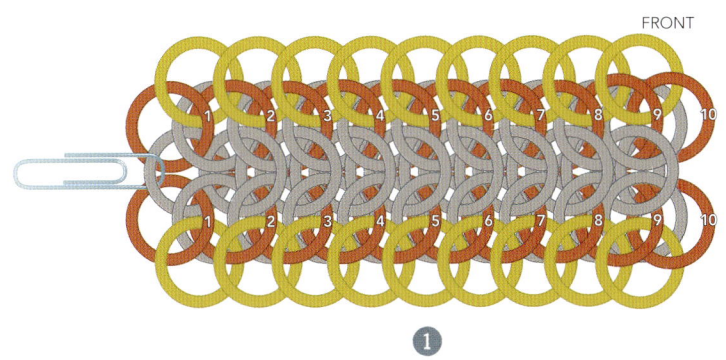

FRONT

1

Hybrid Weaves **87**

4. Repeat Steps 1–3 on the opposite edge of the front of the chain. Your piece should resemble **Fig. 1**.

5. Flip the weave over as you would a pancake.

Second Row of Edge Jump Rings on Back of Weave (see **Fig. 3**).

6. Thread 1 open (orange) jump ring through side (fuchsia) jump rings 1 and 2 on one edge of the Interwoven 4-1 chain (TE connection). Close the open jump ring.

7. Thread 1 open (orange) jump ring through side (fuchsia) jump rings 2 and 3 on the same edge of the Interwoven 4-1 chain (TE connection). Close the open jump ring.

8. Continue in this manner until you've added edge jump rings through all the pairs of side jump rings on one edge of the back side of the chain.

9. Repeat Steps 6–8 on the opposite edge of the back of the chain.

10. To even the piece, you may need to weave additional (orange) jump rings through the last side (fuchsia) jump rings on the left and right edges of the chain (as in **Fig. 2**). Your completed piece should resemble **Fig. 3**.

11. Flip the weave over as you would a pancake.

Third Row of Edge Jump Rings on Front of Weave (see **Fig. 6**).

12. Thread 1 open (fuchsia) jump ring through previously added edge (yellow) jump rings 1 and 2, on one edge of the Interwoven 4-1 chain (TE connection). Close the open jump ring.

13. Thread 1 open (fuchsia) jump ring through previously added edge (yellow) jump rings 2 and 3, on the same edge of the Interwoven 4-1 chain (TE connection). Close the open jump ring.

14. Continue in this manner until you've added edge jump rings through all pairs of previously added edge jump rings on one edge of the front side of the chain.

15. Repeat Steps 12–14 on the opposite edge of the front of the chain.

16. To even the piece, you may need to weave additional (fuchsia) jump rings through the first and last edge (yellow) jump rings on the left and right edges of the chain (as in **Fig. 4**, finishing end, and **Fig. 5**, beginning end). Your completed piece should resemble **Fig. 6**.

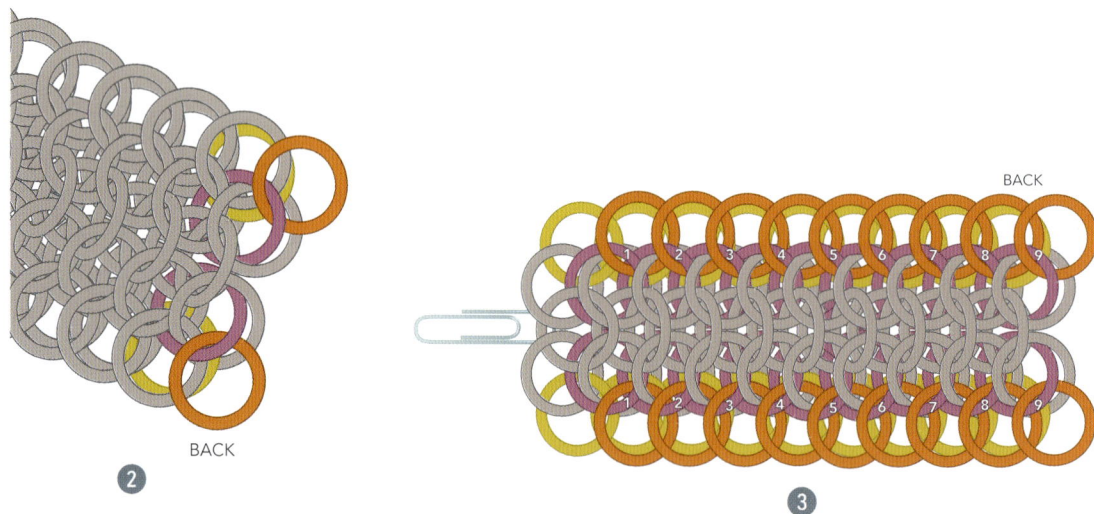

88 ADVANCED CHAIN MAILLE JEWELRY WORKSHOP

Connect Front- and Back-Edge Jump Rings on Both Sides of the Weave

Working with the back side of the weave facing up, you will use 1 open jump ring to connect sets of 4 edge jump rings—2 on the front of the piece and 2 on the back—along the right and left edges of the piece.

You will weave from the finishing end of the chain to the beginning end of the chain (where the paper clip is) on both the right and left edges of the weave. This direction is important.

When working in this direction, each connecting jump ring added sits in front of the previously added connecting jump ring. If you were to work in the opposite direction (from the beginning end of the chain to the finishing end), each new connecting jump ring would have to connect 4 edge jump rings and be tucked behind the previously added connecting jump ring, which is a bit more difficult to accomplish.

Hold the piece so that the front-edge (fuchsia) jump rings are on the bottom.

Depending on the length of your initial Interwoven 4-1 chain and how you evened the ends, this step may also require you to connect fewer than 4 jump rings at either or both ends to keep them even. The exact steps required will vary for each individual piece. **Figures 9 and 12** show one example of this and illustrate the basic idea behind the concept. To determine how many jump rings to connect at the ends of your weave to keep your edges even, take cues from adjacent rows on your base piece.

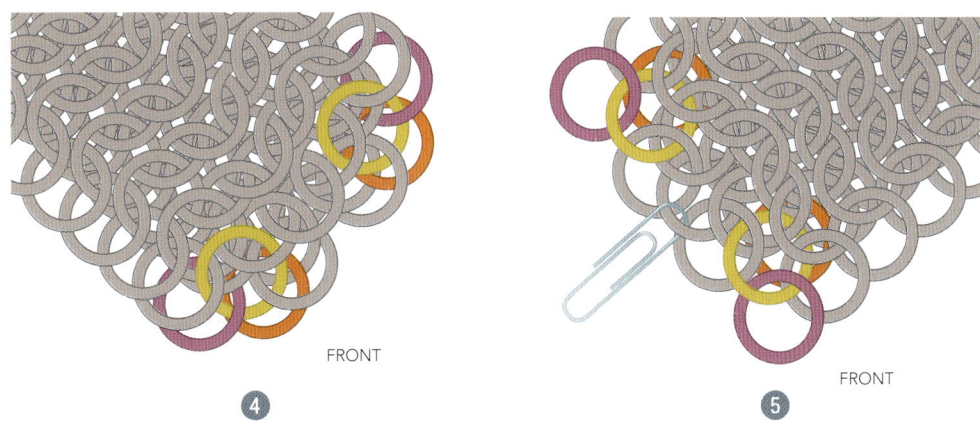

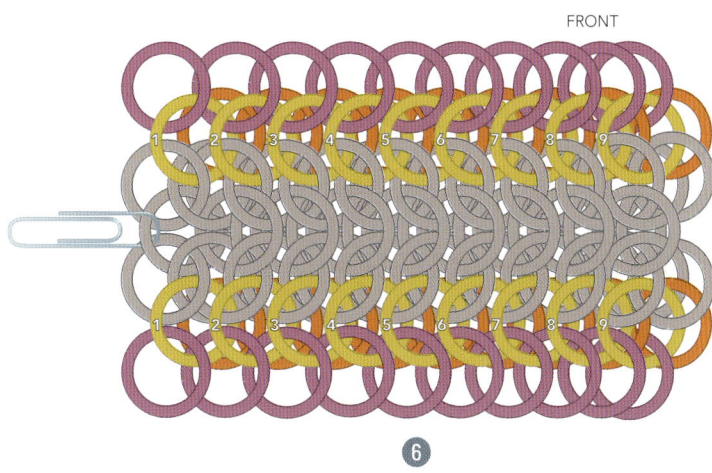

Hybrid Weaves

NOTES

The front-edge (fuchsia) jump rings are connected using an AE connection and the back-edge (orange) jump rings are connected using a TE connection.

In this example, the last set of 4 edge jump rings is "incomplete"—the last back-edge (orange) jump ring is "missing" (see **Figs. 9 and 12**). To even the end, thread 1 open (yellow) jump ring through the second front-edge (fuchsia) jump ring from the end, the last back-edge (orange) jump ring, and then the last front-edge (fuchsia) jump ring to complete the side.

Connect Sets of Front- and Back-Edge Jump Rings on the Left Edge of the Weave

17. Following the path in **Fig. 7**, thread 1 open (green) jump ring through the front-edge (fuchsia) jump ring 1, through back-edge (orange) jump rings 1 and 2, and then through front-edge (fuchsia) jump ring 2. Close the open jump ring.

18. Following the path in **Fig. 8**, thread 1 open (blue) jump ring through front-edge (fuchsia) jump ring 2, through back-edge (orange) jump rings 2 and 3, and then through front-edge (fuchsia) jump ring 3. Close the open jump ring.

19. Continue weaving in this manner until you have connected all of front and back-edge jump rings.

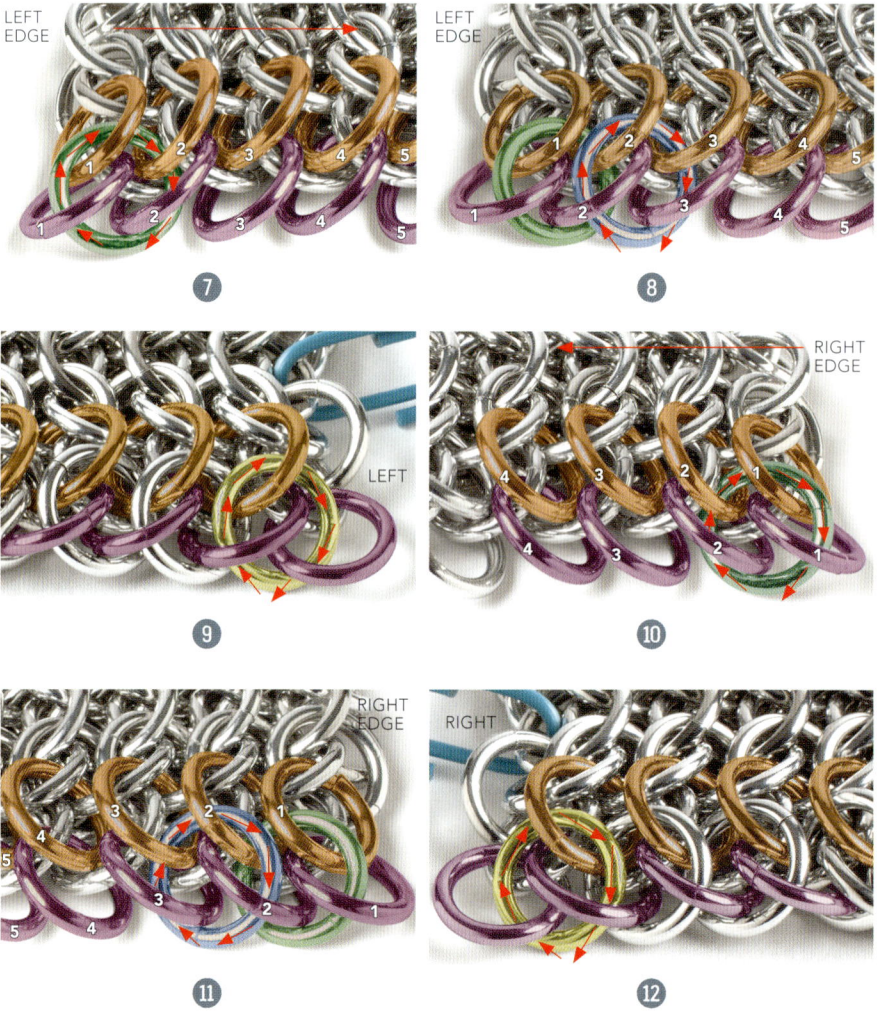

90 ADVANCED CHAIN MAILLE JEWELRY WORKSHOP

Connect Sets of Front- and Back-Edge Jump Rings on the Right Edge of the Weave

20. Connect the edge jump rings on the right edge of the weave in a manner similar to that used on the left edge, but work in the opposite direction. (See **Figs. 10** and **11** for weaving path and direction.)

METHOD 3

In Method 2, you work on both edges of the weave to produce a sheet that is equal to 2 connected Interwoven 4-1 chains (same result as Method 1). You work Method 3 almost exactly the same way as you would work Method 2. The difference between the two methods is that in Method 3, you work asymmetrically, on only one edge of the weave (either the right or the left, your choice). Therefore, you need to make two passes on that one edge (instead of one pass on two edges as in Method 2) to get the same result. If you made only one pass on one edge, it would be like connecting one and a half Interwoven 4-1 chains. A pass consists of adding all 3 rows of edge jump rings (both front and back) and then connecting those edge jump rings and ensuring even ends (see Method 2).

The important part for either method is that you change your working direction after each pass. Therefore, when working Method 2, weaving on two edges with each edge requiring only one pass, we work each edge in the same direction. With Method 3, we are making two passes on one edge, so the second pass has to be worked in the opposite direction from the first pass.

If you wish to widen your sheet using either method, you need to change your working direction on each additional pass.

Make an Interwoven 4-1 Chain

Follow the instructions to make an Interwoven 4-1 chain (page 82).

Prepare Jump Rings

Open your jump rings for weaving.

Add 3 Rows of Edge Jump Rings to the Front and Back Sides of the Weave

1. Add 3 rows of edge jump rings to one edge (left or right) of the weave on both the front and back sides. Work *from the beginning end* of the chain (where the paper clip is) *to the finishing end* of the chain. For details, refer to Method 2, Steps 1–16, omitting the steps to repeat on the opposite edge of the chain.

Connect Front- and Back-Edge Jump Rings on Your Chosen Edge of the Weave

2. Connect the front- and back-edge jump rings just added. Work *from the finishing end* of the chain *to the beginning end* of the chain (where the paper clip is). For details, refer to Method 2, Steps 17–19.

3. Even the ends if necessary: refer to Method 2, **Figs. 9 and 12**.

Repeat Step 1

4. Repeat Step 1 on the same edge of the weave. This time, work *from the finishing end* of the chain *to the beginning end* of the chain (where the paper clip is).

TIP

You can widen your Interwoven Sheet weave by repeating Steps 1–20. Note that each time you add 3 edge rows and a connecting row, you must work in the opposite direction from the previous pass. Also, as you continue to widen your sheet, the steps for keeping the edges even will differ slightly from the previous pass. There may be different configurations of "incomplete sets" at the ends of rows, or you may need to add or omit jump rings at the ends of rows. To determine when to add or omit a connection on the ends of sheet weaves to keep them uniform, remember to take cues from pattern repeats in adjacent rows.

Repeat Step 2

5. Repeat Step 2 on the same edge of the weave. This time, work *from the beginning end* of the chain (where the paper clip is) *to the finishing end* of the chain.

6. Repeat Step 3 if necessary.

Continue in this manner until your weave reaches the desired width.

Dragonback Weave

Originally created by Milorad Milenovici (known online as Fenrir).

Jump Ring Chart

	16 GAUGE			18 GAUGE		
METAL	ID	RPI	AR	ID	RPI	AR
Sterling Silver (AWG)	6.5 mm	36	5.0	5 mm	42	4.9
Bright Aluminum (SWG)						
The Ring Lord	5/16"	27	5.2	7/32"	39	4.7
C&T Designs	19/64"	33	5.0	15/64"	39	4.90
Metal Designz	5/16"	27	5.4	7/32"	39	5.1

The name "Dragonback" reflects the profile of the weave whose ridged side evokes the sinuous spine of a dragon. I like to wear this weave with the ridge facing out to show off the "dragon's backbone." The ridge side of this weave flexes differently from the flat side. If you make the weave tight, it flexes more on the ridge side, meaning that your piece will bend with the ridge side in and the flat side out. Therefore, if you want to wear it with the ridge side out, you may need to experiment with the jump rings you plan to use to get the look you desire.

Both Dragonback and Persian Dragonscale are European/Persian hybrid weaves. The construction of both weaves is identical until the final step of closing the weave. The Dragonback weave produces a chain that is flat with one smooth side and one ridged side. Persian Dragonscale is also called Oval Chain because the chain has an oval profile. Both sides of the oval-shaped chain are smooth.

Start both weaves either by using a base piece of European 4-in-1 (E41) or by using 2 mirror-image Half Persian 3-in-1 (HP31) chains of equal length. Both methods are described in the text that follows. I prefer the E41 method, while some of my students prefer the other. Try both to see what works best for you.

METHOD 1

Start with an E41 base.

Prepare Jump Rings

E41 jump rings:

Prepare your jump rings for E41 as directed in the Review Material, page 20. Make your base E41 piece longer than you think you need it. As you weave into the base piece to make Dragonback, it will reduce by about one-third of its original length. Your results may vary: therefore, some experimentation will be required to arrive at the appropriate length.

Remaining jump rings:

Open all remaining jump rings.

Build the E41 Base

Make your E41 base piece (see instructions in Review Material, page 20) and orient it as in **Fig. 1**. The center row of the E41 base piece will become the ridge (dragon's backbone). You may wish to weave this row with jump rings of a contrasting color or metal to highlight this feature of the weave.

Weave a Half Persian 3-in-1 (HP31) Edge

Add an HP31 edge to the top edge of the piece (see instructions in Review Material, page 26) (**Figs. 2**–**4**).

Add Mirror-Image HP31 Edge

First, rotate the piece 180°. Now, add a mirror-image HP31 edge to the other side of the piece (see instructions in Review Material, page 28) (**Figs. 5**–**7**).

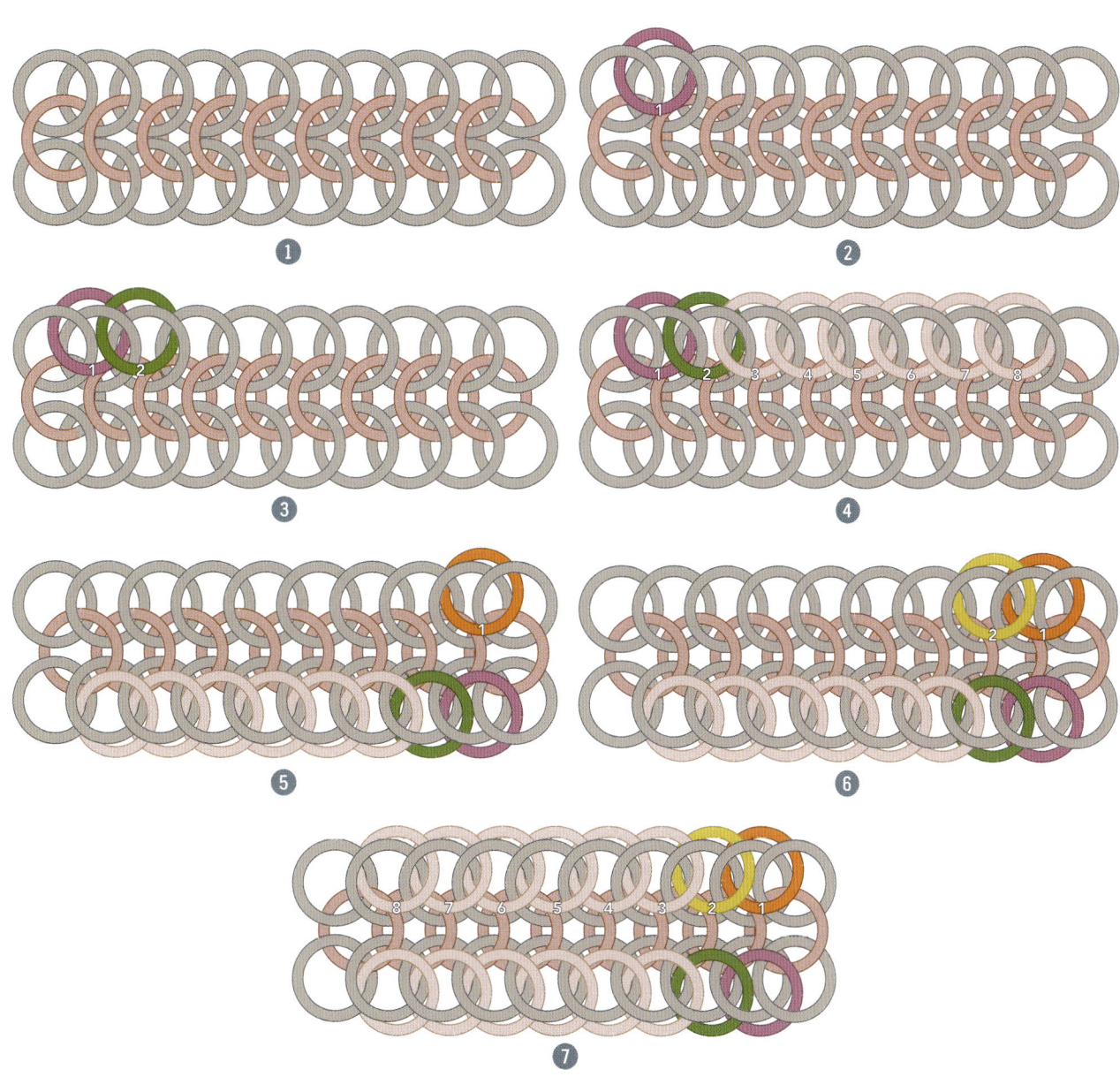

Hybrid Weaves

Close the Piece

Close the piece from end to end as follows:

1. Rotate the piece 180°.

2. Thread 1 open (turquoise) jump ring through 4 HP31 edge jump rings, 1 and 2 on the bottom edge and 2 and 1 on the top edge. Thread down into bottom HP31 edge jump rings 1 and 2 from above using a TE connection and then thread up through top HP31 edge jump rings 2 and 1 from below using a TE connection (see weaving path, **Fig. 8**). Close the open jump ring.

3. Thread 1 open (orange) jump ring through 4 HP31 edge jump rings, 2 and 3 on the bottom edge and 3 and 2 on the top edge. Thread down into bottom HP31 edge jump rings 2 and 3 from above using a TE connection and then thread up through top HP31 edge jump rings 3 and 2 from below using a TE connection (**Fig. 9**). Close the open jump ring.

Continue adding an open jump ring through 4 HP31 edge jump rings until the piece is closed. This is the flat side of the weave (**Fig. 10**). Flip the piece over to reveal ridge side (**Fig. 11**).

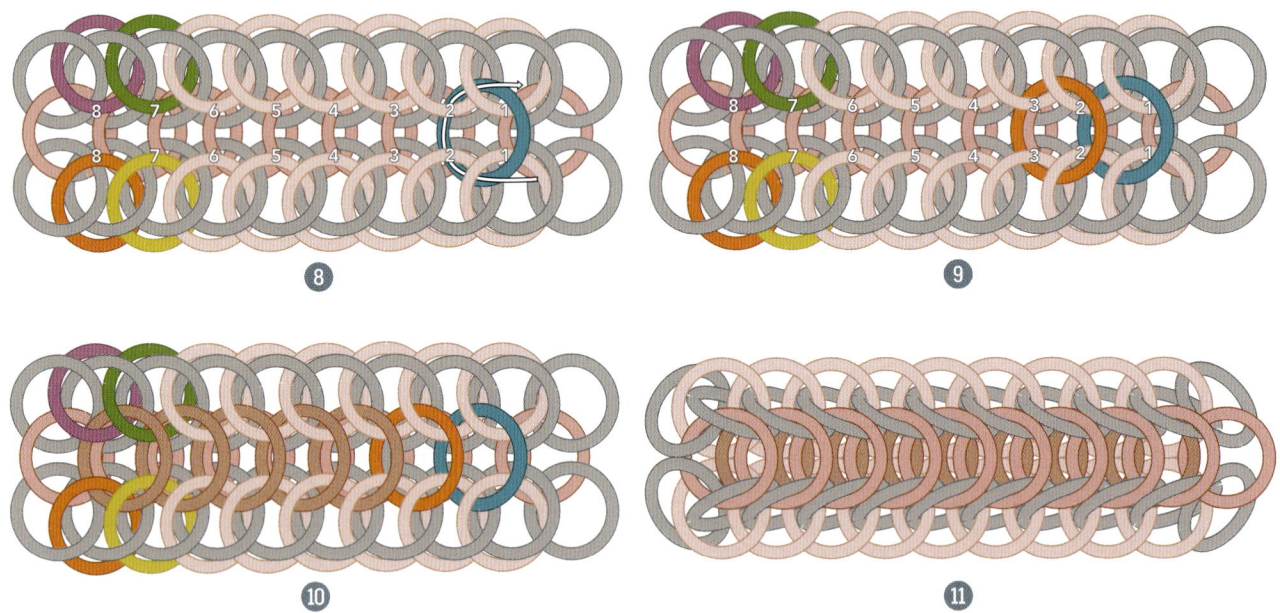

94 ADVANCED CHAIN MAILLE JEWELRY WORKSHOP

METHOD 2

Start with 2 mirror-image chains of HP31 of equal length.

Prepare Jump Rings

Prepare jump rings for both HP31 chains as in Review Material, page 26, and open the rest of the jump rings for weaving Dragonback.

Build an HP31 Chain

Make an HP31 chain to your desired length (Review Material, page 26).

Build a Mirror-Image HP31 Chain

Make a mirror-image HP31 chain that is the same length as the previous chain (See Review Material, page 28).

Connect the Mirror-Image HP31 Chains

1. Line up your chains side by side, concave side facing up and oriented as in **Fig. 1**.

2. Thread 1 open (turquoise) jump ring through 4 HP31 inner-edge jump rings, 1 and 2 on the bottom chain and 2 and 1 on the top chain. Thread down into HP31 inner-edge jump rings 1 and 2 on the bottom chain from above using a TE connection and then thread up through HP31 inner-edge jump rings 2 and 1 on the top chain from below using a TE connection (see weaving path, **Fig. 2**). Close the open jump ring.

3. Thread 1 open (fuchsia) jump ring through 4 HP31 inner-edge jump rings, 2 and 3 on the bottom chain and 3 and 2 on the top chain. Thread down into HP31 inner-edge jump rings 2 and 3 on the bottom chain from above using a TE connection and then weave up through HP31 inner-edge jump rings 3 and 2 on the top chain from below using a TE connection (**Fig. 3**). Close the open jump ring.

Continue adding an open jump ring through 4 HP31 inner-edge jump rings (2 on each chain) until the chains are fully connected (**Fig. 4**).

This row of connecting jump rings will become the ridge (dragon's backbone). You may wish to weave this row with jump rings of a contrasting color or metal to highlight this feature of the weave.

Close the Piece

4. Flip the weave over as you would a pancake (north to south).

5. Close the piece following the closure instructions in Method 1 (page 94), but do NOT rotate the piece 180°. (If you flip from east to west, you will need to rotate the piece 180°.)

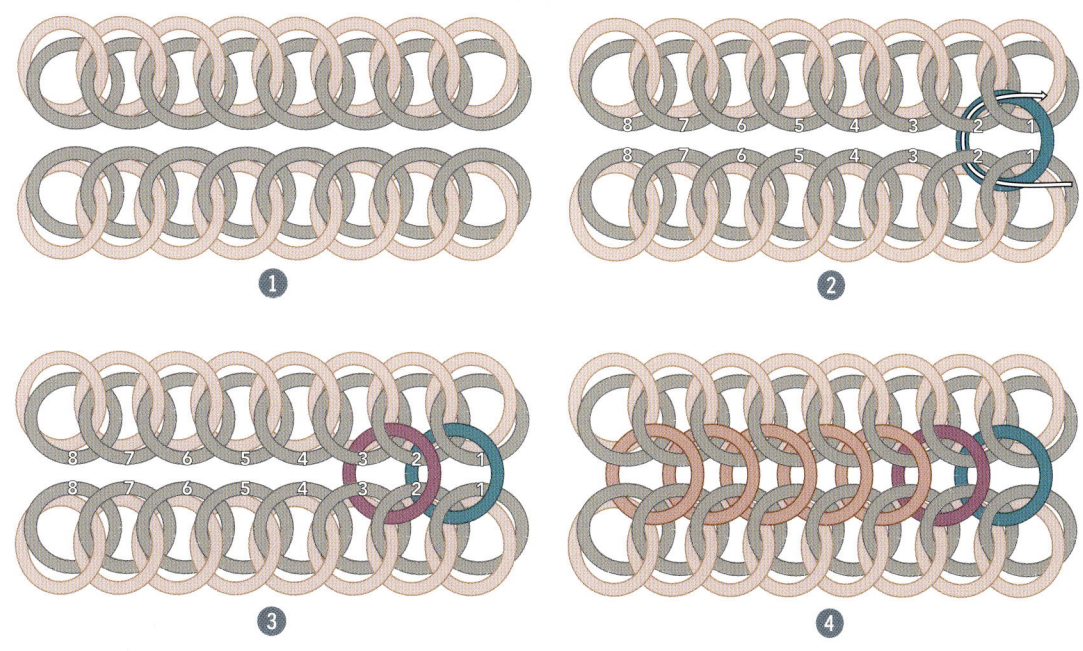

Hybrid Weaves

Persian Dragonscale Weave

Jump Ring Chart

METAL	16 GAUGE ID	RPI	AR	18 GAUGE ID	RPI	AR
Sterling Silver (AWG)	6.5 mm	36	5.0	5 mm	42	4.9
Bright Aluminum (SWG)						
The Ring Lord	5/16"	24	5.2	1/4"	30	5.5
C&T Designs	9/32"	30	4.61	7/32"	42	4.65
Metal Designz	9/32"	33	4.5	13/64"	42	4.6

Persian Dragonscale weave (also known as Oval or Euro/Persian Hybrid) is constructed in much the same way as Dragonback. The process differs only in the closing; therefore, you can refer to the instructions for Dragonback weave until it is time to close.

METHOD 1

Start with an E41 base.

Prepare Jump Rings
Same as for Method 1, Dragonback weave.

Build the E41 Base
Same as for Method 1, Dragonback weave.

Weave a Half Persian 3-in-1 (HP31) Edge
Same as for Method 1, Dragonback weave.

Add Mirror-Image HP31 Edge
Same as for Method 1, Dragonback weave.

Close the Piece

1. Rotate the piece 180° (**Fig. 1**).

2. Flip the piece over (north to south) as you would a pancake (**Fig. 2**).

3. Roll the edges in toward the middle (**Fig. 3**).

Close the piece from end to end as follows:

4. Thread 1 open (turquoise) jump ring through 4 HP31 edge jump rings, 1 and 2 on the bottom edge and 2 and 1 on the top edge. Thread down into bottom HP31 edge jump rings 1 and 2 from above using a TE connection, then thread up through top HP31 edge jump rings 2 and 1 from below using a TE connection (see weaving path, **Fig. 4**). Close the open jump ring.

1

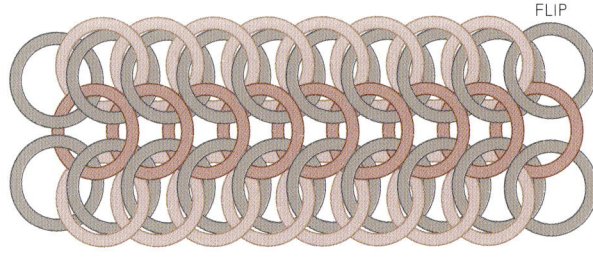

2

96 ADVANCED CHAIN MAILLE JEWELRY WORKSHOP

5. Thread 1 open (fuchsia) jump ring through 4 HP31 edge jump rings, 2 and 3 on the bottom edge and 3 and 2 on the top edge. Thread down into bottom HP31 edge jump rings 2 and 3 from above using a TE connection, then thread up through top HP31 edge jump rings 3 and 2 from below using a TE connection (**Fig. 5**). Close the open jump ring.

Continue adding an open jump ring through 4 HP31 edge jump rings until the piece is closed (**Fig. 6**).

METHOD 2

Start with 2 mirror-image chains of HP31 of equal length.

Prepare Jump Rings

Same as for Method 2, Dragonback weave.

Build an HP31 Chain to the Desired Length

Same as for Method 2, Dragonback weave.

Build a Mirror-Image HP31 Chain to the Desired Length

Same as for Method 2, Dragonback weave.

Connect the Mirror-Image HP31 Chains

Same as for Method 2, Dragonback weave.

Close the Piece

Close the piece following the closing instructions in Method 1 of Persian Dragonscale, Steps 3–5.

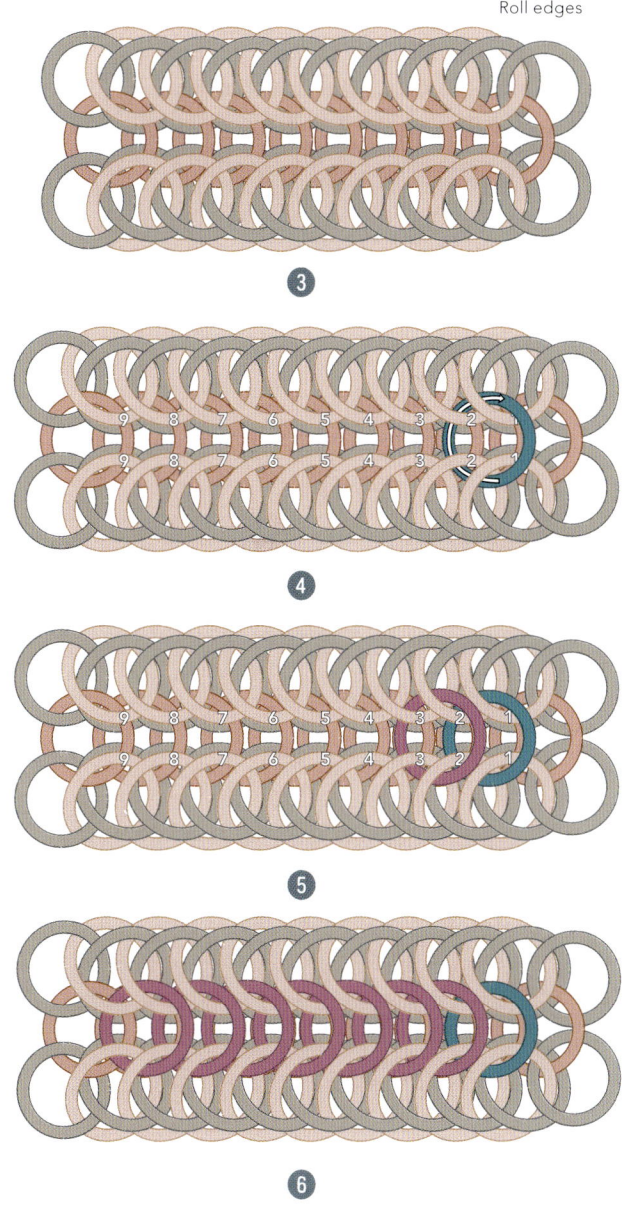

Roll edges

Hybrid Weaves 97

SUPPLIES

- 120 sterling silver jump rings, 22g (AWG), 3.25 mm ID
- 24 gold-filled jump rings, 22g (AWG), 3.25 mm ID

FINISHED SIZE

- Approximate Woman's U.S. Ring Size = a tight 7

DRAGONBACK RING

Gold-filled jump rings highlight the dragon's backbone in this sterling silver Dragonback ring.

Refer to Dragonback weave directions in Hybrid Weaves (page 92).

1. Follow the instructions in Review Material, page 20, to prepare jump rings and weave a strip of E41 (1 jump ring at the start and at the end of the strip) that consists of 24 gold-filled jump rings in the center row and 23 silver jump rings on each edge.

2. Close the strip just completed, using 2 open silver jump rings, following the E41 closing directions in Review Material, page 24.

3. Open the remaining silver jump rings.

4. Begin working anywhere on the outside of the band. Follow the directions in the Dragonback Weave section, Method 1 (page 92), to complete the Dragonback weave using the remaining silver jump rings. You will first create the Half Persian edges along the top and bottom edges of the strip and then join them to create the ridge, as follows:

- Weave the HP31 edge on the top edge of the band. Threading the final jump ring is tricky. Place it in the weave, in pattern. It will lie above the last HP31 edge jump ring added and below the first HP31 edge jump ring added on the top edge.

- Weave the mirror-image HP31 edge on the bottom edge of the band. Threading the final jump ring is tricky. Place it in the weave, in pattern. It will lie above the last HP31 edge jump ring added and below the first HP31 edge jump ring added on the bottom edge.

- Weave jump rings down the center of the weave to connect the HP31 edges as in Dragonback, Method 1, Closing, Steps 2–3, (page 94) (see note that follows).

> **NOTE**
>
> You need to turn the ring inside out and perform the joining steps on the inside of the band: if you join the Half Persian edges on the outside of the band, the ridge will begin to form on the *inside* of the band. Depending on the length of your E41 starting strip, you may be able to begin weaving the joining rings on the outside of the band. However, the weave will tighten as you continue, eventually preventing you from turning the work inside out to bring the ridge to the *outside* (where it belongs). Therefore, try to work on the outside for as long as you can, frequently testing the band's flexibility, until you are forced to turn the ring inside out and finish the weaving on the *inside* of the band. This is a bit tricky—especially threading the final jump ring!

SUPPLIES
- 69 bright aluminum jump rings, saw-cut, 16g (SWG), 9/32" ID
- 69 rubber O-rings, 12 × 8 × 2 mm

FINISHED LENGTH
- 6¼" (16 cm) flat length before closing

INTERWOVEN STRETCH CUFF

Add some color and stretch to your chain maille with a claspless Interwoven 4-1 cuff made with colorful rubber O-rings!

1. Open all of your aluminum jump rings.

2. Follow the instructions in Review Material (page 20) to speed-weave a strip of E41 (2 jump rings at the start and end of the strip) that consists of 22 aluminum jump rings in the center row and 23 rubber O-rings on each edge.

3. Close the strip just completed, using 1 open aluminum jump ring, following the alternate E41 closing directions in Review Material (page 24).

Stop here and you've got a stretchy E41 bracelet (although it will be a bit large as the base E41 piece is made longer than necessary to allow for shrinkage when completing Interwoven).

4. Follow the speed weaving Interwoven 4-1 directions to complete the cuff (page 85). Use aluminum jump rings for the open jump rings and rubber O-rings for the preclosed jump rings. Begin anywhere along the edge of the piece. Make the following pattern adjustments:

- Pick up 2 closed jump rings on your first open jump ring and thread as directed.

- Thread the second open jump ring through top-edge jump rings 1 and 2 and also through the 2 closed jump rings added in the first step.

- Ignore the rightmost closed jump ring added in the first step (just pretend it's not there) and continue the weave as directed.

- At the end, you are left with 2 open jump rings. Weave them, in pattern, as follows:

  » 1 open jump ring must pass through the first and last edge jump rings on the bottom edge of the weave and the first and last center (closed) jump rings.

  » The other open jump ring must pass through the first and last edge jump rings on the top edge of the weave and the first and last center (closed) jump rings.

CHALLENGE

Now that you can close this weave, try making a ring! I recommend 22g (AWG), 2.75 mm sterling silver jump rings. I'm wearing one now! Hint: My ring (approximate size 7) begins with a strip of E41 that uses the same number of jump rings as in these instructions.

SCALE MAILLE

Scale maille, an ancient armor technique, is becoming a very popular trend in chain maille jewelry. Scales are most commonly woven together in a staggered, overlapping pattern to form sheets with a surface that resembles fish scales. Traditionally these sheets formed protective battle armor. Today, these same sheets are transformed into statement jewelry pieces such as cuffs and dramatic collars.

Traditional Weaving Method

In this section, we will learn how to weave scales in the traditional staggered overlapping configuration. We will learn how to weave both straight across and in a diagonal fashion.

SUPPLIES REQUIRED FOR THE FOLLOWING TECHNIQUES:

- Small anodized aluminum scales, 9/16" × 7/8" (1.4 × 2.2 cm), 0.22" hole
- Anodized aluminum saw-cut jump rings, 18g (SWG), 3/16" (4.76 mm) ID

WORKING WITH SCALES (TRADITIONAL WEAVING)

Scales have two distinct sides: the concave (back) side (**Fig. 1**) and the convex (front) side (**Fig. 2**). The back or concave side of the piece faces you while you weave.

To connect 2 scales, thread 1 jump ring through the first scale from back to front, then through second scale from front to back (**Fig. 3**). Alternatively, you can weave through the first scale from the front to the back, then through the second scale from back to front.

Except along the edges, each scale is held in the weave by 4 jump rings.

Weaving scales in the traditional manner can be tricky. The scale weave tends to be very loose, causing the scales to shift and making it difficult to determine placement of the next scale. Therefore, it is helpful to use tape to secure the scales in place as you weave. (I like blue painter's tape because it leaves no sticky residue.)

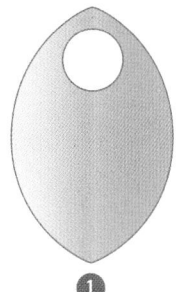

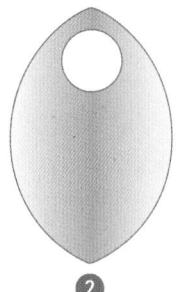

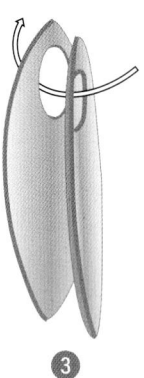

WEAVING STRAIGHT ACROSS

You can create square or rectangular forms by weaving rows of scales in straight lines across from left to right.

Prepare Jump Rings

Open all the jump rings.

Start the Weave

To start the weave, you can weave a long line of scales together, then use tape to secure the staggered position (creating the first 2 scale rows). Or you can weave and position 1 scale at a time. I prefer the latter method, as it is easier to gauge finished length this way. Therefore, the instructions that follow describe the latter method.

Weave the First 2 Rows

Weave as follows, forming 2 staggered horizontal rows until you arrive at the length you desire.

1. Connect 3 scales using 2 jump rings (**Fig. 1**).

2. Tuck the outer scales behind the center scale (**Fig. 2**) and secure with tape. Place the odd-numbered scales above and behind the even-numbered scales. The first (bottom) row consists of the even-numbered scales: the second (top) row consists of the odd-numbered scales.

3. Connect a fourth scale to the third scale using 1 jump ring (**Fig. 3**).

4. Position the fourth scale as in **Fig. 4** (low and in front). Secure with tape.

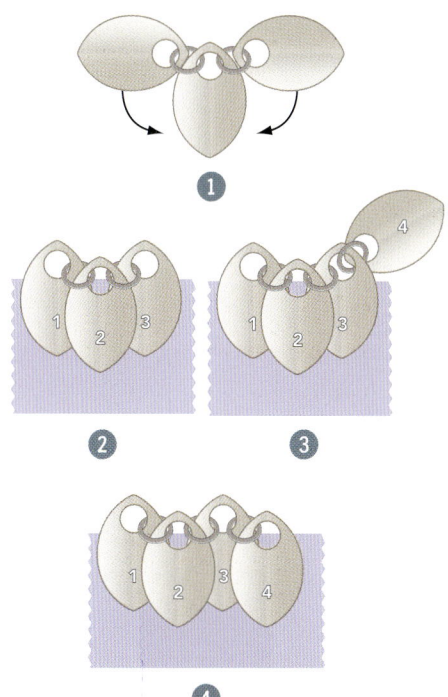

Scale Maille

Join a fifth scale to the fourth scale using 1 jump ring (**Fig. 5**).

5. Position the fifth scale (high and behind) and secure with tape (**Fig. 6**).

Continue in this manner until you reach your desired length, 2 rows completed (**Fig. 7**).

Weave the Pattern

Weave the Third Row

6. Connect 1 scale to the first and second scales of the top row using 2 (dark orange) jump rings (**Fig. 8**).

7. Connect another scale to the second and third scales of the top row using 2 (dark orange) jump rings (**Fig. 9**).

Continue adding scales until you reach the end of the row and secure with tape as needed. The third row is now completed (**Fig. 10**).

Weave the Fourth Row

8. Connect 1 scale to the first and second scales of the top row using 2 (dark orange) jump rings (**Fig. 11**).

9. Connect another scale to the second and third scales of the top row using 2 (dark orange) jump rings (**Fig. 12**).

Continue adding scales until you reach the end of the row and secure with tape as needed (**Fig. 13**).

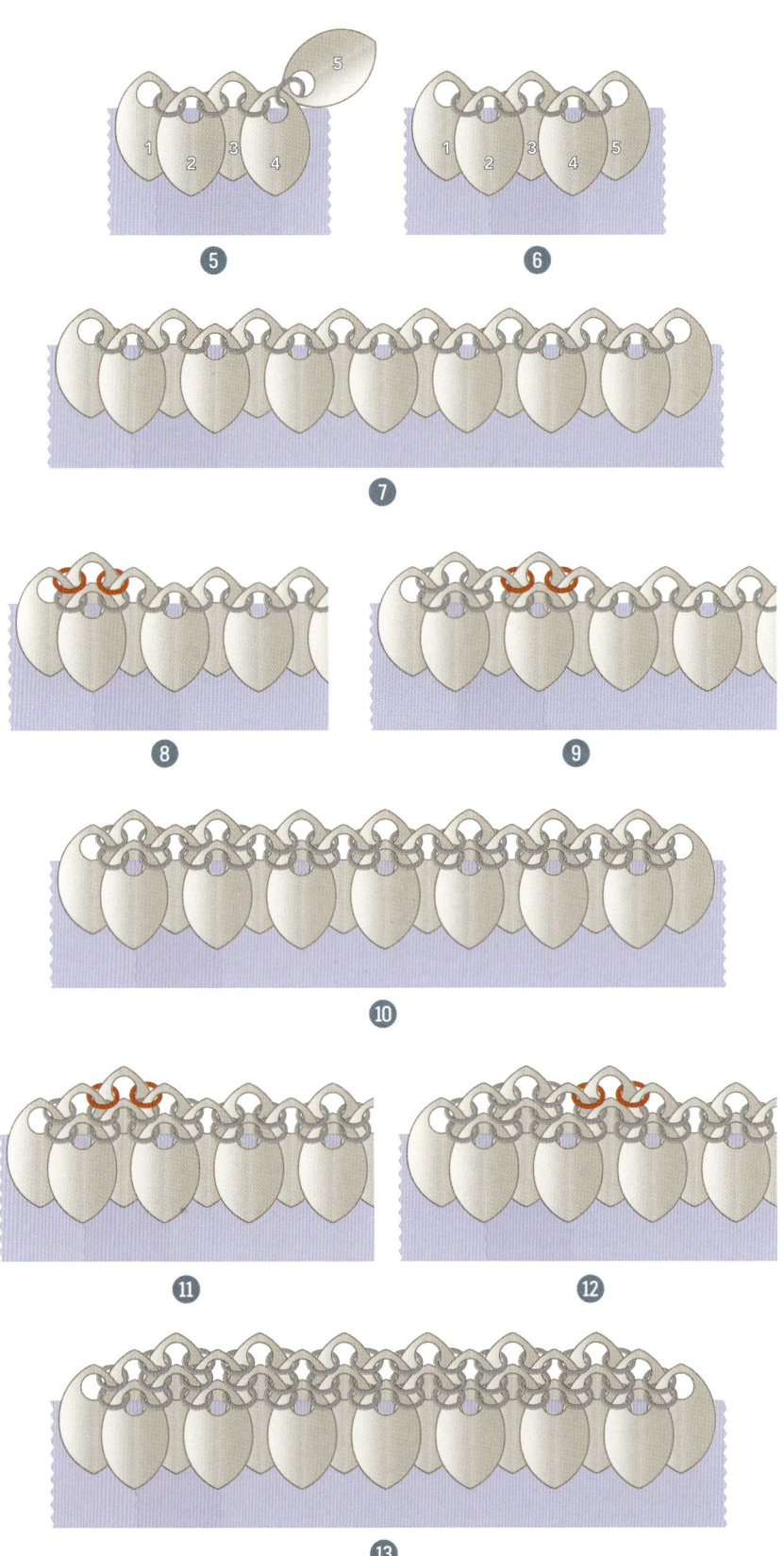

106 ADVANCED CHAIN MAILLE JEWELRY WORKSHOP

Complete the Fourth Row

Add 1 scale to each end. This completion step is to be performed on every other row.

10. Connect 1 scale to the first scale of the top row using 1 (dark orange) jump ring (**Fig. 14**). Position the scale just added high and behind the first scale of the top row and secure with tape (**Fig. 15**).

11. Repeat Step 10 on the other end as follows: Connect 1 scale to the last scale of the top row using 1 jump ring. Position the scale just added high and behind the last scale of the top row and secure with tape.

Add additional rows by repeating directions for weaving the third row and then the fourth row, until your piece is the size you desire.

Stabilizing

The traditional staggered overlapping scale weave produces pieces in which the scales tend to shift along the outer edges. To remedy this, I always stabilize the sides of the weave by adding jump rings. This helps keep the piece from shifting quite a bit. Often, but not always, I stabilize the top edge by working the extra jump rings along the front of the weave, which also adds a decorative touch. Depending on my design, I may or may not stabilize the bottom edge. Sometimes I prefer the jingly movement of unstabilized scales and leave the bottom-edge scales free.

Sides

The steps that follow show how to stabilize the left side of the piece; repeat on right side. Work on the back side of the piece.

12. Add 1 (fuchsia) jump ring to each end-scale of every even-numbered scale row (**Fig. 16**).

13. Add 1 (dark orange) jump ring to the end-scale of Row 1 (**Fig. 16**).

14. Connect the (fuchsia) jump rings just added in Step 12 to the lower outer (dark orange) jump rings in the end-scales of each odd-numbered scale row using open (turquoise) jump rings. Thread the open (turquoise) jump rings through the (fuchsia) jump rings added in Step 12 and the lower outer (dark orange) jump rings of the end-scales of the odd-numbered scale rows (**Fig. 17**).

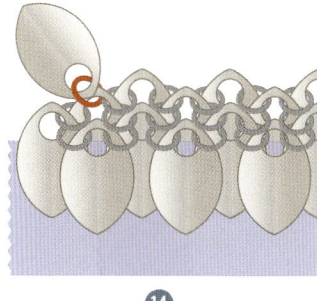

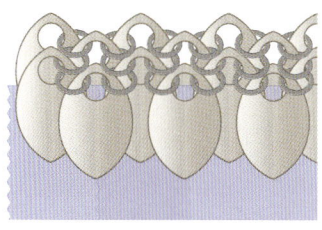

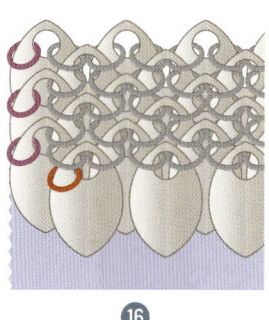

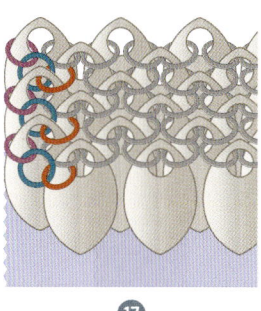

Scale Maille 107

Top Edge

15. Working on the front of the piece, thread (dark orange) jump rings through the pairs of jump rings connecting the scales along the top row for added detail. This decorative treatment will also help to stabilize the weave (**Fig. 18**).

Bottom Edge

16. Working on the back side of the piece, add 2 (dark orange) jump rings to each scale in the bottom row so that each one has 4 jump rings attached to it (**Fig. 19**).

17. Connect the (dark orange) jump rings just added using open (green) jump rings (**Fig. 20**).

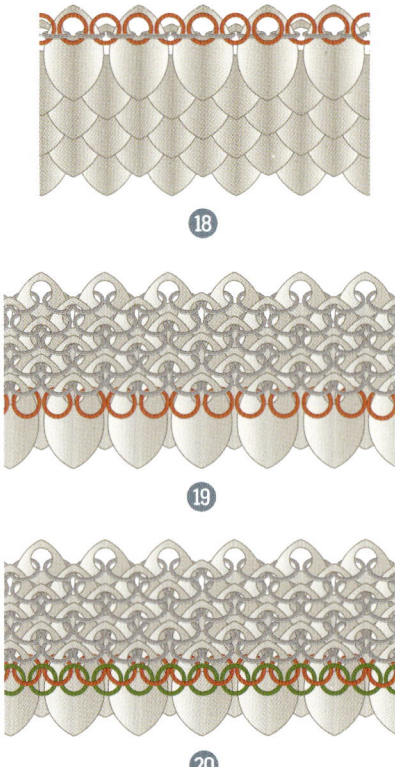

WEAVING DIAGONALLY

You can also weave scales diagonally to produce diamond- or triangle-shaped forms. To make a triangle shape, simply weave half of a diamond shape.

Prepare Jump Rings

Open all the jump rings.

Weave Diamond Shape

First expand the weave and then contract it to achieve a diamond shape. This is similar to creating a European 4-in-1 (E41) diamond shape as shown in my *Chain Maille Jewelry Workshop* book.

Expand the Weave

Weave the first 2 rows of the diamond shape.

1. Attach 3 scales using 2 open jump rings (**Fig. 1**).

2. Tuck the outer scales behind the center scale and push up as in **Fig. 2** (first 2 rows of diamond completed: Row 1 contains 1 scale, Row 2 contains 2 scales). Secure with tape.

Create the third row of the diamond shape (contains 3 scales).

3. Attach 1 scale to the right scale of Row 2 using 1 open jump ring (**Fig. 3**). Flip the scale into position as directed by the arrow and secure it between the 2 scales of Row 2 with tape (**Fig. 4**).

4. Attach the scale just added to the left scale in Row 2 using 1 open (dark orange) jump ring (**Fig. 5**).

5. Attach 1 scale to the right scale of Row 2 using 1 open jump ring (**Fig. 6**). Tuck the scale into position as directed by the arrow and secure it with tape (**Fig. 7**).

6. Attach 1 scale to the left scale of Row 2 using 1 open jump ring (**Fig. 8**). Tuck the scale into position as directed by the arrow and secure it with tape (**Fig. 9**, third row of scales completed).

Create the fourth row of the diamond shape (contains 4 scales).

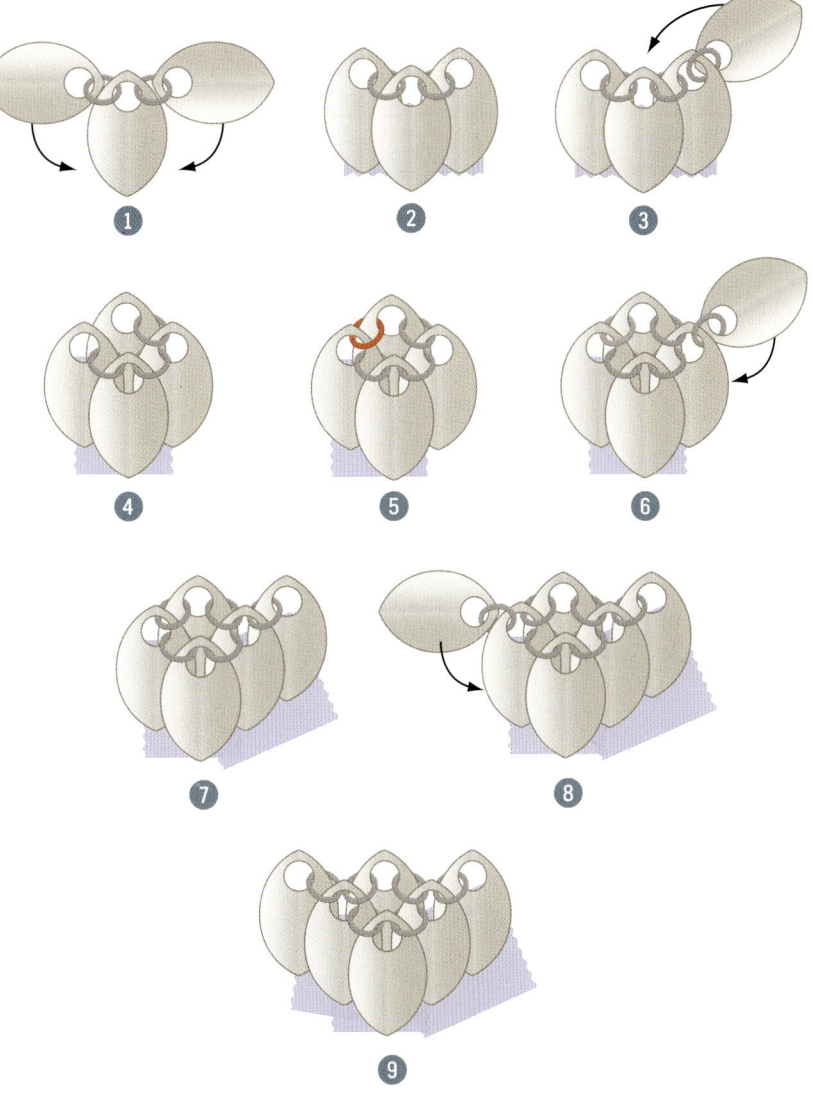

Scale Maille 109

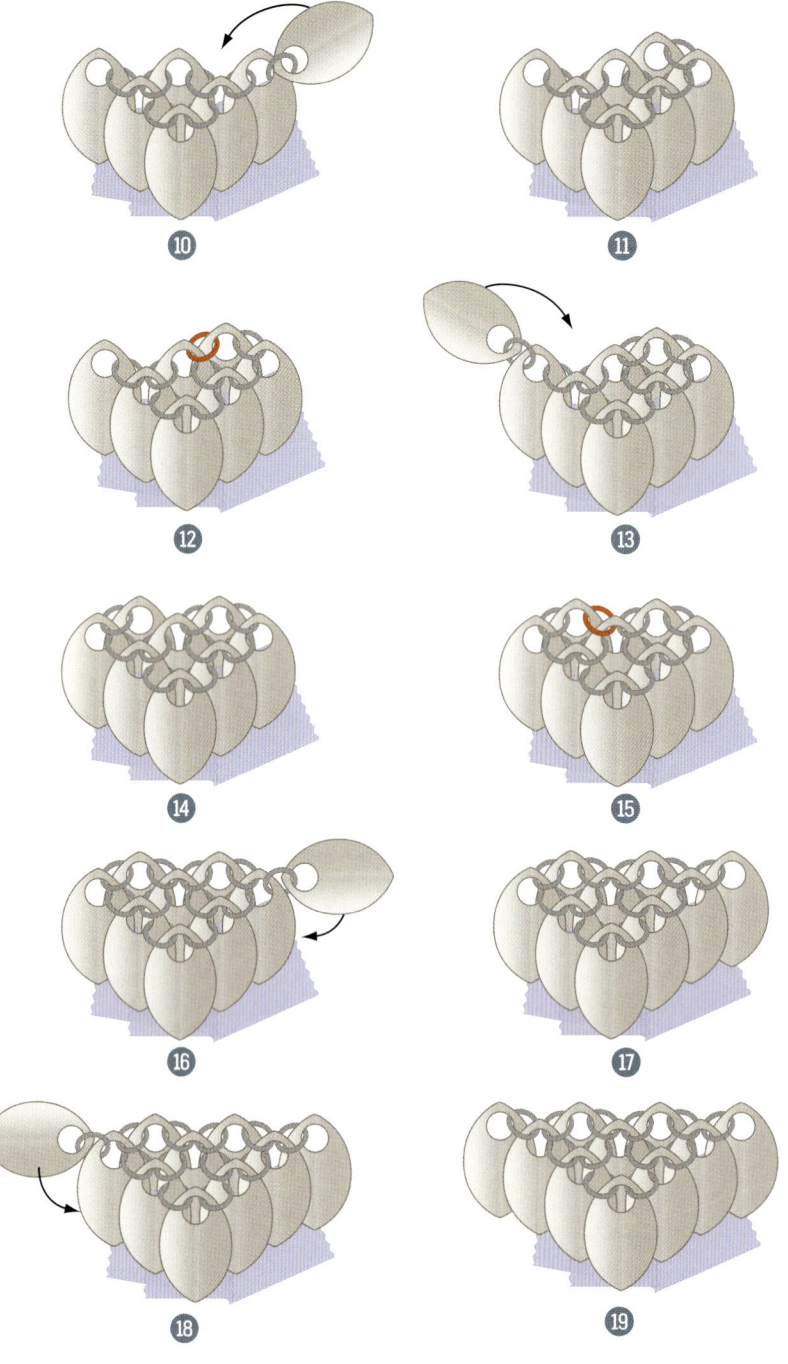

7. Attach 1 scale to the right scale of Row 3 using 1 open jump ring (**Fig. 10**). Flip the scale into position as directed by the arrow and secure it between the right and center scales of Row 3 with tape (**Fig. 11**).

8. Attach the scale just added to the center scale of Row 3 using 1 open (dark orange) jump ring (**Fig. 12**).

9. Attach 1 scale to the left scale of Row 3 using 1 open jump ring (**Fig. 13**). Flip the scale into position as directed by the arrow and secure it between the left and center scales of Row 3 with tape (**Fig. 14**).

10. Attach the scale just added to the center scale of Row 3 using 1 open (dark orange) jump ring (**Fig. 15**).

11. Attach 1 scale to the right scale of Row 3 using 1 open jump ring (**Fig. 16**). Tuck the scale into position as directed by the arrow and secure with tape (**Fig. 17**).

12. Attach 1 scale to the left scale of Row 3 using 1 open jump ring (**Fig. 18**). Tuck the scale into position as directed by the arrow and secure with tape (**Fig. 19**, fourth row of scales completed).

You can continue adding rows of scales in this manner (Row 5 will consist of 5 scales, Row 6 will consist of 6 scales, etc.) until your diamond shape reaches the desired width. To finish the diamond, contract the weave using the steps that follow.

110   ADVANCED CHAIN MAILLE JEWELRY WORKSHOP

Contract the Weave

Weave the first decrease row (Row 5) of the diamond shape.

13. Attach 1 scale to the right scale of Row 4 using 1 open jump ring (**Fig. 20**). Flip the scale into position as directed by the arrow and secure it between the right and center/right scales of Row 4 with tape (**Fig. 21**).

14. Attach the scale just added to the center/right scale in Row 4 using 1 open (dark orange) jump ring (**Fig. 22**).

15. Attach 1 scale to the center/right scale of Row 4 using 1 open jump ring (**Fig. 23**). Flip the scale into position as directed by the arrow and secure it between the center/right and center/left scales of Row 4 using tape (**Fig. 24**).

16. Attach the scale just added to the center/left scale in Row 4 using 1 open (dark orange) jump ring (**Fig. 25**).

17. Attach 1 scale to the left scale of Row 4 using 1 open jump ring (**Fig. 26**). Flip the scale into position as directed by the arrow and secure it between the left and center/left scales of Row 4 with tape (**Fig. 27**).

18. Attach the scale just added to the center/left scale in Row 4 using 1 open (red) jump ring.

Your first decrease row is now completed (**Fig. 28**).

Weave the next decrease row (Row 6) of the diamond shape.

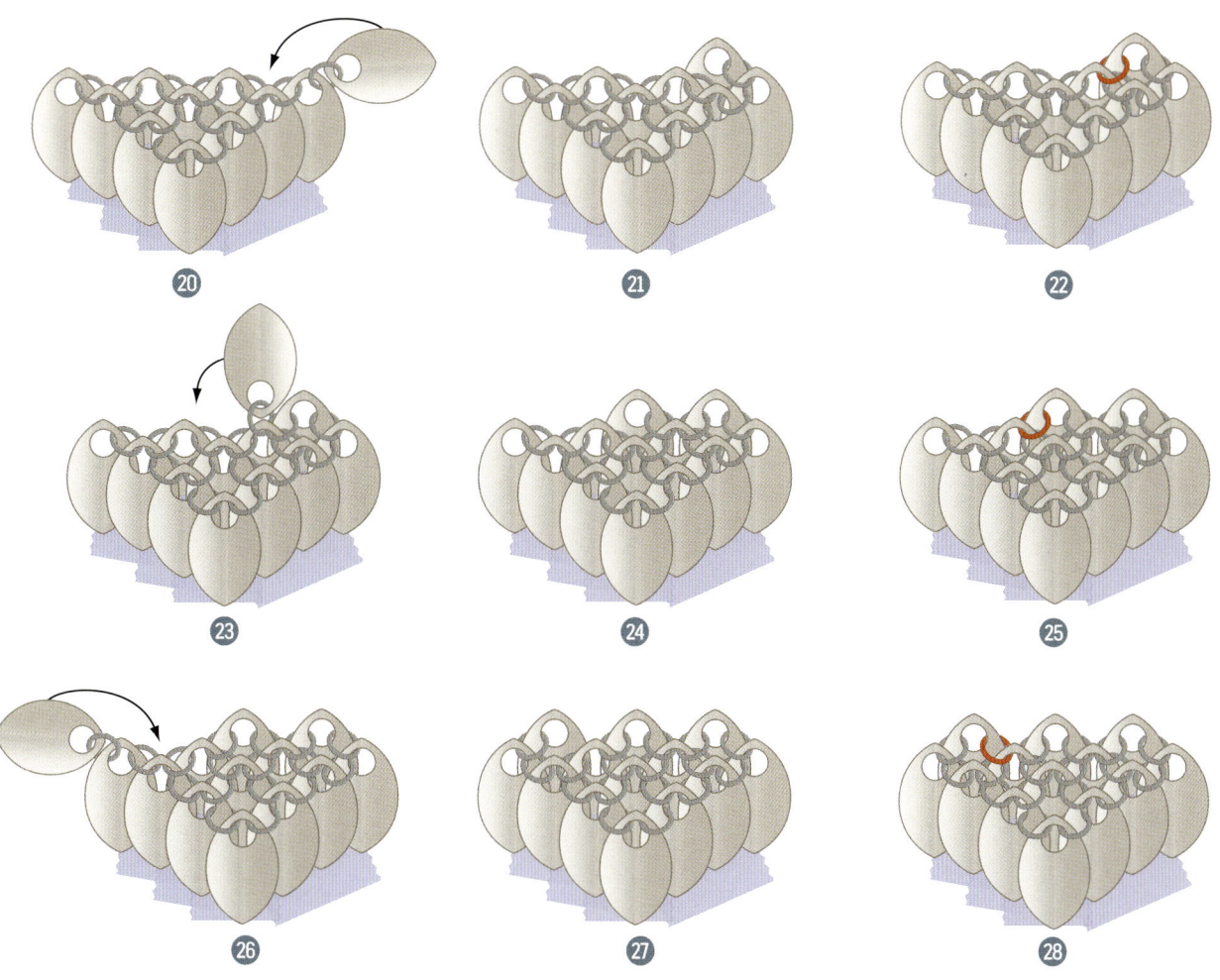

Scale Maille 111

19. Attach 1 scale to the right scale of Row 5 using 1 open jump ring (**Fig. 29**). Flip the scale into position as directed by the arrow and secure it between the right and center scales of Row 5 with tape (**Fig. 30**).

20. Attach the scale just added to the center scale in Row 5 using 1 open (dark orange) jump ring (**Fig. 31**).

21. Attach 1 scale to the left scale of Row 5 using 1 open jump ring (**Fig. 32**). Flip the scale into position as directed by the arrow and secure it between the left and center scales of Row 5 with tape (**Fig. 33**).

22. Attach the scale just added to the center scale in Row 5 using 1 open (dark orange) jump ring.

Your second decrease row is now completed (**Fig. 34**).

Create the last decrease row (Row 7) of the diamond shape.

23. Attach 1 scale to the right scale of Row 6 using 1 open jump ring (**Fig. 35**). Flip the scale into position as directed by the arrow and secure it between the scales of Row 6 with tape (**Fig. 36**).

24. Attach the scale just added to the left scale in Row 6 using 1 open (red) jump ring.

Your diamond shape is now complete (**Fig. 37**)!

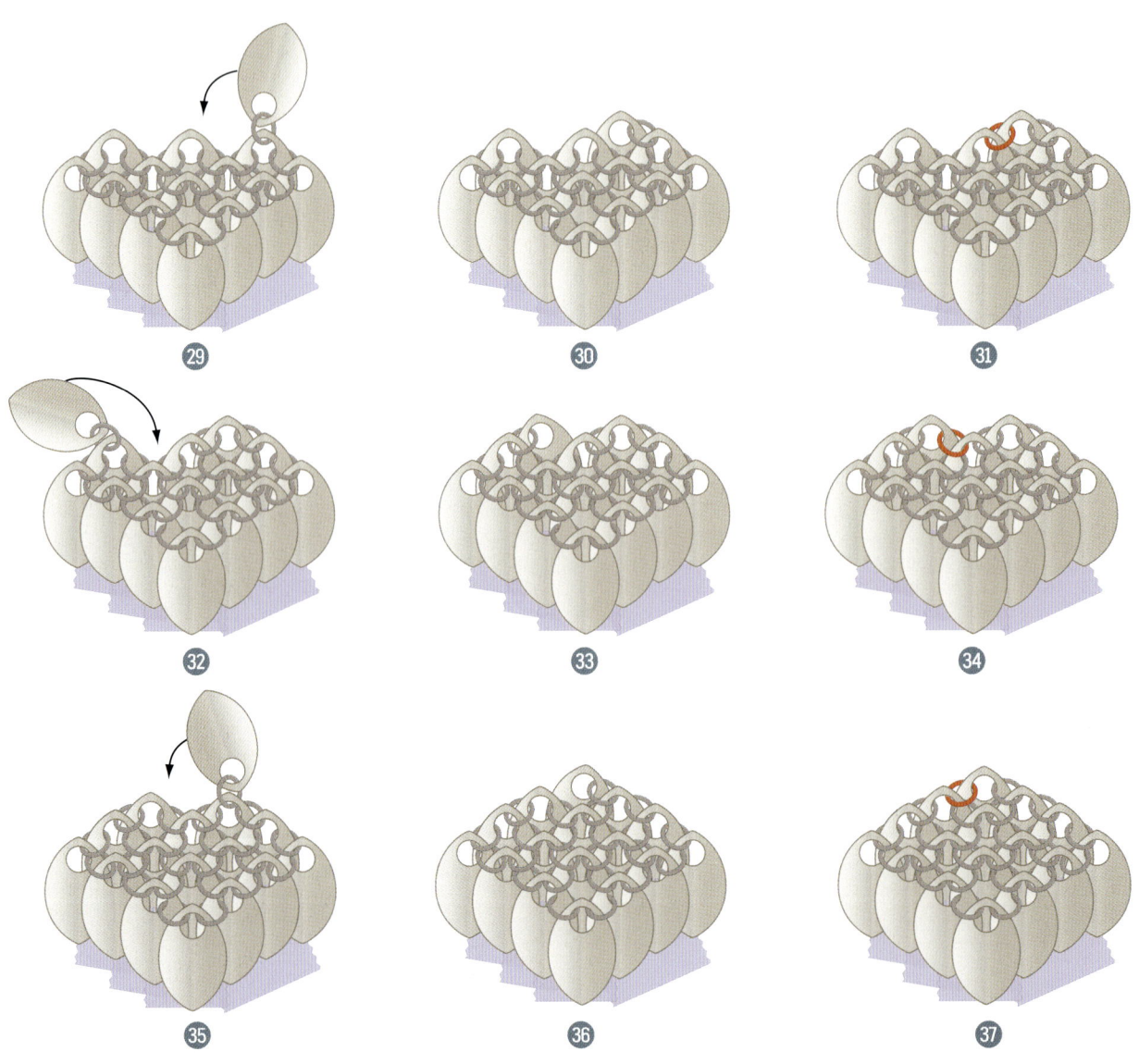

112   ADVANCED CHAIN MAILLE JEWELRY WORKSHOP

Stabilizing

If desired, you can add stabilizing jump rings to the top and bottom diagonal edges of the diamond-shaped piece.

Bottom Edges

25. Add 1 (dark orange) jump ring to the outer edge of each scale along the bottom edges of the piece (**Fig. 38**).

26. Beginning at the corner scales, one at a time, thread open (turquoise) jump rings through the (dark orange) jump rings just added and the 2 outer (gray/dark orange) jump rings of the scale diagonally below. Each open (turquoise) jump ring added is threaded through 3 jump rings. Close each open jump ring (**Fig. 39**).

27. Thread 1 open (fuchsia) jump ring through the 2 (dark orange) jump rings added to the bottom scale in Step 25. Close the open jump ring (**Fig. 40**).

Top Edges

28. Working on the front of the piece, thread (dark orange) jump rings through the pairs of jump rings connecting the scales along the top edges for added detail (**Fig. 41**).

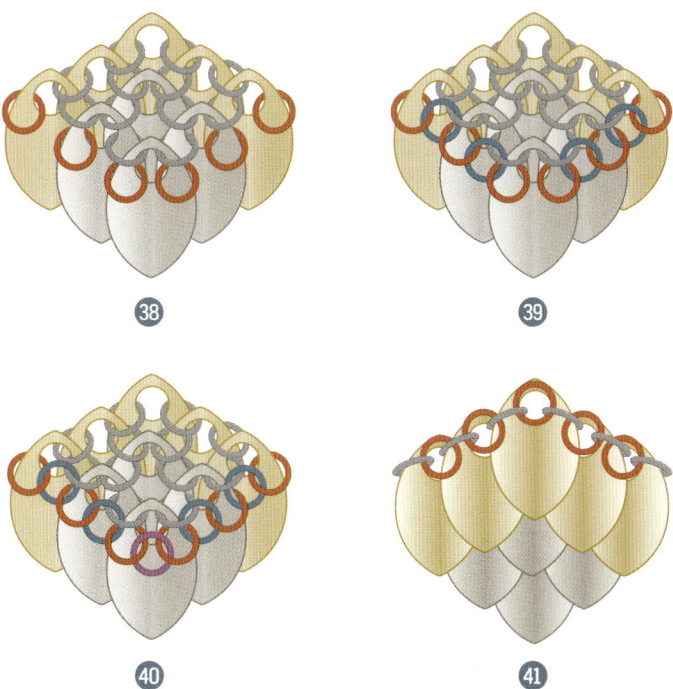

Scale Maille 113

Linear Weaving Method

When scales are joined in a linear fashion, the texture produced is reminiscent of feathers. These formations can be used as is, joined together, or combined with other maille techniques to make bold jewelry.

In this section, we will learn how to incorporate scales into the Box Chain and the Half Persian 3-in-1 (HP31) and Dragonback weaves and how to approach the linear weave to achieve the desired drape and level of "spikiness." We'll also learn how to incorporate the European 4-in-1 weave into linear rows of scales.

SUPPLIES REQUIRED FOR THE FOLLOWING TECHNIQUES:

- Small anodized aluminum scales, 9/16" × 7/8" (1.4 × 2.2 cm), 0.22" (5.8 mm) hole

- Anodized aluminum or bright aluminum saw-cut jump rings:

    18g (SWG), 3/16" (4.76 mm) ID—for Box chain, E41, and HP31* applications

    19g (SWG), 3/16" (4.76 mm) ID—for HP31* applications

    18g (SWG), 7/32" (5.6 mm) ID—for Dragonback*

*Using 18g, 3/16" (4.76 mm) ID jump rings to make an HP31 edging makes for a close fit. Jump rings can vary from batch to batch. Therefore, sometimes this size works and sometimes it can be too tight. In tight situations, I've substituted 19g, 3/16" (4.76 mm) ID jump rings. If you are making Dragonback, create your entire piece with 18g, 7/32" (5.6 mm) ID jump rings.

WORKING WITH SCALES (LINEAR FORMS)

Scales have two distinct sides: the concave (back) side (**Fig. 1**) and the convex (front) side (**Fig. 2**).

To position scales for weaving a linear chain, nest 1 scale behind the other (**Fig. 3** or **5**). You can determine the texture of the chain by the way you choose to nest the scales for weaving. Nest the scales with back (concave) sides facing you (**Fig. 3**) to produce a chain where the scales have a smoother, flatter

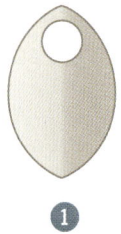
1

2

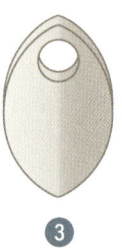
3

114 ADVANCED CHAIN MAILLE JEWELRY WORKSHOP

appearance (**Fig. 4**). Nest the scales with front (convex) sides facing you (**Fig. 5**) to produce a chain where the scales appear rougher and a bit spiky (**Fig. 6**).

Once connected, position the back scale by pushing it up (**Fig. 7**) to facilitate weaving the next scale. The side facing you while weaving is the back of the piece. Except along the edges, each scale is held in the weave by 4 jump rings.

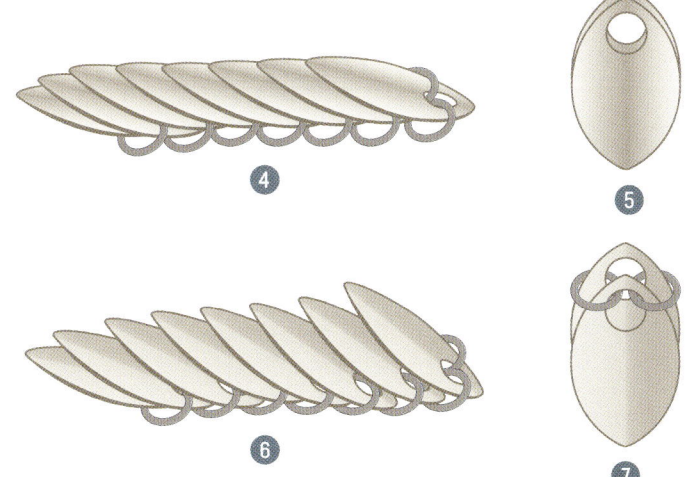

Weave the Basic Linear Chain of Scales

1. Using 2 scales, nest 1 scale behind the other scale.

2. Thread 1 open jump ring through the 2 scales, close it, and position it to the right (**Fig. 1**).

Thread another open jump ring through the same 2 scales, close it, and position it to the left (**Fig. 2**).

3. Position the scale in back by pushing it up (**Fig. 3**).

4. Nest another scale behind the scale that was just pushed up (**Fig. 4**).

5. Thread 1 open jump ring through those 2 scales, close it, and position it to the right (**Fig. 5**).

6. Thread another open jump ring through the same 2 scales, close it, and position it to the left (**Fig. 6**). Position the scale in back by pushing it up (**Fig. 7**).

Continue to add scales in this manner until you reach your desired length.

In essence, what you have just created (the basic linear form) is a strip of European 4-in-1 (E41), where the center jump ring is now a scale instead (**Fig. 8**). This strip can be used much like any other piece of E41.

TIP

Make your basic linear scale chain to your desired length if using as is. If joining together or combining with other techniques discussed in the following text (i.e., Box Chain, HP31, Dragonback, etc.), make your chain of scales longer than you will need, as it will contract (by as much as 25 percent or so, depending on the technique) as you add additional scales/jump rings to complete your piece.

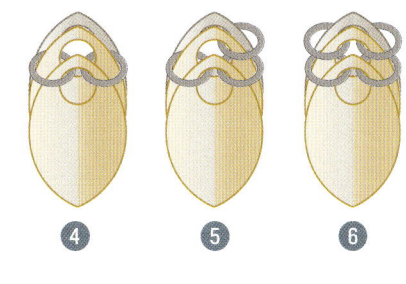

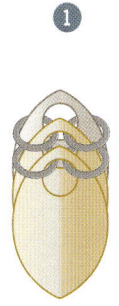

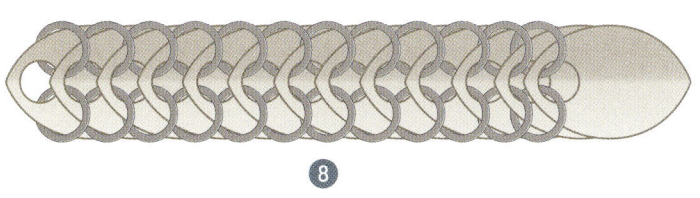

Scale Maille 115

Attaching Linear Scale Strips

1. Line up 2 scale strips side by side, back sides facing you (**Fig. 1**). You will work on the inner edges of each strip.

2. Thread 1 open (turquoise) jump ring through the first pair of jump rings of one strip and through the first pair of jump rings on the other strip (TE connections). Then, close the open jump ring (**Fig. 2**).

3. Thread another open (dark orange) jump ring through the second and third jump rings of the first strip and through the second and third jump rings of the other strip (TE connections). Then, close the open jump ring (**Fig. 3**).

4. Thread another open jump ring through the third and fourth jump rings of the first strip and through the third and fourth jump rings of the other strip (TE connections). Then, close the open jump ring.

Continue in this manner down the length of the strips until all pairs of jump rings have been connected.

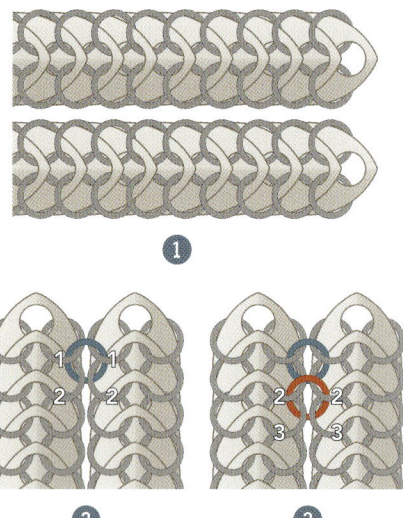

LINEAR SCALE MAILLE NECKLACE WITH CRYSTAL

I thought of this design while connecting two scale strips for another project. I combined two colors of scales simply because I did not have enough of one color in my stash. The crystal focal bead was just sitting in my stash looking for a purpose (moral: embrace serendipity).

1. Make 2 basic linear scale strips, each consisting of 32 scales. Nest the scales with back (concave) sides facing you, alternating the gold and champagne colors. Follow the instructions for attaching 2 linear scale strips. You will make only a partial join at the beginning end of the chains using 3 (dark orange) jump rings, ³⁄₁₆" (4.76 mm) (**Fig. 1**).

2. Attach the crystal to the first joining jump ring using the silver (yellow) jump ring (**Fig. 1**).

3. Attach each half of the clasp to each end of each scale strip as shown in Termination Options for Scale Maille (page 135).

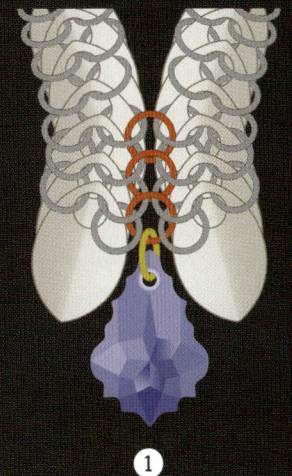

①

SUPPLIES

- 64 gold and champagne small anodized aluminum scales, ⁹⁄₁₆" × ⁷⁄₈" (1.4 × 2.2 cm), 0.22" (5.8 mm) hole (32 of each color)
- 128–132 champagne anodized aluminum saw-cut jump rings, 18g (SWG), ³⁄₁₆" (4.76 mm) ID
- 1 sterling silver* jump ring, 18g (AWG), 6 mm ID to attach crystal
- 1 Swarovski Baroque Crystal 22 mm Pendant (color Crystal AB)
- 1 pewter 22 mm toggle clasp

*I used one sterling silver jump ring in this aluminum project because that is what I had on hand. If you've got an appropriate aluminum ring, feel free to use it instead.

FINISHED LENGTH

- 14" (35.5 cm) not including clasp

Adding E41 Maille to a Linear Scale Strip

This technique is basically the same as the technique for widening E41 sheet maille from *Chain Maille Jewelry Workshop* (page 63).

1. Thread 1 open (dark orange) jump ring through the first pair of jump rings on one side of the strip (TE connection) and then close the open jump ring (**Fig. 1**).

2. Thread another open (green) jump ring through the second and third jump rings on the same side of the strip (TE connection) and then close the open jump ring (**Fig. 2**).

3. Thread another open jump ring through the third and fourth jump rings on the same side of the strip (TE connection), then close the open jump ring.

Proceed in this manner down the length of the strip until all pairs of jump rings have been connected (**Fig. 3**). To widen the maille, one at a time, thread open jump rings through the pairs of jump rings just added (first and second, second and third, third and fourth, . . .) on the edge of the strip (TE connections: **Figs. 4–6**). Continue adding rows to make the maille as wide as desired. To keep the maille even on both ends, for every additional odd-numbered row woven, thread a jump ring through the first and last jump rings of the preceding row.

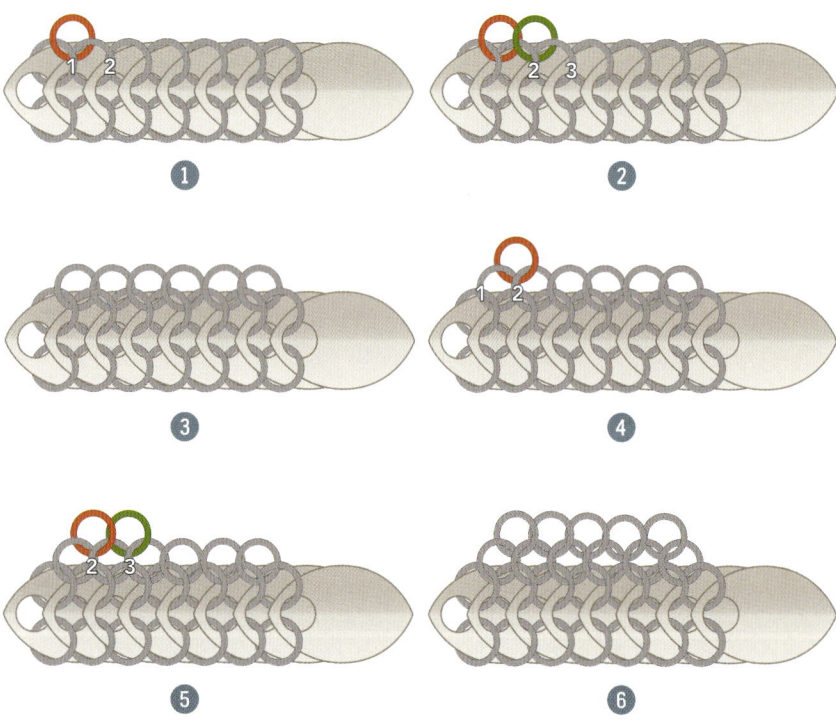

118 ADVANCED CHAIN MAILLE JEWELRY WORKSHOP

Box Chain

The box chain with integrated scales works well in the form of a necklace. This technique is basically the same as the technique of closing E41 from side to side to form round maille from *Chain Maille Jewelry Workshop* (page 68).

Start with a basic linear scale strip. Make your strip of scales a bit longer than you will need as it will contract slightly as you add additional jump rings to complete the box chain.

1. Pinch together the 2 rows of jump rings to form a line of nested Vs along the length of the scale strip (**Fig. 1**).

2. Hold the strip so that the pointy ends of the Vs point north (**Fig. 2**).

3. Thread 1 open (fuchsia) jump ring through the first 2 jump rings on the right side of the scale strip, then through the first 2 jump rings on the left side of the scale strip, following the path in **Fig. 3** (TE connections). Close the open jump ring.

4. Thread 1 open (blue) jump ring through jump rings 2 and 3 on the right side of the scale strip and then through jump rings 3 and 2 on the left side of the scale strip, following the path in **Fig. 4** (TE connections). Close the open jump ring.

Continue in this manner (next thread through jump rings 3 and 4 on both sides, then 4 and 5 on both sides . . .) until you have completed the box chain.

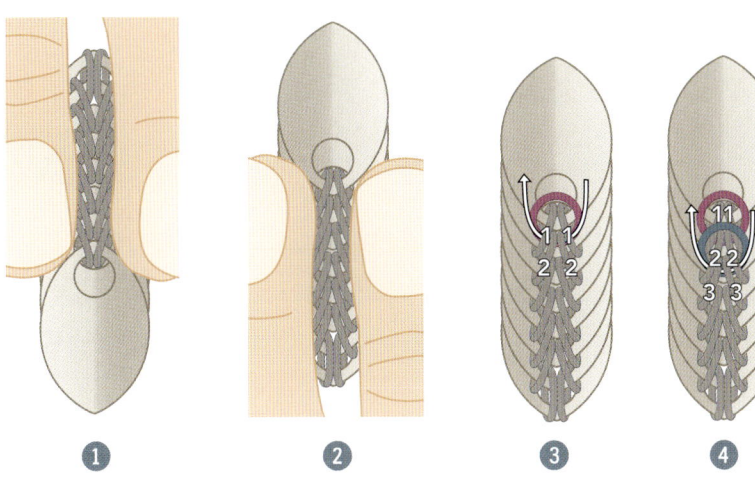

❶ ❷ ❸ ❹

Scale Maille 119

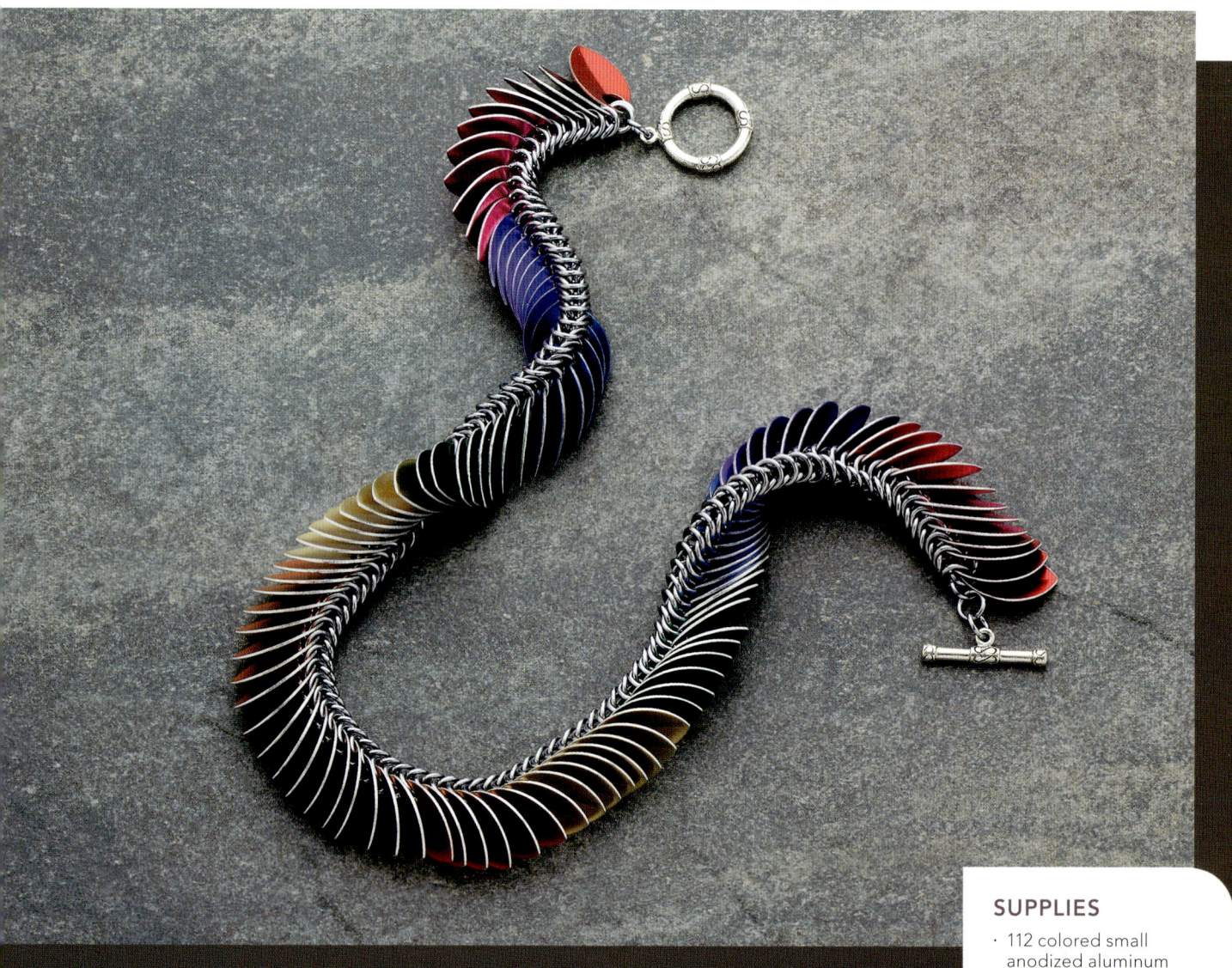

COLORFUL SCALE AND BOX CHAIN NECKLACE

This simple design elicits lots of attention because of the lively color combinations. I also made a version in subtle colors, which attracts its share of compliments as well.

1. Make a basic linear scale strip. Nest the scales with front (convex) sides facing you and arrange the colors as follows: 4 red, 8 pink, 8 purple, 8 blue, 8 green, 8 gold, 8 orange, 8 red, 8 orange, 8 gold, 8 green, 8 blue, 8, purple, 8, pink, 4 red.

2. Follow instructions to create the box chain along the length of the scale strip.

3. Attach each half of the clasp to each end of the box chain as directed in Termination Options for Scale Maille (page 135).

SUPPLIES

- 112 colored small anodized aluminum scales (16 of each color: red, pink, purple, blue, green, gold, orange), 9/16" × 7/8" (1.4 × 2.2 cm), 0.22" (5.8 mm) hole
- 340–345 black ice anodized aluminum saw-cut jump rings, 18g (SWG), 3/16" (4.76 mm) ID
- 1 pewter 15 mm toggle clasp

FINISHED LENGTH

- 16 ½" (42 cm) not including clasp

Half Persian 3-in-1

To produce a piece with a curved edge for a collar, use the HP31 weave on one side of your linear scale chain. To create a tighter scale strip or to begin Dragonback, use the HP31 weave on both sides of your linear scale chain.

Down One Side

Thread open jump rings down the line of jump rings on one edge of the scale strip to create the Half Persian 3-in-1 weave as follows:

1. Orient your linear scale strip as in the figures that follow (end of scale strip to the left, first edge jump ring sits in front of second, and so on down the length).

2. Thread 1 open (blue) jump ring through (TE connection) jump rings 3 and 2 from behind and then through (AE connection) jump ring 1 from the front, following the path in **Fig. 1**. Close the open jump ring. (For left-handers, reverse direction as shown in Fig. 4.)

3. Thread 1 open (fuchsia) jump ring through (TE connection) jump rings 4 and 3 from behind and then through (AE connection) jump ring 2 from the front, following the path in **Fig. 2**. Close the open jump ring. It should sit above the previously added jump ring.

4. Thread 1 open (yellow) jump ring through (TE connection) jump rings 5 and 4 from behind and then through (AE connection) jump ring 3 from the front, following the path in **Fig. 3**. Close the open jump ring. It should sit above the previously added jump ring.

Continue weaving down the length of the scale chain.

Down Two Sides

When working on the second side, you need to work in the opposite direction of the first side, producing mirror image HP31 chains on each side of the piece.

1. Orient your linear scale strip as in the figures that follow (end of scale strip to the right, first edge jump ring sits in front of second, and so on down the length).

2. Thread 1 open (blue) jump ring through jump ring 1 from behind and then AE (of 1 and 2) and through jump rings 2 and 3 (TE connection) from the front, following the path in **Fig. 5**. Close the open jump ring. (For left-handers, reverse direction as shown in Fig. 7.)

3. Thread 1 open (fuchsia) jump ring through jump ring 2 from behind and then AE (of 2 and 3) and through jump rings 3 and 4 (TE connection) from the front, following the path in **Fig. 6**. Close the open jump ring. It should sit above the previously added jump ring.

Continue weaving down the length of the scale strip.

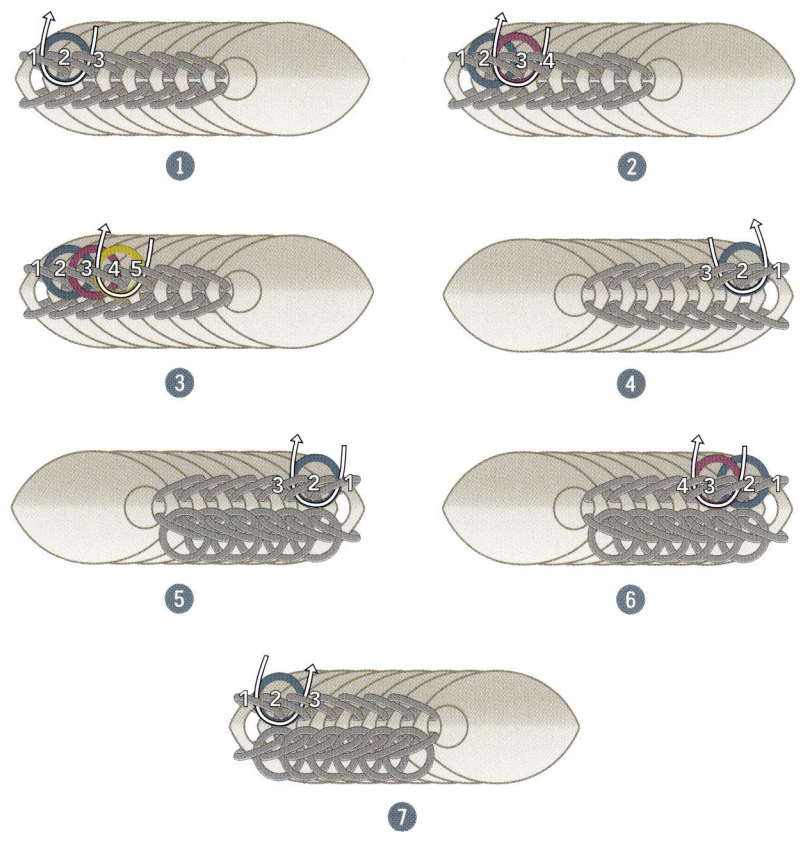

Scale Maille

Dragonback

1. Begin with a basic linear scale strip woven with 18g, 7/32" (5.6 mm) ID jump rings.

2. Weave 2 lines of mirror image HP31 along each edge of the chain as shown previously.

Connect the 2 lines of HP31 along the length of the scale chain to create the Dragonback weave as follows:

3. Orient your piece as in the figures that follow (inner jump ring 1 overlaps in front of inner jump ring 2, and so on down the length).

4. Thread 1 open (orange) jump ring down through inner jump rings 1 and 2 (TE connection) on the bottom line of HP31 from above and then up through inner jump rings 2 and 1 (TE connection) on the top line of HP31 from underneath, following the path in **Fig. 1**. Close the open jump ring.

5. Thread 1 open (green) jump ring down through inner jump rings 2 and 3 (TE connection) on the bottom line of HP31 from above and then up through inner jump rings 3 and 2 (TE connection) on the top line of HP31 from underneath, following the path in **Fig. 2**. Close the open jump ring.

Continue weaving down the length of the scale chain. **Fig. 3** shows left-handed weaving.

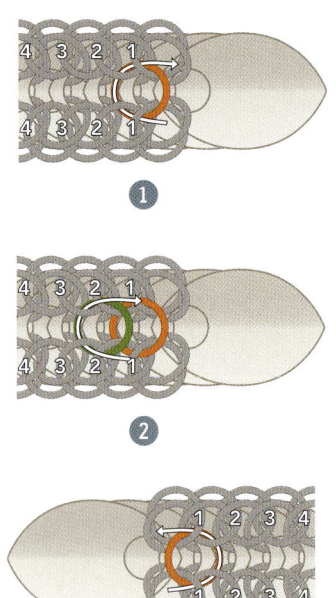

DRAGONBACK BRACELET WITH SCALES

This bracelet is simply a Dragonback chain (see page 92), where the scales take the place of the ridge jump rings in the weave.

1. Make basic linear scale strip using the 39 scales. Nest the scales with back (concave) sides facing you.

2. Follow the instructions for making the Dragonback weave from the basic linear scale strip.

3. Attach each half of a 2-strand clasp to each end of the bracelet using black ice jump rings as directed in Termination Options for Scale Maille, page 135.

SUPPLIES

- 39 champagne small anodized aluminum scales, 9/16" × 7/8" (1.4 × 2.2 cm), 0.22" (5.8 mm) hole
- 190–195 bright aluminum saw-cut jump rings, 18g (SWG), 7/32" (5.6 mm) ID
- 4 black ice anodized aluminum saw-cut jump rings, 18g (SWG), 5/32" (4 mm) ID, to attach clasp
- 1 silver-plated brass 2-strand slide clasp

FINISHED LENGTH

- 7½" (19 cm) not including clasp

SUPPLIES

- 146 small bronze anodized aluminum scales, 9/16" × 7/8" (1.4 × 2.2 cm), 0.22" (5.8 mm) hole
- 275 (approximate count) champagne anodized aluminum saw-cut jump rings, 18g (SWG), 3/16" (4.8 mm) ID
- 1 pewter 21 mm toggle clasp

FINISHED LENGTH

- 16½" (42 cm) not including clasp

TAPERED BRONZE SCALE MAILLE COLLAR

This collar uses the traditional scale weaving method. It is built from the center and out toward the ends by beginning with a diagonally woven diamond shape.

Weave the Tapered Right Side of the Collar

Add 1 row of 4 scales to the right side of the diamond as follows:

1. Make a diamond-shaped scale base consisting of 16 scales as directed in the Traditional Scale Weave/Diagonal section.

2. Attach 1 (green, first scale added) scale using 1 open jump ring to the right scale in the second row from the top of the diamond shape (**Fig. 1**).

3. Tuck the scale into position as directed by the arrow (**Fig. 2**) and secure with tape.

4. Attach 1 (yellow, second scale added) scale to the first (green) scale added using 1 open jump ring (**Fig. 3**).

5. Flip the scale into position as directed by the arrow (**Fig. 3**) and secure with tape (**Fig. 4**).

> **TIP**
> Use a paper clip to mark the center/top scale of the diamond. It will help you to keep your place when adding the sides of the collar.

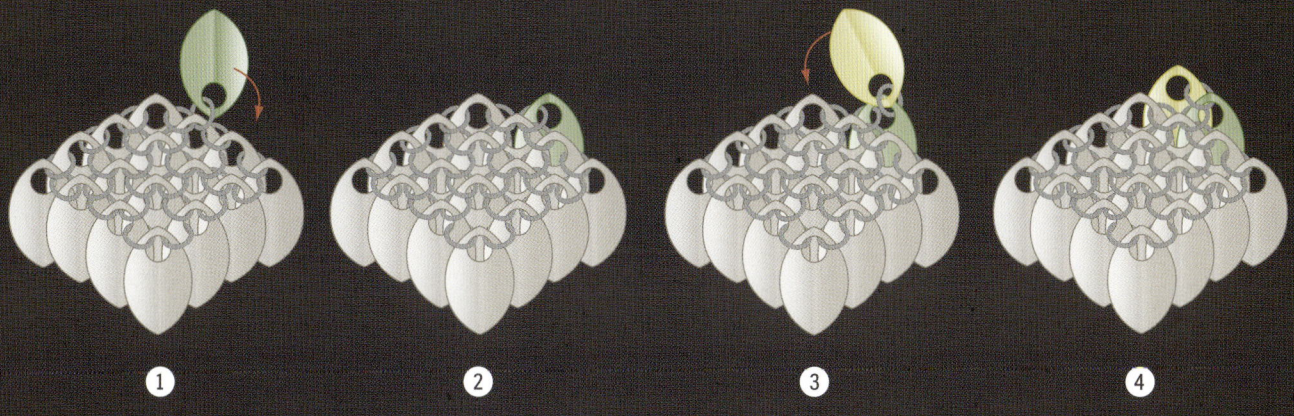

6. Attach the (yellow) scale just added to the top center scale of the diamond using 1 open (orange) jump ring (**Fig. 5**).

7. Attach 1 (turquoise, third scale added) scale to the first (green) scale added using 1 open jump ring (**Fig. 6**).

8. Attach the (turquoise) scale just added to the right scale in the third row from the top of the diamond shape using 1 open (orange) jump ring (**Fig. 7**).

9. Tuck the scale into position as directed by the arrow (**Fig. 7**) and secure with tape (**Fig. 8**).

10. Attach 1 (orange, fourth scale added) scale to the third (turquoise) scale added using 1 open jump ring (**Fig. 9**).

11. Attach the (orange) scale just added to the right scale in the fourth row from the top of the diamond shape using 1 open (orange) jump ring (**Fig. 10**).

12. Tuck the scale into position as directed by the arrow (**Fig. 10**). Secure with tape (**Fig. 11**).

13. In the same manner, add another row of 4 (pink) scales to the row just added (**Fig. 12**).

14. Continue adding rows of 4 scales in the same manner until 11 rows of 4 scales have been added to the right side of the collar.

15. To create the taper, add 5 rows of 3 scales and then 3 rows of 2 scales to the right side of the collar.

Weave the Tapered Left Side of the Collar

16. Create the tapered left side by following instructions for the tapered right side.

17. Add stabilizing jump rings at each end of the chain and where the weave transitions from rows of 4 scales to rows of 3 scales and rows of 3 scales to rows of 2 scales (**Fig. 13**), following directions for stabilizing sides of a straight weave (page 107).

18. Attach each half of the clasp to each end of the collar using a total of 4 (orange) jump rings, as shown (**Figs. 14** and **15**).

> **NOTE**
> To weave a row of 3 scales, follow instructions for a row of 4 scales, omitting the addition of the fourth scale. To weave a row of 2 scales, follow instructions for a row of 4 scales, omitting the addition of the third and fourth scales.

Scale Maille | Tapered Bronze Scale Maille Collar

SUPPLIES

- 84 champagne small anodized aluminum scales, 9/16" × 7/8" (1.4 × 2.2 cm), 0.22" (5.8 mm) hole

- 560 (approximate count) champagne anodized aluminum saw-cut jump rings, 18g (SWG), 3/16" (4.76 mm) ID

- 15 champagne anodized aluminum saw-cut jump rings, 20g (SWG), 5/32" (4 mm) ID, used to attach beads

- 15 smoky topaz pressed-glass dagger beads, 5 × 16 mm

- 1 pewter 15 mm toggle clasp

FINISHED LENGTH

- 13" (33 cm) not including clasp

128 ADVANCED CHAIN MAILLE JEWELRY WORKSHOP

BEADED LINEAR SCALE AND MAILLE COLLAR

This collar begins with a linear strip of scales that is shaped around the neck using the HP31 edge technique on one side. The other side is embellished with chain maille and accented with beads.

1. Make a linear scale strip using 84 scales and 166 18g jump rings, following the directions in the Linear Scale section (page 115).

2. Create a Half Persian edge on one edge of your strip using 81 18g jump rings, following the directions in the Linear Scale/Half Persian 3-in-1 section (page 121).

3. On the other edge of the strip, weave European 4-in-1 maille along the length of the edge, using 306 18g jump rings, following the directions in the Linear Scale/E41 Maille section (page 118). Thread the 306 jump rings through pairs of jump rings along the edge, using TE connections as follows:

- Weave 82 jump rings along the edge of the scale strip, opposite the HP31 edge.
- Weave 81 jump rings through the 82 jump rings just added.
- Weave 80 jump rings through the 81 jump rings just added.
- Weave 18 jump rings, centered in the row of 80 jump rings just added.
- Weave 15 jump rings, centered in the row of 18 jump rings just added.
- Weave 12 jump rings, centered in the row of 15 jump rings just added.
- Weave 9 jump rings, centered in the row of 12 jump rings just added.
- Weave 6 jump rings, centered in the row of 9 jump rings just added.
- Weave 3 jump rings, centered in the row of 6 jump rings just added.

4. Attach beads to collar using 20g jump rings as follows:

- Attach 3 beads, 1 to each of the last 3 jump rings added.
- Attach 2 beads, 1 to each end jump ring in the previous 5 rows of jump rings added (total of 10 beads added).
- Attach 2 beads to the row of 80 jump rings added, 1 on each side of the centered maille section.

5. Attach each half of the clasp to each of the ends of the linear scale strip using 4 or 5 jump rings (see finishing examples in Termination Options for Scale Maille, page 135).

Terminations, Attachments, and Finishing Touches

This chapter includes all of the information you'll need to turn your weaves into wearable jewelry. First, you'll get tips for making the ends of your weaves neat and even and for attaching clasps to various end configurations. Next, you'll find topics to help you improve the appearance and value of your chain maille jewelry, such as jump ring quality, closures, flex, and fit. You'll also receive helpful tips for sizing rings and bracelets and for choosing proper findings. Design suggestions are sprinkled throughout. This section concludes with a discussion on tumbling, cleaning, and storing your pieces to ensure that you can achieve and maintain a sparkling finish to your beautiful chain maille jewelry.

Termination Options for Chain Maille Weaves

To transform your weave into finished jewelry, you'll need to attach some sort of finding to make it a wearable piece (clasp, bail, ear wire, etc.). To do this, you first need to ensure the finished ends of your chain maille weaves are neat and even. Achieving this can be especially complicated for weaves created from a base piece and for sheet weaves. Each weave presents its own challenges.

With some weaves, the method of construction you choose to employ and how wide and long you decide to make your piece will alter the jump ring configurations at the finishing end. Each piece needs to be evaluated individually. In addition, several of these weaves have a directional grain, causing the beginning end to differ slightly from the finishing end and making clasp attachment a bit tricky. Although there is not room to present specific examples for every possible termination option, the suggestions that follow should provide you with the guidance needed to attach various findings.

Generally, I begin finishing the ends of my pieces by removing any leftover jump rings from extra-long base pieces. I examine both ends to make sure they are the same (or at least similar, as some directional weaves produce slightly different starting and finishing ends). If jump rings at the ends appear loose or don't seem to be fully integrated in the weave, I remove them. To determine if there seem to be any incomplete sections, I take cues from adjacent jump rings and pattern repeats. To correct any incompleteness, I add jump rings accordingly.

MAKING NEAT ENDINGS

Persian Weaves

GSG, GSG Sheet, Arkham, and Vertical Arkham Sheet Weaves

These weaves basically finish themselves. When you reach your desired length and have finished your last row, just stop weaving and the ends will be uniform. GSG and Arkham have ends consisting of 2 adjacent jump rings. GSG Sheet and Vertical Arkham Sheet have ends consisting of 3 adjacent jump rings—or more if you make a wider sheet.

Crotalus and Viperscale Weaves

You can stop weaving at various times in the weaving process to create a chain that ends in a single jump ring, 2 jump rings, or 3 jump rings. If you decide to end your weave with 3 jump rings, no other steps are required. If, however, you decide to end with 1 or 2 jump rings, you will need to remove jump rings from the starting end of the weave to make both ends match. Removing the right and left jump rings at the starting end will leave you with a single jump ring at that end. If you remove that single jump ring, you will have a pair of jump rings at that end.

HP31S6 and Horizontal Arkham Sheet Weaves

If you make your base HP31 chain longer than necessary, you will need to remove any extra jump rings. If, instead, you make it to size, there should be no additional steps required to finish the ends. The ends of these weaves consist of pairs of crossed jump rings. The number of crossed pairs depends on the width of the finished piece.

Elf-Based Weaves

Elfweave, Elfsheet, and Tiffany Weave

These weaves all begin with a base weave (1-by-1 chain or Elfweave). Depending on the method of construction you choose to weave the sheet versions and how wide and long you decide to make them, the ends will comprise different jump ring configurations. In addition, all Elf-based weaves have a directional grain, so the beginning end will differ slightly from the finishing end, making it more challenging to attach the clasp. If you make your base chain longer than necessary, you will need to remove any extra jump rings. Then you will need to study your ends to determine whether to add any jump rings (in pattern) or remove some to make the ends neat and even and ready for findings.

Hybrid Weaves

Interwoven Weave

Interwoven begins with a base weave (E41). It has a directional grain. Thus, the beginning end will differ slightly from the finishing end, making it more challenging to attach the clasp. If you make your base chain longer than necessary, you will need to remove any extra jump rings, as well as any other seemingly loose jump rings. The finished ends will consist of 2 pairs of crossed jump rings.

Interwoven Sheet

Interwoven Sheet also begins with a base weave (Interwoven 4-1). Depending on the method of construction you choose and how wide and long you decide to make the weave, the ends will comprise different configurations of jump rings. In addition, this weave has a directional grain. Thus, the beginning end will differ slightly from the finishing end, making it more challenging to attach the clasp.

If you make your base chain longer than necessary, you will need to remove any extra jump rings. Then you will need to study your ends to determine whether to add any jump rings (in pattern) or remove some to make the ends neat and even and ready for findings.

Dragonback and Persian Dragonscale

These Hybrid weaves both begin with a base weave (E41 or HP31) and, because their construction is so similar, they end in a comparable manner. Depending on the method of construction you choose and how long you decide to make the weave, the ends will comprise different configurations of jump rings. You will need to remove any extra jump rings from the original base chain, as well as any other seemingly loose jump rings. The finished ends will consist of 2 pairs of crossed jump rings.

Attachment Options for Findings

Once the ends look neat, you need to choose appropriate findings. Many options exist. You can buy simple utilitarian findings, fancy decorative and embellished findings, or you can make your own distinctive clasps and ear wires using wire, sheet, metal clay, beads, gems, or other unique materials. This is where you can really make your design stand out from the crowd.

To attach clasps and other findings to chain maille weaves, simply use additional jump rings. I generally try to choose jump rings that are 18g or 20g and of the smallest inner diameter possible to ensure a secure connection. Another way to increase security is to use 2 jump rings for each connection instead of just one. Split rings (similar to key rings) are another option that can be used to increase security.

1 JUMP RING ON THE ENDS

If the ends of your piece consist of a single jump ring, you can simply attach a single-strand clasp, such as a lobster clasp, a hook-style clasp, or toggle clasp, to the end of your piece. You can open the end jump ring(s) of your piece and slide the clasp directly onto the end jump ring(s), or you can use other jump rings to attach the clasp to the end jump ring(s). Based on the orientation of the clasp's attachment loop, you may need to use an additional jump ring(s) to attach the clasp. Depending on the clasp style you choose, the single-end jump ring at the opposite end of your piece can function as the catch for the clasp. Another option for a single-loop clasp is to remove the existing single-end jump ring and replace it (in pattern) with a larger jump ring.

A larger jump ring makes a handy and easily accessible catch for a clasp.

2 ADJACENT JUMP RINGS ON THE ENDS

Single and multistrand clasps can be used on ends consisting of 2 jump rings.

Single-Strand Clasps

To use a single-strand clasp, use jump rings to connect the clasp through the eye formed by the 2 adjacent jump rings at the end of the weave. You can make the connection more decorative and secure by threading several small (gold) jump rings through the clasp's loop and then through both end (purple/green) jump rings and the eye formed by the 2 end jump rings (**Fig. 1**).

If you need to create a catch for your single-loop clasp, you can attach a large jump ring (which will serve as your catch) to the end of your piece using small jump ring(s) woven through the large jump ring and the 2 end jump rings and/or the eye formed by the 2 end jump rings. You can also connect the large jump ring directly to the end of your piece by weaving it around the eye formed by the 2 end jump rings.

Terminations, Attachments, and Finishing Touches 133

Multistrand Clasps

Two-strand and 3-strand clasps work well when the weave ends in 2 jump rings. Attach a 2-strand clasp by threading a small jump ring through 1 loop of the clasp and 1 end jump ring. Close the jump ring just added and repeat the process to connect the second loop of the clasp to the second end jump ring. Attach a 3-strand clasp to the end of your piece by threading 1 small jump ring through the center loop of the clasp and then through the eye formed by the 2 end jump rings. Close this jump ring. One at a time, thread 1 small jump ring through each of the outer loops of the clasp and then through each end jump ring to complete the clasp attachment.

3 ADJACENT JUMP RINGS ON THE ENDS

Connecting a 3-strand clasp to weaves ending in 3 jump rings would seem to be the most logical choice. However, the number of jump rings at the end of your piece is not the only factor to consider. The 2 outer end jump rings on Vertical Arkham Sheet, Crotalus, and Viperscale tend to be a bit loose. Therefore, I do not recommend connecting a 3-strand clasp to the 3 jump rings at the ends (even though that does seem like the most logical choice). There is simply not enough stability there. Depending on the gauge/size of the jump rings used to construct the piece, 2-strand and 4-strand clasps can work well for a piece ending in 3 jump rings, as the TE connections used to attach these clasps help to make the ends more stable.

For GSG Sheet, only 1 outer end jump ring (the TE-only jump ring) is a bit loose, especially if the piece is constructed using an AR on the larger side. For added stability, I still prefer a clasp that attaches through the eyes, as opposed to attaching directly to the 3 end jump rings.

Attach a 2-strand clasp by threading a small jump ring through 1 loop of the clasp and 1 of the eyes formed by the 3 end jump rings. Close the jump ring just added and repeat the process to connect the second loop of the clasp to the second eye.

Attach a 4-strand clasp to the end of your piece by threading a small jump ring through each of the 2 center loops of the clasp and then through each of the 2 eyes formed by the 3 end jump rings. Add and close 1 jump ring before proceeding to add the next. One at a time, thread 1 small jump ring through each of the outer loops of the clasp and through each outer end jump ring. Close 1 jump ring before adding the next to complete the clasp attachment.

PAIRS OF CROSSED JUMP RINGS ON THE ENDS

The simplest way to attach a clasp to a weave with pairs of crossed jump rings at each end is to use a multistrand clasp that has corresponding loops for each pair of crossed jump rings at the end of the weave. One at a time, thread a small (gold) jump ring through each loop of the clasp and then through each crossed pair of (orange/gray) jump rings (**Fig. 2**).

You can also use a clasp with a single connection at the ends of weaves with pairs of crossed jump rings. Simply thread a larger (dark orange) jump ring through all the pairs of crossed jump rings by threading it through the side of the weave (**Fig. 3**). A single-loop clasp can be attached to this new jump ring as described above, or the jump ring can function as a catch.

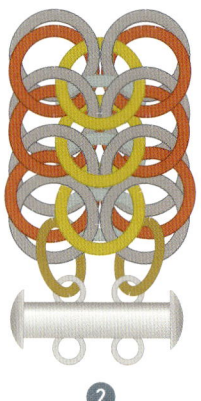

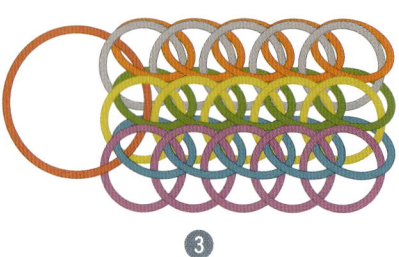

MORE COMPLEX END CONFIGURATIONS

Elfweave Chain

The starting end of the Elfweave chain is comprised of 1 jump ring, while the finishing end is comprised of 2, making it difficult to decide how to proceed.

I like to terminate my Elfweave chains with a single-loop clasp as follows:

- On the starting end, I reopen the center jump ring (the one with the paper clip attached to it), thread the clasp loop onto it, and close it.

- On the finishing end, I weave a larger jump ring through the 2 jump rings at the end of the chain: the larger jump ring serves as a catch for my clasp.

Interwoven 41 and Elfweave

The sheet versions of Interwoven 41 and Elfweave present a bigger challenge. Even after the ends have been made neat and even, the jump rings at the ends of these weaves overlap and sit at different angles, instead of sitting side by side in a more uniform fashion. In addition, these weaves are slightly different at the starting and finishing ends, making things even more complicated.

Depending on the method of construction used, the width of each sheet, and how you choose to neaten the ends of these weaves, single or multistrand options are possible. You can taper the ends of the weaves down to create a place for a single-loop clasp, or you can use various multistrand clasps (2-strand, 3-strand, 4-strand, etc.), attaching each loop through different combinations of end jump rings and the eyes formed by the end jump rings. Examples are shown in **Figs. 4–6**. **Fig. 4** shows a single attachment on a Tiffany weave. **Fig. 5** shows a 4-strand clasp on an Elfsheet weave. **Fig. 6** shows a 5-strand clasp on an Interwoven Sheet weave.

Many attachment solutions are possible for these weaves. For example, you could use 2 or 3 single clasps in place of a multistrand clasp. Don't be afraid to get creative by experimenting!

4

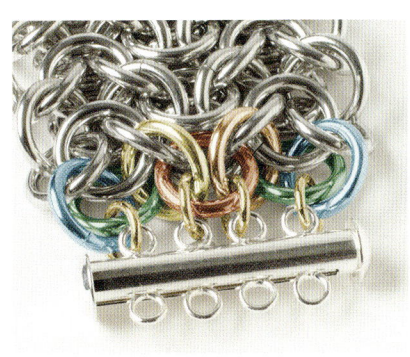

5

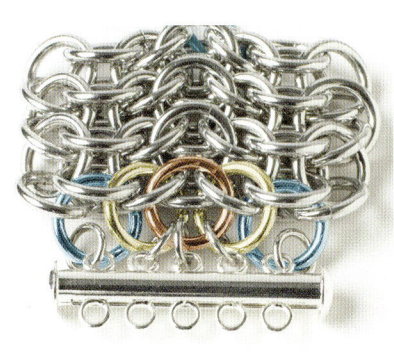

6

Termination Options for Scale Maille Weaves

Attaching findings to scale maille pieces is similar to attaching findings to chain maille pieces. Various options exist, depending on the finished item. You can use many styles of clasps and findings, either purchased or handmade.

TRADITIONAL SCALE MAILLE OPTIONS

Weaving Straight Across

If you are weaving wide (horizontal), you can attach a multistrand clasp to the sides of the piece by threading open jump rings to the outer stabilizing jump rings added to the end-scales of each even-numbered scale row and each loop of a multistrand clasp. If you are weaving long (vertical), you can attach a multistrand clasp by using open jump rings to connect the clasp to the scales across the top of the piece and then to the stabilizing jump rings at the bottom of the weave.

You can also taper the finishing end (follow instructions to contract a diagonal weave) to create a place to attach a single clasp. To create a single attachment spot at the starting end of the weave, taper the maille as shown (red/fuchsia jump rings) in **Fig. 7**.

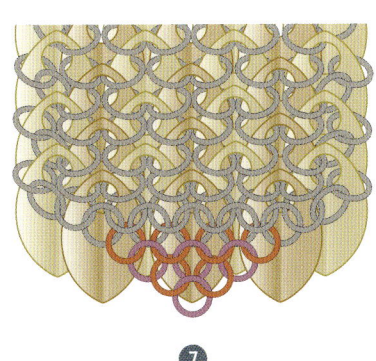

7

Terminations, Attachments, and Finishing Touches **135**

Weaving Diagonally

The diagonal form is usually just a starting point for making pieces of various shapes. Therefore, how you attach a clasp depends on the final item. The Tapered Bronze Scale Maille Collar is an example of a piece that begins with a diagonal form.

LINEAR SCALE MAILLE OPTIONS

Basic Linear Scale Strip

Using a single attachment–style clasp, attach each half of your clasp to each end of the scale chain using 1 or more jump ring(s). You can attach half of the clasp to the scale at the finishing end and the other half of the clasp to the jump rings on the starting end.

Box Chain with Scales

Using a single attachment–style clasp, attach each half of your clasp to the pair of jump rings at each end of the box chain using 1 or more jump rings, depending on the clasp style chosen.

Dragonback with Scales

Use small jump rings to attach each loop of each half of a 2-strand clasp to each pair of crossed jump rings at the ends of the chain (similar to attaching a clasp to the Dragonback chain maille weave).

Connected Linear Strips

The simplest solution for connecting linear strips is to use a multistrand clasp: attach each loop of each half of the clasp to the jump rings at the beginning and finishing ends of the weave. For a fancier finish, use the European 4-in-1 weaving technique to taper the ends of connected strips (3 connected strips pictured **Fig. 8**), providing a place to attach a single clasp. On the finishing end of the weave, taper the maille by threading the jump rings through the stabilizing jump rings on the front of the weave as in **Fig. 8**. On the beginning end of the weave, taper

the maille by threading jump rings through the stabilizing jump rings on the back of the weave (in similar fashion to that shown in **Fig. 7**).

Edged with Maille

Maille can be added to the edges of scale strips in a variety of ways to produce pieces with assorted uses. Therefore, clasp attachment would depend on the piece created and how the piece will be worn.

Finishing Touches

There are some important things you can do throughout the entire process of making your piece to achieve professional-quality jewelry, not just in the finishing stages.

1. Quality of Jump Rings—If you are making your own jump rings, *practice in order to perfect your results.* Your cuts must be straight, flush, and burr-free and your jump rings consistent in size and sufficiently strong. If you choose to purchase your jump rings instead (which is my choice), buy quality jump rings from a reliable vendor. (See Resources for recommendations.)

2. Quality of Closures—When constructing pieces, be sure you close your jump rings so that each closure is flush and tight.

JUMP RING CLOSING TIPS

Closing your jump rings properly is the key to making durable chain maille jewelry with a professional look. Proper closing technique takes practice. As you close your jump rings, inspect each closure from both a vertical (**Fig. 1**) and a horizontal (**Fig. 2**) angle before you move on. The seam should be tight, allowing no light to shine through, and the

ends should be perfectly aligned so the closed jump ring appears almost seamless.

If you have trouble seeing your joins, run your finger over them. You can feel the raw edges of an improperly closed seam, which is why a piece of jewelry containing poorly closed jump rings can irritate the skin and be uncomfortable to wear.

Closing Jump Rings

1. Hold the jump ring with the cut end in a 12 o'clock position (**Fig. 3**).

2. Position your pliers on the left and right sides of the jump ring. Make sure that the jaws of your pliers are parallel to the surface of the jump ring (**Fig. 4**).

3. Apply inward pressure evenly to both sides of the jump ring as you bring the ends of the jump ring together to close it. Use sufficient pressure so that the ends of the jump ring overlap when brought together. This creates tension in the wire, ensuring a tight and secure closure.

4. Release the pressure and wiggle the jump ring ends back and forth with your pliers. This often produces a satisfying clicking sound. Wiggle until the edges of the jump ring are perfectly aligned.

When weaving with sterling silver, I like to perform the above steps in both directions to build the tension evenly and work-harden the jump rings.

Common Jump Ring Closing Issues and Solutions

Gaps: When a coil of wire is cut to make a jump ring, the saw blade removes a small amount of metal, causing a slight gap between the cut ends. This is why it is important to apply inward pressure evenly to both sides of the jump ring when closing. If you can see light through the seam, try closing again to ensure that you are applying adequate inward pressure (**Fig. 5**).

Misalignment (horizontal view): If you notice, from a horizontal perspective, that the ends of your jump ring are misaligned, adjust the seam by wiggling the ends of the jump ring back and forth with your pliers until you achieve proper alignment (**Fig. 6**).

Misalignment (vertical view): This misalignment is more difficult to correct. It is the result of inward pressure that is unevenly applied to each side of the jump ring. To correct the overhang, repeat the closing steps, this time applying more inward pressure to the high side and less to the low side of the jump ring. **Never** try to remedy this situation by squeezing down the high side; you will likely distort the shape of the jump ring, necessitating a replacement (**Fig. 7**).

Warping: This error is most frequently caused by wrist-twisting or improperly positioned pliers (not placed parallel to jump ring's surface). If left in the piece, warped jump rings will adversely affect the chain's flexibility and fluidity. Replace warped jump rings and add them to your refining scrap (**Fig. 8**).

Marring: If you grasp your pliers too tightly, you can create dents and scratches in your jump rings. Also, the anodized colors on aluminum and niobium jump rings are merely a layer of oxidation on the metal's surface and can be scratched off by the pliers if you are not careful. Marred jump rings detract from the beauty of the finished piece and should be replaced and added to your refining scrap. You cannot rely on a tumbler to remove deep scratches, dents, and gouges in your precious metals. It will polish out superficial surface marks only.

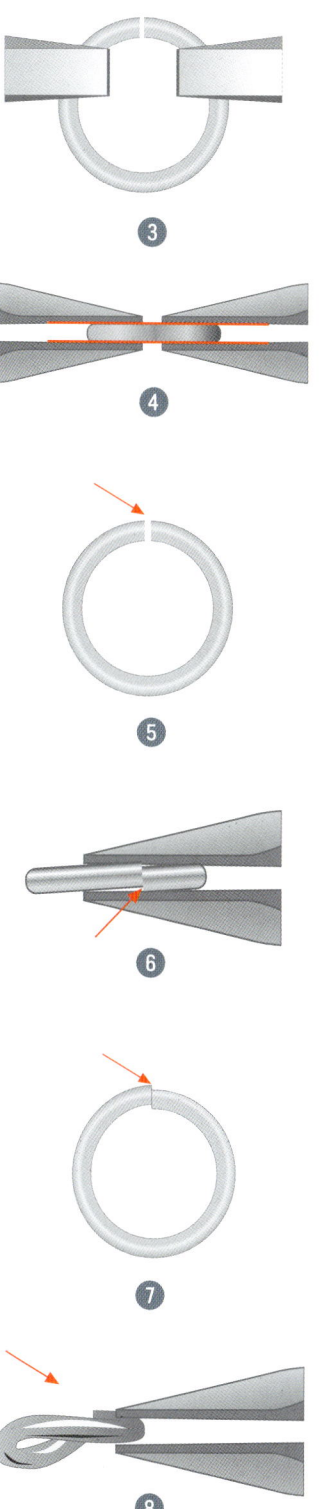

Terminations, Attachments, and Finishing Touches

People use various solutions to cover and coat the jaws of their pliers to reduce the possibility of marring jump rings. Some solutions are tape (all kinds), moleskin, cut bits of plastic drinking straws, liquid tool dip, etc. I prefer not to use any of the above. The coverings and coatings add thickness to the jaws of my pliers, affecting my control. It reminds me of trying to tie my shoes with gloves on. However, if marring is a real problem for you, feel free to try one of these solutions: you may find it helpful.

When you get a new pair of pliers, the edges can be sharp and the surface of the jaws may be rough. I use wet/dry sandpaper and polishing papers to refine the jaws of my pliers before I work on projects with them. This must be done carefully. Do not over-sand your pliers—you do not want to alter their shape or render them useless! You just want to gently smooth out the rough spots. Run your finger along the edges and surfaces of your plier jaws to gauge smoothness. Refining the jaws will not totally eliminate marring, but I've found that it cuts down on how often and how seriously it occurs. I find that smoothing the plier jaws and gripping pliers properly when working with them are very effective ways to avoid marring.

Proper flex and fit: You need to make sure your maille piece flexes properly and fits well. Weave flexibility is determined by aspect ratio (AR). As explained in the beginning of the book, the recommended jump ring sizes that are provided are based on the simplest form, a bracelet. If you wish to make an item that needs to flex differently—for example, a collar that requires flexibility on the edges, you will need to experiment and then adjust the jump ring size to achieve just the flex you desire.

With earrings, fit is not an issue. People's preferences regarding earrings usually involve style, size, or weight. For necklaces, the most common range of lengths is 16"–24" (40.5–61 cm) for women and 18"–24" (45.5–61 cm) for men. Chokers, collars, rings, and bracelets can be more difficult to fit.

- Collars and chokers: These can be tricky. For choker styles [13"–15" (33–38 cm)], try adding an extender chain to the clasp to make the length adjustable. Collars need to encircle the neck without drooping or puckering along the inner edge. Therefore, it is sometimes necessary to weave additional jump rings around the inner edge to create a curve that lies smoothly around the neck, as shown in the Beaded Linear Scale and Maille Collar project on page 128.

- Chain maille rings: These are even trickier to fit properly. When sizing a solid metal ring, the band can be slightly expanded, or a tiny bit of metal can be removed to make the band smaller, providing a wide range of sizing options. However, when adjusting the size of a chain maille ring, you must either add or remove one row or one pattern repeat (which may involve two or more rows). Therefore, precision sizing adjustments cannot be made. You may have to wear a ring on a finger other than your ring finger, for example. The standard U.S. ring size for women is 7, and for men the standard size is 10.

- Bracelets: Sizing bracelets can also be challenging. Wrists come in many shapes and sizes. The U.S. standard bracelet length is based on a wrist measurement of 7" (18 cm) for women and 8" (20.5 cm) for men.

SIZING RINGS AND BRACELETS

My students often ask me, "How long do you make your bracelets?" My answer is usually, "I don't know." That response makes them crazy! The real answer is, "Every piece is different. It depends on the weave and the size of the jump rings being used." People's wrists and fingers are simply not uniform in size. Also, the width, thickness, flexibility, and style (closed or clasped) of the piece will affect the length requirement. What follow are some key factors in sizing:

The thicker the weave, the longer it has to be to encircle an object (like a wrist or a finger). A closed band that is wide requires a bit of additional length to enable it to pass over the knuckle.

For those who are mathematically inclined, here are a couple of basic formulas that can be used to determine the length needed to surround a round- or an oval-shaped object. These can help you estimate the weave length you need for rings and bracelets:

Round: Weave Length = (Inside Diameter + Weave Thickness) × π

Oval: Weave Length = (Oval Length + Oval Width) ÷ 2 + Weave Thickness) × π

I choose to avoid the math for a few reasons:

- I don't really like to do math.
- There are lots of variables and therefore lots of opportunities to mess up the calculation.

- Mathematical calculations are based on numbers and not real objects. When working with decimals and fractions and rounding (Oh my!) there will be some loss of precision, so the result is basically just an estimate.

Because the length requirement will vary based on thickness, width, flexibility, and style of a maille piece, I don't think in terms of length. I prefer working around a three-dimensional object that gives me a good visual idea of how the weave will fit. Because of this, I use a mandrel instead of a flat ruler. My ring mandrel is steel and has the ring sizes marked on it. My bracelet mandrel is plain wood. I use a cloth or plastic tailor's tape measure to find the proper working spot on the bracelet mandrel and then mark it with a rubber band. For example, if I want to make a bracelet for a person with a standard 7" (18 cm) wrist, I use a tailor's tape measure to find the spot on the mandrel that is 7" (18 cm) around and then place a rubber band at this spot.

If you are making a bracelet or ring for yourself, you don't need a mandrel or a ruler. Simply use your own wrist or finger to measure. After all, you've always got them handy, and they're exactly the right size. In fact, when doing custom work, I prefer to have fittings. Fittings are the most accurate way to ensure the fit is perfect. Mandrels are not shaped exactly like the human body, which is pliable and somewhat irregularly shaped. Instead, mandrels are rigid and perfectly symmetrical. However, if your recipient is not available for fittings, mandrels are the next best option.

If you are making a bracelet or ring for a person who is not available for fittings, ask the person for their ring size or wrist measurement. If you are making items with no particular person in mind, you can use the standard sizes/measurements. Work around a ring mandrel at the spot showing the desired ring size or use a tailor's tape measure on a bracelet mandrel to determine the proper working spot for the desired length. As you weave, periodically stop and try the piece on the mandrel to test the size. When sizing bracelets, the wearer's preference needs to be considered. Some people like snug-fitting, fairly stationary bracelets, while others like them to be a bit loose with some movement. Keep this in mind as well when determining the final size.

The ring projects in this book can be especially tricky to fit. Each starts with a base weave (E41 or 1-by-1 chain) that, in theory, should be closed before additional weaving steps are performed. The hard part is to figure out how long the base chain should be, as the additional weaving steps required will cause the base chain to shrink. My approach to achieving the correct ring size is to begin by making the base chain a bit longer than required. I do *not* close the base chain at this time. I begin to perform the additional weaving steps, leaving a short tail of unwoven base chain at *both* ends. This way, I can easily add more base chain if the weave begins to shrink too much. If not, I can just remove the extra jump rings. After all, it is much easier to remove extra jump rings than it is to figure out where to add more in the pattern. While weaving, I frequently stop to test the size on my finger (or mandrel). When the ring seems to fit about right, I close the ends of the base chain and perform the last of the additional weaving steps to complete the ring.

> **NOTE**
>
> π = Pi = 3.142
>
> Inside Diameter (ID) = Inner Circumference* ÷ π
>
> *Inner Circumference represents the measurement around the body part.
>
> For a ring, if the band width will be greater than 4 mm wide, add 0.5 mm to the length.
>
> **NOTE**
>
> If you don't want too snug a fit on a cuff or bracelet, you can add about 4–8 mm to your wrist measurement* to achieve your level of comfort.
>
> *If making a closed, claspless-style bracelet, you cannot use your wrist measurement, as the bracelet needs to slide over your entire hand. To get a useable measurement, hold your hand straight out and squish your fingers together, touching your thumb to your pinky as you would when slipping on a bangle bracelet. Now, use a tailor's tape measure to measure around the thickest part of your hand.

If I want to make more rings of the same size, no problem. I now know how long the base chain needs to be, so I can just make the base chain to the proper length, close it, and then finish the weave without having to stop and test the fit. I can also use that base length as an estimating tool to make rings a bit larger or a bit smaller.

APPROPRIATE FINDINGS

Findings (ear wires, bails, clasps, etc.) can, literally, make or break your jewelry. Always consider the style, size/weight, type of metal, and wearer for your creation when selecting findings. Choose a style that complements your piece, such as pairing a sleek weave with modern-style findings or an intricate weave with something more decorative. You can also express a theme with the findings you choose. For example, pair a Dragonback chain with a serpent-themed clasp. Hefty pieces require findings that can bear weight, while small findings will suit a delicate piece.

When deciding which metal to use, I take my cues from the piece. I would not use a cheap base metal clasp on a sterling silver bracelet: I use precious metal findings on precious metal pieces and plated or base metal findings on nonprecious metal pieces. Some supply outlets offer a limited variety of findings in enameled and anodized metals, which allows you to accent a color scheme, either matching or complementary.

The finding must also suit the wearer. If the finding is difficult to operate or makes the jewelry uncomfortable to wear, it won't be worn; for example, a necklace that keeps flipping over due to the wrong type of clasp or earrings that are too heavy to wear. Plus, many people have preferences regarding ear wires and clasps.

Ear wires: Ear wires come in many sizes and styles, including hooks, leverbacks, and posts. Keep in mind that some people are allergic to base metals such as nickel, but it's usually safe to stick to precious metals such as sterling silver and gold. Or you can try a hypoallergenic metal such as niobium or titanium.

I like leverback ear wires best because they provide both comfort and security. However, I prefer the look of hook-style ear wires. They are available in lots of cool shapes, and they are very comfortable, but it is easy for the earrings to fall out of your earlobes. I've lost some of my favorite earrings this way! You can remedy this easily by fitting the ear wire ends with clear rubber ear nuts, available at most jewelry supply outlets. For me, posts are uncomfortable (they often poke my neck). Also, should you lose the ear nut for a post, you may not be able to wear the earring if you can't find another that fits and matches. (You can, of course, simply replace the posts.)

Clasps: Clasps come in a variety of sizes and types—toggles, lobsters, hooks, S-clasps, slide clasps, magnetic clasps, multistrand clasps, and so many more.

I like large lobster clasps. The large ones are much easier to operate than the smaller sizes. Lobster clasps also spring shut for security. However, they don't have much style. I also like well-designed toggle clasps. They, too, are easy to operate and are available in fun shapes and styles as well. However, you need to make sure that the bar of the toggle clasp is long enough so that it won't easily slip back out through the loop. (Some toggle clasps are poorly designed, with bars that are too short—and that is how bracelets are lost.)

S-hooks or hook-and-eye clasps are easy to operate and work well for necklaces (where gravity helps keep the chain in position). But because they don't actually close (just connect), I don't feel they are secure enough for bracelets. Magnetic clasps are another option. They can be very strong. In fact, I bought a magnetic clasp that is so strong, I have trouble pulling it apart (which can also be a problem). I like box-style clasps with safety latches, but these can be quite expensive. On flat chains or sheet weaves, I like to use multistrand slide clasps because they help to keep flat chains from flipping.

Different types of clasps require varying degrees of manual dexterity to operate, so in addition to considering which clasp will function and look best with your piece, think about the wearer of your jewelry. For example, if you are designing for someone with arthritis, larger clasps are usually easier to operate than smaller clasps. Also, you may want to use a hook or a toggle instead of a tightly sprung lobster clasp. Or you can go claspless.

When purchasing clasps, pay attention to the orientation of the connecting loops: make sure the loops are in the proper plane for connecting to your weave.

Jump rings for attachment: Because you will typically attach findings to your jewelry with jump rings, it's nice to have several sizes of them on hand. For security, I recommend using jump rings of the thickest gauge that seem appropriate for the scale of your piece, keeping in mind how much stress a piece of jewelry may absorb when worn. A bracelet clasp, for example, would need to be attached with a stronger jump ring than, say, a lightweight earring finding. A small inner diameter also increases security as does using multiple jump rings to make attachments. Split rings are another alternative.

It's All in the Details

Sometimes it's the little things that give your jewelry design an edge. For example, when making earrings from weaves with a directional grain, it's nice to weave them in mirror image to create a pleasing symmetrical frame around the face. Sometimes, a jeweled clasp or a hammered ear wire or other special finding will make your piece stand out.

FINAL FINISH

You want to make sure the finish on your designs is attractive. To keep my bright aluminum and anodized aluminum and niobium pieces clean and shiny, I simply handwash the pieces with mild dish soap and warm water and dry them well with a soft cloth. It can be difficult to dry scale maille pieces with a cloth, so I often use my blow dryer to help dry between the scales. If you do this, put the dryer on a low setting and be careful, as the metal can get very hot!

For precious metals, nothing makes a piece of jewelry look quite so impressive as an incredibly bright shine, so I like to tumble-polish my finished sterling silver, silver-filled, and gold-filled pieces. The tumbling process doesn't really remove metal, but rather it is as if the jewelry is being hit by lots of tiny hammers that smooth the surface to make it shine. The tumbling process also helps to work-harden the jump rings, adding strength to the finished piece.

Do be very careful about what you put into the tumbler. Certain types of beads or stones should never be put into the tumbler, as they may crack or discolor. I've tumbled dichroic glass cabochons and uncoated Swarovski crystals without incident, but it's a good idea to test a spare bead or stone by tumbling it alone before you tumble the actual piece, just to be safe. When tumbling pieces with inclusions, like beads, I usually reduce my tumbling time. Of course, a hidden flaw in a bead may cause it to break when tumbled as well. Therefore, whenever possible,

I remove beads and dangles before tumbling and replace when done. If an embellishment cannot be removed and I am not sure if it is safe to tumble, then I don't. My advice: When in doubt, leave it out!

Although tumbling is a fairly gentle process, you must use common sense when loading the tumbler. To avoid damage to delicate or soft items, don't place heavy or hard items in with them. Fine chains are prone to tangling around themselves or other items in the tumbler. If I tumble jump rings or chain maille beads, I first string them on a bit of wire for easy retrieval.

Inspect your chain maille when it comes out of the tumbler. Sometimes a stray piece of shot can lodge in the chain maille weave and will need to be removed. Occasionally, tumbling can cause the jump rings in a piece of chain maille to shift position in the weave, necessitating a quick repair.

To tumble-polish your jewelry, you'll need a rotary tumbler, some tumbling media (shot), dish soap or a burnishing liquid, and water. There are many fine brands of tumblers on the market, some quite modestly priced. Buy one based on your needs and your wallet. The tumbler, the shot for polishing, and burnishing compound can be purchased through jewelry supply outlets (see Resources). I recommend mixed stainless-steel shot, which contains a variety of shapes, perfect for fitting into nooks and crannies. The mixes I use to tumble my chain maille do not contain pins, the long, thin pointy shapes that often become buried in the weaves.

I have a Lortone 33B double-barrel rotary tumbler. Each barrel has a 3-pound capacity. My tumbling recipe is:

- Stainless-steel mixed shot, 2 lb of shot per 3-lb barrel
- One moderate handful of precious metal jewelry per barrel
- Rio Grande's Super Sunsheen burnishing compound mixed with water as per product directions

Fill barrel with mixture, about ½" (1.3 cm) over the level of the contents. I tumble each load for 2 to 3 hours. I prefer the result I get when tumbling with Rio's Super Sunsheen as opposed to dishwashing liquid.

I JUST WASHED MY WEAVE AND I CAN'T DO A THING WITH IT!

I have to tell you about a weird phenomenon that I can't explain logically. Sometimes, after washing or tumbling a piece, the weave gets tighter—it kind of shrinks in the wash. Once dry, a gentle chain "massage" usually helps to loosen it back up. However, on occasion I've washed aluminum test patches that were dense yet quite fluid before washing, but locked tight after washing. Even after being fully dried, the weaves remained solidly immoveable. I couldn't even massage the stiffness out of them. So, I recommend that you make a small test piece of your weave in the jump ring size you plan to use and finish it as you intend to finish your actual jewelry to see if the weave remains flexible after finishing.

If you like the look of oxidized metal, you can use liver of sulfur on your silver pieces to give them that aged, ancient look. Use caution when oxidizing a piece that contains beads or stones and, in general, when working with chemicals.
You can find liver of sulfur at most jewelry supply outlets as well.

MAINTENANCE AND STORAGE

With sterling silver, tarnish is always an issue. When a silver piece begins to look a bit dingy, I simply throw it into the tumbler if I've got an hour or two. If I've got only 10 or 15 minutes, I do one of two things:

(1) Gently burnish the piece with a jeweler's soft brass brush and lots of dish soap and water; or (2) Make a paste of baking soda and water and, with an old soft toothbrush, gently scrub the piece with the paste.

These quick methods produce a softer satin finish, as opposed to the high polish achieved through tumbling. Use care cleaning around beads and stones to prevent scratching them. Lastly, rinse the piece with water and dry it well with a soft cloth. Using a silver polishing cloth is another quick solution to remove tarnish.

To help avoid tarnish on silver in the first place, I store my pieces in plastic zip-lock bags. This minimizes their exposure to the atmospheric compounds that promote oxidation. I do the same with my anodized metal pieces. When I take off my silver jewelry at night, I use rubbing alcohol on a cotton pad to wipe off any perfumes, oils, lotions, makeup, or sweat that may have transferred from my body to the jewelry. If you choose to do this, avoid getting alcohol on beads or stones as it might be detrimental to the finish. When in doubt, just wipe with a soft cloth. Of course, commonsense practices such as removing jewelry before sleeping, swimming, showering, or exercising will help to keep it like new.

142 ADVANCED CHAIN MAILLE JEWELRY WORKSHOP

Resources

There is a vibrant and active maille community online. Maillers are generous people who are passionate about their craft and about sharing knowledge.

For informative articles, tutorials, and helpful links, check out the Maille Artisans International League website (mailleartisans.org). They are an online international community of chain maille artisans whose mission is to share and archive chain maille information.

For tutorials, cgmaille.com (Phong's Chainmaille Tutorials), complete with beautiful computer-generated illustrations, is the place to go.

For technical data and charts, articles, and a few tutorials, check out chainmailbasket.com.

In addition, Urban Maille (urbanmaille.com) and The Ring Lord (theringlord.com) have lots of useful chain maille information posted on their websites.

Taking classes is a wonderful way to learn. Many bead shops offer classes in chain maille techniques, and you also may find classes at local art centers, museums, or universities that have metals programs. I teach chain maille classes at Metalwerx, a metal arts school that offers classes, workshops, and studio space for working artists. I hope to see you there!

Metalwerx School for Jewelry and Metal Arts
50 Guinan St.
Waltham, MA 02451
(781) 891-3854; fax (781) 891-3857
metalwerx.com

Jewelry supplies are available at bead stores, retail shops, and from online retailers. I encourage you to support your local bead shops whenever possible. Here is a list of some of my favorite online sources for jump rings and jewelry tools and supplies:

JUMP RINGS, TOOLS, AND SUPPLIES

Chain Maille Suppliers

C&T Designs
Jump rings, scales, kits, tools, findings
4756 N. Chestnut St. (retail store)
Colorado Springs, CO 80907
(719) 638-4631
(855) 2-MAILLE [(855) 262-4553)]
candtdesigns.com

Metal Designz
Jump rings, scales, rubber O-rings, kits, tools, findings, classes
832 Broadway Ave.
Saskatoon, SK, Canada S7N 1B6
(306) 343-1892, (866) 349-RING
metaldesignz.com

The Ring Lord
Jump rings, scales, rubber O-rings, wire, tools, kits, findings
290C RR9
Saskatoon, SK, Canada S7K 1P3
(855) 746-4567; fax (877) 297-8199
theringlord.com

Urban Maille
Jump rings, findings, tools, kits
PO Box 682
Pine, CO 80470
(303) 838-7432
urbanmaille.com

Bead Supply Outlets

Fire Mountain Gems and Beads
Beads, rubber O-rings, findings
1 Fire Mountain Wy.
Grants Pass, OR 97526
(800) 355-2137
firemountaingems.com

Fusion Beads
Beads, findings
3830 Stone Wy. N. (retail store)
Seattle, WA 98103
(206) 782-4595
fusionbeads.com

Jewelry and Tool Supply Outlets

Contenti
Tools, supplies
515 Narragansett Park Dr.
Pawtucket, RI 02861
(401) 305-3000; fax (800) 651-1887
contenti.com

Kingsley North, Inc.
Tumbling equipment, supplies
910 Brown St. (or PO Box 216)
Norway, MI 49870
(800) 338-9280
kingsleynorth.com

Otto Frei
Tools, supplies
126 2nd St.
Oakland, CA 94607
(800) 772-3456
ottofrei.com

Rio Grande Jewelers' Supply
Jump rings, wire, findings, tools, and supplies
7500 Bluewater Rd. NW
Albuquerque, NM 87121
(800) 545-6566
riogrande.com

Warg Enamel and Tool Center
Tuff Brake, tools, classes
10 Oak Hill Plaza
Scarborough, ME 04074
(855) 885-9382
wargetc.com

Abbreviations

AE around-the-eye connection

AR aspect ratio

AWG American Wire Gauge

cm centimeter

E41 European 4-in-1 weave

g gauge

HP31 Half Persian 3-in-1 weave

HP31S6 Half Persian 3-in-1 Sheet 6 weave

HP41 Half Persian 4-in-1 weave

ID inner diameter

mm millimeter

OD outer diameter

RPI rings per inch

SWG British Standard Wire Gauge

TE through-the-eye connection

WD wire diameter

Aspect Ratio Charts

The figures in the following charts are merely mathematical calculations. Differences in manufacturing of actual jump rings are not considered. In addition, as conversions from different measuring systems are made and numbers are rounded, precision is lost. Therefore, the figures contained in these charts are to be used as guidelines for estimation only.

ASPECT RATIO FOR AMERICAN WIRE GAUGE (AWG)

10-Gauge Wire (AWG)

WD (mm)	ID (mm)	OD (mm)	AR	Rounded AR
2.588	1.00	6.2	0.386	0.4
2.588	1.25	6.4	0.483	0.5
2.588	1.50	6.7	0.580	0.6
2.588	1.75	6.9	0.676	0.7
2.588	2.00	7.2	0.773	0.8
2.588	2.25	7.4	0.869	0.9
2.588	2.50	7.7	0.966	1.0
2.588	2.75	7.9	1.062	1.1
2.588	3.00	8.2	1.159	1.2
2.588	3.25	8.4	1.256	1.3
2.588	3.50	8.7	1.352	1.4
2.588	3.75	8.9	1.449	1.4
2.588	4.00	9.2	1.545	1.5
2.588	4.25	9.4	1.642	1.6
2.588	4.50	9.7	1.739	1.7
2.588	4.75	9.9	1.835	1.8
2.588	5.00	10.2	1.932	1.9
2.588	5.25	10.4	2.028	2.0
2.588	5.50	10.7	2.125	2.1

10-Gauge Wire (AWG) Cont'd.

WD (mm)	ID (mm)	OD (mm)	AR	Rounded AR
2.588	5.75	10.9	2.222	2.2
2.588	6.00	11.2	2.318	2.3
2.588	6.25	11.4	2.415	2.4
2.588	6.50	11.7	2.511	2.5
2.588	6.75	11.9	2.608	2.6
2.588	7.00	12.2	2.705	2.7
2.588	7.25	12.4	2.801	2.8
2.588	7.50	12.7	2.898	2.9
2.588	7.75	12.9	2.994	3.0
2.588	8.00	13.2	3.091	3.1
2.588	8.25	13.4	3.187	3.2
2.588	8.50	13.7	3.284	3.3
2.588	8.75	13.9	3.381	3.4
2.588	9.00	14.2	3.477	3.5
2.588	9.25	14.4	3.574	3.6
2.588	9.50	14.7	3.670	3.7
2.588	9.75	14.9	3.767	3.8
2.588	10.00	15.2	3.864	3.9
2.588	10.25	15.4	3.960	4.0

10-Gauge Wire (AWG) Cont'd.

WD (mm)	ID (mm)	OD (mm)	AR	Rounded AR
2.588	10.50	15.7	4.057	4.1
2.588	10.75	15.9	4.153	4.2
2.588	11.00	16.2	4.250	4.2
2.588	11.25	16.4	4.347	4.3
2.588	11.50	16.7	4.443	4.4
2.588	11.75	16.9	4.540	4.5
2.588	12.00	17.2	4.636	4.6
2.588	13.00	18.2	5.023	5.0
2.588	14.00	19.2	5.409	5.4
2.588	15.00	20.2	5.795	5.8
2.588	16.00	21.2	6.182	6.2

12-Gauge Wire (AWG)

WD (mm)	ID (mm)	OD (mm)	AR	Rounded AR
2.052	1.00	5.1	0.487	0.5
2.052	1.25	5.4	0.609	0.6
2.052	1.50	5.6	0.731	0.7
2.052	1.75	5.9	0.853	0.9
2.052	2.00	6.1	0.975	1.0
2.052	2.25	6.4	1.096	1.1
2.052	2.50	6.6	1.218	1.2
2.052	2.75	6.9	1.340	1.3
2.052	3.00	7.1	1.462	1.5
2.052	3.25	7.4	1.584	1.6
2.052	3.50	7.6	1.705	1.7
2.052	3.75	7.9	1.827	1.8
2.052	4.00	8.1	1.949	1.9
2.052	4.25	8.4	2.071	2.1
2.052	4.50	8.6	2.193	2.2
2.052	4.75	8.9	2.314	2.3
2.052	5.00	9.1	2.436	2.4
2.052	5.25	9.4	2.558	2.6
2.052	5.50	9.6	2.680	2.7
2.052	5.75	9.9	2.802	2.8
2.052	6.00	10.1	2.924	2.9
2.052	6.25	10.4	3.045	3.0
2.052	6.50	10.6	3.167	3.2
2.052	6.75	10.9	3.289	3.3
2.052	7.00	11.1	3.411	3.4

12-Gauge Wire (AWG) Cont'd.

WD (mm)	ID (mm)	OD (mm)	AR	Rounded AR
2.052	7.25	11.4	3.533	3.5
2.052	7.50	11.6	3.654	3.7
2.052	7.75	11.9	3.776	3.8
2.052	8.00	12.1	3.898	3.9
2.052	8.25	12.4	4.020	4.0
2.052	8.50	12.6	4.142	4.1
2.052	8.75	12.9	4.263	4.3
2.052	9.00	13.1	4.385	4.4
2.052	9.25	13.4	4.507	4.5
2.052	9.50	13.6	4.629	4.6
2.052	9.75	13.9	4.751	4.8
2.052	10.00	14.1	4.873	4.9
2.052	10.25	14.4	4.994	5.0
2.052	10.50	14.6	5.116	5.1
2.052	10.75	14.9	5.238	5.2
2.052	11.00	15.1	5.360	5.4
2.052	11.25	15.4	5.482	5.5
2.052	11.50	15.6	5.603	5.6
2.052	11.75	15.9	5.725	5.7
2.052	12.00	16.1	5.847	5.8
2.052	13.00	17.1	6.334	6.3
2.052	14.00	18.1	6.822	6.8
2.052	15.00	19.1	7.309	7.3
2.052	16.00	20.1	7.796	7.8

14-Gauge Wire (AWG)

WD (mm)	ID (mm)	OD (mm)	AR	Rounded AR
1.628	1.00	4.3	0.614	0.6
1.628	1.25	4.5	0.768	0.8
1.628	1.50	4.8	0.921	0.9
1.628	1.75	5.0	1.075	1.1
1.628	2.00	5.3	1.228	1.2
1.628	2.25	5.5	1.382	1.4
1.628	2.50	5.8	1.535	1.5
1.628	2.75	6.0	1.689	1.7
1.628	3.00	6.3	1.843	1.8
1.628	3.25	6.5	1.996	2.0
1.628	3.50	6.8	2.150	2.1
1.628	3.75	7.0	2.303	2.3

Aspect Ratio Charts

14-Gauge Wire (AWG) Cont'd.

WD (mm)	ID (mm)	OD (mm)	AR	Rounded AR
1.628	4.00	7.3	2.457	2.5
1.628	4.25	7.5	2.610	2.6
1.628	4.50	7.8	2.764	2.8
1.628	4.75	8.0	2.917	2.9
1.628	5.00	8.3	3.071	3.1
1.628	5.25	8.5	3.225	3.2
1.628	5.50	8.8	3.378	3.4
1.628	5.75	9.0	3.532	3.5
1.628	6.00	9.3	3.685	3.7
1.628	6.25	9.5	3.839	3.8
1.628	6.50	9.8	3.992	4.0
1.628	6.75	10.0	4.146	4.1
1.628	7.00	10.3	4.299	4.3
1.628	7.25	10.5	4.453	4.5
1.628	7.50	10.8	4.606	4.6
1.628	7.75	11.0	4.760	4.8
1.628	8.00	11.3	4.914	4.9
1.628	8.25	11.5	5.067	5.1
1.628	8.50	11.8	5.221	5.2
1.628	8.75	12.0	5.374	5.4
1.628	9.00	12.3	5.528	5.5
1.628	9.25	12.5	5.681	5.7
1.628	9.50	12.8	5.835	5.8
1.628	9.75	13.0	5.988	6.0
1.628	10.00	13.3	6.142	6.1
1.628	10.25	13.5	6.296	6.3
1.628	10.50	13.8	6.449	6.4
1.628	10.75	14.0	6.603	6.6
1.628	11.00	14.3	6.756	6.8
1.628	11.25	14.5	6.910	6.9
1.628	11.50	14.8	7.063	7.1
1.628	11.75	15.0	7.217	7.2
1.628	12.00	15.3	7.370	7.4
1.628	13.00	16.3	7.985	8.0
1.628	14.00	17.3	8.599	8.6
1.628	15.00	18.3	9.213	9.2
1.628	16.00	19.3	9.827	9.8

16-Gauge Wire (AWG)

WD (mm)	ID (mm)	OD (mm)	AR	Rounded AR
1.290	1.00	3.6	0.775	0.8
1.290	1.25	3.8	0.969	1.0
1.290	1.50	4.1	1.163	1.2
1.290	1.75	4.3	1.356	1.4
1.290	2.00	4.6	1.550	1.6
1.290	2.25	4.8	1.744	1.7
1.290	2.50	5.1	1.938	1.9
1.290	2.75	5.3	2.131	2.1
1.290	3.00	5.6	2.325	2.3
1.290	3.25	5.8	2.519	2.5
1.290	3.50	6.1	2.713	2.7
1.290	3.75	6.3	2.906	2.9
1.290	4.00	6.6	3.100	3.1
1.290	4.25	6.8	3.294	3.3
1.290	4.50	7.1	3.488	3.5
1.290	4.75	7.3	3.681	3.7
1.290	5.00	7.6	3.875	3.9
1.290	5.25	7.8	4.069	4.1
1.290	5.50	8.1	4.263	4.3
1.290	5.75	8.3	4.456	4.5
1.290	6.00	8.6	4.650	4.7
1.290	6.25	8.8	4.844	4.8
1.290	6.50	9.1	5.038	5.0
1.290	6.75	9.3	5.231	5.2
1.290	7.00	9.6	5.425	5.4
1.290	7.25	9.8	5.619	5.6
1.290	7.50	10.1	5.813	5.8
1.290	7.75	10.3	6.006	6.0
1.290	8.00	10.6	6.200	6.2
1.290	8.25	10.8	6.394	6.4
1.290	8.50	11.1	6.588	6.6
1.290	8.75	11.3	6.781	6.8
1.290	9.00	11.6	6.975	7.0
1.290	9.25	11.8	7.169	7.2
1.290	9.50	12.1	7.363	7.4
1.290	9.75	12.3	7.556	7.6
1.290	10.00	12.6	7.750	7.8

16-Gauge Wire (AWG) Cont'd.

WD (mm)	ID (mm)	OD (mm)	AR	Rounded AR
1.290	10.25	12.8	7.944	7.9
1.290	10.50	13.1	8.138	8.1
1.290	10.75	13.3	8.331	8.3
1.290	11.00	13.6	8.525	8.5
1.290	11.25	13.8	8.719	8.7
1.290	11.50	14.1	8.913	8.9
1.290	11.75	14.3	9.106	9.1
1.290	12.00	14.6	9.300	9.3
1.290	13.00	15.6	10.075	10.1
1.290	14.00	16.6	10.850	10.9
1.290	15.00	17.6	11.625	11.6
1.290	16.00	18.6	12.400	12.4

18-Gauge Wire (AWG)

WD (mm)	ID (mm)	OD (mm)	AR	Rounded AR
1.024	1.00	3.0	0.977	1.0
1.024	1.25	3.3	1.221	1.2
1.024	1.50	3.5	1.465	1.5
1.024	1.75	3.8	1.710	1.7
1.024	2.00	4.0	1.954	2.0
1.024	2.25	4.3	2.198	2.2
1.024	2.50	4.5	2.442	2.4
1.024	2.75	4.8	2.687	2.7
1.024	3.00	5.0	2.931	2.9
1.024	3.25	5.3	3.175	3.2
1.024	3.50	5.5	3.419	3.4
1.024	3.75	5.8	3.663	3.7
1.024	4.00	6.0	3.908	3.9
1.024	4.25	6.3	4.152	4.2
1.024	4.50	6.5	4.396	4.4
1.024	4.75	6.8	4.640	4.6
1.024	5.00	7.0	4.885	4.9

18-Gauge Wire (AWG) Cont'd.

WD (mm)	ID (mm)	OD (mm)	AR	Rounded AR
1.024	5.25	7.3	5.129	5.1
1.024	5.50	7.5	5.373	5.4
1.024	5.75	7.8	5.617	5.6
1.024	6.00	8.0	5.862	5.9
1.024	6.25	8.3	6.106	6.1
1.024	6.50	8.5	6.350	6.4
1.024	6.75	8.8	6.594	6.6
1.024	7.00	9.0	6.838	6.8
1.024	7.25	9.3	7.083	7.1
1.024	7.50	9.5	7.327	7.3
1.024	7.75	9.8	7.571	7.6
1.024	8.00	10.0	7.815	7.8
1.024	8.25	10.3	8.060	8.1
1.024	8.50	10.5	8.304	8.3
1.024	8.75	10.8	8.548	8.5
1.024	9.00	11.0	8.792	8.8
1.024	9.25	11.3	9.037	9.0
1.024	9.50	11.5	9.281	9.3
1.024	9.75	11.8	9.525	9.5
1.024	10.00	12.0	9.769	9.8
1.024	10.25	12.3	10.013	10.0
1.024	10.50	12.5	10.258	10.3
1.024	10.75	12.8	10.502	10.5
1.024	11.00	13.0	10.746	10.7
1.024	11.25	13.3	10.990	11.0
1.024	11.50	13.5	11.235	11.2
1.024	11.75	13.8	11.479	11.5
1.024	12.00	14.0	11.723	11.7
1.024	13.00	15.0	12.700	12.7
1.024	14.00	16.0	13.677	13.7
1.024	15.00	17.0	14.654	14.7
1.024	16.00	18.0	15.631	15.6

20-Gauge Wire (AWG)

WD (mm)	ID (mm)	OD (mm)	AR	Rounded AR
0.813	1.00	2.6	1.230	1.2
0.813	1.25	2.9	1.538	1.5
0.813	1.50	3.1	1.845	1.8
0.813	1.75	3.4	2.153	2.2
0.813	2.00	3.6	2.461	2.5
0.813	2.25	3.9	2.768	2.8
0.813	2.50	4.1	3.076	3.1
0.813	2.75	4.4	3.383	3.4
0.813	3.00	4.6	3.691	3.7
0.813	3.25	4.9	3.999	4.0
0.813	3.50	5.1	4.306	4.3
0.813	3.75	5.4	4.614	4.6
0.813	4.00	5.6	4.921	4.9
0.813	4.25	5.9	5.229	5.2
0.813	4.50	6.1	5.536	5.5
0.813	4.75	6.4	5.844	5.8
0.813	5.00	6.6	6.152	6.2
0.813	5.25	6.9	6.459	6.5
0.813	5.50	7.1	6.767	6.8
0.813	5.75	7.4	7.074	7.1
0.813	6.00	7.6	7.382	7.4
0.813	6.25	7.9	7.689	7.7
0.813	6.50	8.1	7.997	8.0
0.813	6.75	8.4	8.305	8.3
0.813	7.00	8.6	8.612	8.6
0.813	7.25	8.9	8.920	8.9
0.813	7.50	9.1	9.227	9.2
0.813	7.75	9.4	9.535	9.5
0.813	8.00	9.6	9.843	9.8
0.813	8.25	9.9	10.150	10.2
0.813	8.50	10.1	10.458	10.5
0.813	8.75	10.4	10.765	10.8
0.813	9.00	10.6	11.073	11.1
0.813	9.25	10.9	11.380	11.4
0.813	9.50	11.1	11.688	11.7
0.813	9.75	11.4	11.996	12.0
0.813	10.00	11.6	12.303	12.3
0.813	10.25	11.9	12.611	12.6
0.813	10.50	12.1	12.918	12.9
0.813	10.75	12.4	13.226	13.2

20-Gauge Wire (AWG) Cont'd.

WD (mm)	ID (mm)	OD (mm)	AR	Rounded AR
0.813	11.00	12.6	13.533	13.5
0.813	11.25	12.9	13.841	13.8
0.813	11.50	13.1	14.149	14.1
0.813	11.75	13.4	14.456	14.5
0.813	12.00	13.6	14.764	14.8
0.813	13.00	14.6	15.994	16.0
0.813	14.00	15.6	17.224	17.2
0.813	15.00	16.6	18.455	18.5
0.813	16.00	17.6	19.685	19.7

22-Gauge Wire (AWG)

WD (mm)	ID (mm)	OD (mm)	AR	Rounded AR
0.643	1.00	2.3	1.556	1.6
0.643	1.25	2.5	1.945	1.9
0.643	1.50	2.8	2.334	2.3
0.643	1.75	3.0	2.723	2.7
0.643	2.00	3.3	3.112	3.1
0.643	2.25	3.5	3.501	3.5
0.643	2.50	3.8	3.890	3.9
0.643	2.75	4.0	4.279	4.3
0.643	3.00	4.3	4.668	4.7
0.643	3.25	4.5	5.057	5.1
0.643	3.50	4.8	5.446	5.4
0.643	3.75	5.0	5.835	5.8
0.643	4.00	5.3	6.225	6.2
0.643	4.25	5.5	6.614	6.6
0.643	4.50	5.8	7.003	7.0
0.643	4.75	6.0	7.392	7.4
0.643	5.00	6.3	7.781	7.8
0.643	5.25	6.5	8.170	8.2
0.643	5.50	6.8	8.559	8.6
0.643	5.75	7.0	8.948	8.9
0.643	6.00	7.3	9.337	9.3
0.643	6.25	7.5	9.726	9.7
0.643	6.50	7.8	10.115	10.1
0.643	6.75	8.0	10.504	10.5
0.643	7.00	8.3	10.893	10.9
0.643	7.25	8.5	11.282	11.3
0.643	7.50	8.8	11.671	11.7

22-Gauge Wire (AWG) Cont'd.

WD (mm)	ID (mm)	OD (mm)	AR	Rounded AR
0.643	7.75	9.0	12.060	12.1
0.643	8.00	9.3	12.449	12.4
0.643	8.25	9.5	12.838	12.8
0.643	8.50	9.8	13.227	13.2
0.643	8.75	10.0	13.616	13.6
0.643	9.00	10.3	14.005	14.0
0.643	9.25	10.5	14.394	14.4
0.643	9.50	10.8	14.783	14.8
0.643	9.75	11.0	15.172	15.2
0.643	10.00	11.3	15.561	15.6
0.643	10.25	11.5	15.950	16.0
0.643	10.50	11.8	16.339	16.3
0.643	10.75	12.0	16.728	16.7
0.643	11.00	12.3	17.117	17.1
0.643	11.25	12.5	17.506	17.5
0.643	11.50	12.8	17.895	17.9
0.643	11.75	13.0	18.285	18.3
0.643	12.00	13.3	18.674	18.7
0.643	13.00	14.3	20.230	20.2
0.643	14.00	15.3	21.786	21.8
0.643	15.00	16.3	23.342	23.3
0.643	16.00	17.3	24.898	24.9

24-Gauge Wire (AWG)

WD (mm)	ID (mm)	OD (mm)	AR	Rounded AR
0.511	1.00	2.0	1.959	2.0
0.511	1.25	2.3	2.448	2.4
0.511	1.50	2.5	2.938	2.9
0.511	1.75	2.8	3.428	3.4
0.511	2.00	3.0	3.917	3.9
0.511	2.25	3.3	4.407	4.4
0.511	2.50	3.5	4.897	4.9
0.511	2.75	3.8	5.386	5.4
0.511	3.00	4.0	5.876	5.9
0.511	3.25	4.3	6.366	6.4
0.511	3.50	4.5	6.855	6.9

24-Gauge Wire (AWG) Cont'd.

WD (mm)	ID (mm)	OD (mm)	AR	Rounded AR
0.511	3.75	4.8	7.345	7.3
0.511	4.00	5.0	7.835	7.8
0.511	4.25	5.3	8.325	8.3
0.511	4.50	5.5	8.814	8.8
0.511	4.75	5.8	9.304	9.3
0.511	5.00	6.0	9.794	9.8
0.511	5.25	6.3	10.283	10.3
0.511	5.50	6.5	10.773	10.8
0.511	5.75	6.8	11.263	11.3
0.511	6.00	7.0	11.752	11.8
0.511	6.25	7.3	12.242	12.2
0.511	6.50	7.5	12.732	12.7
0.511	6.75	7.8	13.221	13.2
0.511	7.00	8.0	13.711	13.7
0.511	7.25	8.3	14.201	14.2
0.511	7.50	8.5	14.690	14.7
0.511	7.75	8.8	15.180	15.2
0.511	8.00	9.0	15.670	15.7
0.511	8.25	9.3	16.159	16.2
0.511	8.50	9.5	16.649	16.6
0.511	8.75	9.8	17.139	17.1
0.511	9.00	10.0	17.628	17.6
0.511	9.25	10.3	18.118	18.1
0.511	9.50	10.5	18.608	18.6
0.511	9.75	10.8	19.097	19.1
0.511	10.00	11.0	19.587	19.6
0.511	10.25	11.3	20.077	20.1
0.511	10.50	11.5	20.566	20.6
0.511	10.75	11.8	21.056	21.1
0.511	11.00	12.0	21.546	21.5
0.511	11.25	12.3	22.035	22.0
0.511	11.50	12.5	22.525	22.5
0.511	11.75	12.8	23.015	23.0
0.511	12.00	13.0	23.505	23.5
0.511	13.00	14.0	25.463	25.5
0.511	14.00	15.0	27.422	27.4
0.511	15.00	16.0	29.381	29.4
0.511	16.00	17.0	31.339	31.3

ASPECT RATIO FOR BRITISH STANDARD WIRE GAUGE (SWG)

10-Gauge Wire (SWG)

WD (mm)	ID (mm)	OD (mm)	AR	Rounded AR
3.251	1.00	7.5	0.308	0.3
3.251	1.25	7.8	0.384	0.4
3.251	1.50	8.0	0.461	0.5
3.251	1.75	8.3	0.538	0.5
3.251	2.00	8.5	0.615	0.6
3.251	2.25	8.8	0.692	0.7
3.251	2.50	9.0	0.769	0.8
3.251	2.75	9.3	0.846	0.8
3.251	3.00	9.5	0.923	0.9
3.251	3.25	9.8	0.100	1.0
3.251	3.50	10.0	1.077	1.1
3.251	3.75	10.3	1.153	1.2
3.251	4.00	10.5	1.230	1.2
3.251	4.25	10.8	1.307	1.3
3.251	4.50	11.0	1.384	1.4
3.251	4.75	11.3	1.461	1.5
3.251	5.00	11.5	1.538	1.5
3.251	5.25	11.8	1.615	1.6
3.251	5.50	12.0	1.692	1.7
3.251	5.75	12.3	1.769	1.8
3.251	6.00	12.5	1.845	1.8
3.251	6.25	12.8	1.922	1.9
3.251	6.50	13.0	1.999	2.0
3.251	6.75	13.3	2.076	2.1
3.251	7.00	13.5	2.153	2.2
3.251	7.25	13.8	2.230	2.2
3.251	7.50	14.0	2.307	2.3
3.251	7.75	14.3	2.384	2.4
3.251	8.00	14.5	2.461	2.5
3.251	8.25	14.8	2.538	2.5
3.251	8.50	15.0	2.614	2.6
3.251	8.75	15.3	2.691	2.7
3.251	9.00	15.5	2.768	2.8
3.251	9.25	15.8	2.845	2.8
3.251	9.50	16.0	2.922	2.9
3.251	9.75	16.3	2.999	3.0
3.251	10.00	16.5	3.076	3.1
3.251	10.25	16.8	3.153	3.2

10-Gauge Wire (SWG) Cont'd.

WD (mm)	ID (mm)	OD (mm)	AR	Rounded AR
3.251	10.50	17.0	3.230	3.2
3.251	10.75	17.3	3.306	3.3
3.251	11.00	17.5	3.383	3.4
3.251	11.25	17.8	3.460	3.5
3.251	11.50	18.0	3.537	3.5
3.251	11.75	18.3	3.614	3.6
3.251	12.00	18.5	3.691	3.7
3.251	13.00	19.5	3.999	4.0
3.251	14.00	20.5	4.306	4.3
3.251	15.00	21.5	4.614	4.6
3.251	16.00	22.5	4.921	4.9

12-Gauge Wire (SWG)

WD (mm)	ID (mm)	OD (mm)	AR	Rounded AR
2.642	1.00	6.3	0.379	0.4
2.642	1.25	6.5	0.473	0.5
2.642	1.50	6.8	0.568	0.6
2.642	1.75	7.0	0.662	0.7
2.642	2.00	7.3	0.757	0.8
2.642	2.25	7.5	0.852	0.9
2.642	2.50	7.8	0.946	0.9
2.642	2.75	8.0	1.041	1.0
2.642	3.00	8.3	1.136	1.1
2.642	3.25	8.5	1.230	1.2
2.642	3.50	8.8	1.325	1.3
2.642	3.75	9.0	1.420	1.4
2.642	4.00	9.3	1.514	1.5
2.642	4.25	9.5	1.609	1.6
2.642	4.50	9.8	1.704	1.7
2.642	4.75	10.0	1.798	1.8
2.642	5.00	10.3	1.893	1.9
2.642	5.25	10.5	1.987	2.0
2.642	5.50	10.8	2.082	2.1
2.642	5.75	11.0	2.177	2.2
2.642	6.00	11.3	2.271	2.3
2.642	6.25	11.5	2.366	2.4
2.642	6.50	11.8	2.461	2.5

12-Gauge Wire (SWG) Cont'd.

WD (mm)	ID (mm)	OD (mm)	AR	Rounded AR
2.642	6.75	12.0	2.555	2.6
2.642	7.00	12.3	2.650	2.6
2.642	7.25	12.5	2.745	2.7
2.642	7.50	12.8	2.839	2.8
2.642	7.75	13.0	2.934	2.9
2.642	8.00	13.3	3.028	3.0
2.642	8.25	13.5	3.123	3.1
2.642	8.50	13.8	3.218	3.2
2.642	8.75	14.0	3.312	3.3
2.642	9.00	14.3	3.407	3.4
2.642	9.25	14.5	3.502	3.5
2.642	9.50	14.8	3.596	3.6
2.642	9.75	15.0	3.691	3.7
2.642	10.00	15.3	3.786	3.8
2.642	10.25	15.5	3.880	3.9
2.642	10.50	15.8	3.975	4.0
2.642	10.75	16.0	4.070	4.1
2.642	11.00	16.3	4.164	4.2
2.642	11.25	16.5	4.259	4.3
2.642	11.50	16.8	4.353	4.4
2.642	11.75	17.0	4.448	4.4
2.642	12.00	17.3	4.543	4.5
2.642	13.00	18.3	4.921	4.9
2.642	14.00	19.3	5.300	5.3
2.642	15.00	20.3	5.678	5.7
2.642	16.00	21.3	6.057	6.1

14-Gauge Wire (SWG)

WD (mm)	ID (mm)	OD (mm)	AR	Rounded AR
2.032	1.00	5.1	0.492	0.5
2.032	1.25	5.3	0.615	0.6
2.032	1.50	5.6	0.738	0.7
2.032	1.75	5.8	0.861	0.9
2.032	2.00	6.1	0.984	1.0
2.032	2.25	6.3	1.107	1.1
2.032	2.50	6.6	1.230	1.2
2.032	2.75	6.8	1.353	1.4
2.032	3.00	7.1	1.476	1.5
2.032	3.25	7.3	1.599	1.6

14-Gauge Wire (SWG) Cont'd.

WD (mm)	ID (mm)	OD (mm)	AR	Rounded AR
2.032	3.50	7.6	1.722	1.7
2.032	3.75	7.8	1.845	1.8
2.032	4.00	8.1	1.969	2.0
2.032	4.25	8.3	2.092	2.1
2.032	4.50	8.6	2.215	2.2
2.032	4.75	8.8	2.338	2.3
2.032	5.00	9.1	2.461	2.5
2.032	5.25	9.3	2.584	2.6
2.032	5.50	9.6	2.707	2.7
2.032	5.75	9.8	2.830	2.8
2.032	6.00	10.1	2.953	3.0
2.032	6.25	10.3	3.076	3.1
2.032	6.50	10.6	3.199	3.2
2.032	6.75	10.8	3.322	3.3
2.032	7.00	11.1	3.445	3.4
2.032	7.25	11.3	3.568	3.6
2.032	7.50	11.6	3.691	3.7
2.032	7.75	11.8	3.814	3.8
2.032	8.00	12.1	3.937	3.9
2.032	8.25	12.3	4.060	4.1
2.032	8.50	12.6	4.183	4.2
2.032	8.75	12.8	4.306	4.3
2.032	9.00	13.1	4.429	4.4
2.032	9.25	13.3	4.552	4.6
2.032	9.50	13.6	4.675	4.7
2.032	9.75	13.8	4.798	4.8
2.032	10.00	14.1	4.921	4.9
2.032	10.25	14.3	5.044	5.0
2.032	10.50	14.6	5.167	5.2
2.032	10.75	14.8	5.290	5.3
2.032	11.00	15.1	5.413	5.4
2.032	11.25	15.3	5.536	5.5
2.032	11.50	15.6	5.659	5.7
2.032	11.75	15.8	5.782	5.8
2.032	12.00	16.1	5.906	5.9
2.032	13.00	17.1	6.398	6.4
2.032	14.00	18.1	6.890	6.9
2.032	15.00	19.1	7.382	7.4
2.032	16.00	20.1	7.874	7.9

Aspect Ratio Charts

16-Gauge Wire (SWG)

WD (mm)	ID (mm)	OD (mm)	AR	Rounded AR
1.626	1.00	4.3	0.615	0.6
1.626	1.25	4.5	0.769	0.8
1.626	1.50	4.8	0.923	0.9
1.626	1.75	5.0	1.077	1.1
1.626	2.00	5.3	1.230	1.2
1.626	2.25	5.5	1.384	1.4
1.626	2.50	5.8	1.538	1.5
1.626	2.75	6.0	1.692	1.7
1.626	3.00	6.3	1.845	1.8
1.626	3.25	6.5	1.999	2.0
1.626	3.50	6.8	2.153	2.2
1.626	3.75	7.0	2.307	2.3
1.626	4.00	7.3	2.461	2.5
1.626	4.25	7.5	2.614	2.6
1.626	4.50	7.8	2.768	2.8
1.626	4.75	8.0	2.922	2.9
1.626	5.00	8.3	3.076	3.1
1.626	5.25	8.5	3.230	3.2
1.626	5.50	8.8	3.383	3.4
1.626	5.75	9.0	3.537	3.5
1.626	6.00	9.3	3.691	3.7
1.626	6.25	9.5	3.845	3.8
1.626	6.50	9.8	3.999	4.0
1.626	6.75	10.0	4.152	4.2
1.626	7.00	10.3	4.306	4.3
1.626	7.25	10.5	4.460	4.5
1.626	7.50	10.8	4.614	4.6
1.626	7.75	11.0	4.767	4.8
1.626	8.00	11.3	4.921	4.9
1.626	8.25	11.5	5.075	5.1
1.626	8.50	11.8	5.229	5.2
1.626	8.75	12.0	5.383	5.4
1.626	9.00	12.3	5.536	5.5
1.626	9.25	12.5	5.690	5.7
1.626	9.50	12.8	5.844	5.8
1.626	9.75	13.0	5.998	6.0
1.626	10.00	13.3	6.152	6.2
1.626	10.25	13.5	6.305	6.3
1.626	10.50	13.8	6.459	6.5
1.626	10.75	14.0	6.613	6.6

16-Gauge Wire (SWG) Cont'd.

WD (mm)	ID (mm)	OD (mm)	AR	Rounded AR
1.626	11.00	14.3	6.767	6.8
1.626	11.25	14.5	6.921	6.9
1.626	11.50	14.8	7.074	7.1
1.626	11.75	15.0	7.228	7.2
1.626	12.00	15.3	7.382	7.4
1.626	13.00	16.3	7.997	8.0
1.626	14.00	17.3	8.612	8.6
1.626	15.00	18.3	9.227	9.2
1.626	16.00	19.3	9.843	9.8

18-Gauge Wire (SWG)

WD (mm)	ID (mm)	OD (mm)	AR	Rounded AR
1.219	1.00	3.4	0.820	0.8
1.219	1.25	3.7	1.025	1.0
1.219	1.50	3.9	1.230	1.2
1.219	1.75	4.2	1.435	1.4
1.219	2.00	4.4	1.640	1.6
1.219	2.25	4.7	1.845	1.8
1.219	2.50	4.9	2.051	2.1
1.219	2.75	5.2	2.256	2.3
1.219	3.00	5.4	2.461	2.5
1.219	3.25	5.7	2.666	2.7
1.219	3.50	5.9	2.871	2.9
1.219	3.75	6.2	3.076	3.1
1.219	4.00	6.4	3.281	3.3
1.219	4.25	6.7	3.486	3.5
1.219	4.50	6.9	3.691	3.7
1.219	4.75	7.2	3.896	3.9
1.219	5.00	7.4	4.101	4.1
1.219	5.25	7.7	4.306	4.3
1.219	5.50	7.9	4.511	4.5
1.219	5.75	8.2	4.716	4.7
1.219	6.00	8.4	4.921	4.9
1.219	6.25	8.7	5.126	5.1
1.219	6.50	8.9	5.331	5.3
1.219	6.75	9.2	5.536	5.5
1.219	7.00	9.4	5.741	5.7
1.219	7.25	9.7	5.947	5.9

18-Gauge Wire (SWG) Cont'd.

WD (mm)	ID (mm)	OD (mm)	AR	Rounded AR
1.219	7.50	9.9	6.152	6.2
1.219	7.75	10.2	6.357	6.4
1.219	8.00	10.4	6.562	6.6
1.219	8.25	10.7	6.767	6.8
1.219	8.50	10.9	6.972	7.0
1.219	8.75	11.2	7.177	7.2
1.219	9.00	11.4	7.382	7.4
1.219	9.25	11.7	7.587	7.6
1.219	9.50	11.9	7.792	7.8
1.219	9.75	12.2	7.997	8.0
1.219	10.00	12.4	8.202	8.2
1.219	10.25	12.7	8.407	8.4
1.219	10.50	12.9	8.612	8.6
1.219	10.75	13.2	8.817	8.8
1.219	11.00	13.4	9.022	9.0
1.219	11.25	13.7	9.227	9.2
1.219	11.50	13.9	9.432	9.4
1.219	11.75	14.2	9.637	9.6
1.219	12.00	14.4	9.843	9.8
1.219	13.00	15.4	10.663	10.7
1.219	14.00	16.4	11.483	11.5
1.219	15.00	17.4	12.303	12.3
1.219	16.00	18.4	13.123	13.1

20-Gauge Wire (SWG)

WD (mm)	ID (mm)	OD (mm)	AR	Rounded AR
0.914	1.00	2.8	1.094	1.1
0.914	1.25	3.1	1.367	1.4
0.914	1.50	3.3	1.640	1.6
0.914	1.75	3.6	1.914	1.9
0.914	2.00	3.8	2.187	2.2
0.914	2.25	4.1	2.461	2.5
0.914	2.50	4.3	2.734	2.7
0.914	2.75	4.6	3.007	3.0
0.914	3.00	4.8	3.281	3.3
0.914	3.25	5.1	3.554	3.6
0.914	3.50	5.3	3.828	3.8

20-Gauge Wire (SWG) Cont'd.

WD (mm)	ID (mm)	OD (mm)	AR	Rounded AR
0.914	3.75	5.6	4.101	4.1
0.914	4.00	5.8	4.374	4.4
0.914	4.25	6.1	4.648	4.6
0.914	4.50	6.3	4.921	4.9
0.914	4.75	6.6	5.195	5.2
0.914	5.00	6.8	5.468	5.5
0.914	5.25	7.1	5.741	5.7
0.914	5.50	7.3	6.015	6.0
0.914	5.75	7.6	6.288	6.3
0.914	6.00	7.8	6.562	6.6
0.914	6.25	8.1	6.835	6.8
0.914	6.50	8.3	7.108	7.1
0.914	6.75	8.6	7.382	7.4
0.914	7.00	8.8	7.655	7.7
0.914	7.25	9.1	7.929	7.9
0.914	7.50	9.3	8.202	8.2
0.914	7.75	9.6	8.476	8.5
0.914	8.00	9.8	8.749	8.7
0.914	8.25	10.1	9.022	9.0
0.914	8.50	10.3	9.296	9.3
0.914	8.75	10.6	9.569	9.6
0.914	9.00	10.8	9.843	9.8
0.914	9.25	11.1	10.116	10.1
0.914	9.50	11.3	10.389	10.4
0.914	9.75	11.6	10.663	10.7
0.914	10.00	11.8	10.936	10.9
0.914	10.25	12.1	11.210	11.2
0.914	10.50	12.3	11.483	11.5
0.914	10.75	12.6	11.756	11.8
0.914	11.00	12.8	12.030	12.0
0.914	11.25	13.1	12.303	12.3
0.914	11.50	13.3	12.577	12.6
0.914	11.75	13.6	12.850	12.8
0.914	12.00	13.8	13.123	13.1
0.914	13.00	14.8	14.217	14.2
0.914	14.00	15.8	15.311	15.3
0.914	15.00	16.8	16.404	16.4
0.914	16.00	17.8	17.498	17.5

22-Gauge Wire (SWG)

WD (mm)	ID (mm)	OD (mm)	AR	Rounded AR
0.711	1.00	2.4	1.406	1.4
0.711	1.25	2.7	1.758	1.8
0.711	1.50	2.9	2.109	2.1
0.711	1.75	3.2	2.461	2.5
0.711	2.00	3.4	2.812	2.8
0.711	2.25	3.7	3.164	3.2
0.711	2.50	3.9	3.515	3.5
0.711	2.75	4.2	3.867	3.9
0.711	3.00	4.4	4.218	4.2
0.711	3.25	4.7	4.570	4.6
0.711	3.50	4.9	4.921	4.9
0.711	3.75	5.2	5.273	5.3
0.711	4.00	5.4	5.624	5.6
0.711	4.25	5.7	5.976	6.0
0.711	4.50	5.9	6.327	6.3
0.711	4.75	6.2	6.679	6.7
0.711	5.00	6.4	7.030	7.0
0.711	5.25	6.7	7.382	7.4
0.711	5.50	6.9	7.733	7.7
0.711	5.75	7.2	8.085	8.1
0.711	6.00	7.4	8.436	8.4
0.711	6.25	7.7	8.788	8.8
0.711	6.50	7.9	9.139	9.1
0.711	6.75	8.2	9.491	9.5
0.711	7.00	8.4	9.843	9.8

22-Gauge Wire (SWG) Cont'd.

WD (mm)	ID (mm)	OD (mm)	AR	Rounded AR
0.711	7.25	8.7	10.194	10.2
0.711	7.50	8.9	10.546	10.5
0.711	7.75	9.2	10.897	10.9
0.711	8.00	9.4	11.249	11.2
0.711	8.25	9.7	11.600	11.6
0.711	8.50	9.9	11.952	12.0
0.711	8.75	10.2	12.303	12.3
0.711	9.00	10.4	12.655	12.7
0.711	9.25	10.7	13.006	13.0
0.711	9.50	10.9	13.358	13.4
0.711	9.75	11.2	13.709	13.7
0.711	10.00	11.4	14.061	14.1
0.711	10.25	11.7	14.412	14.4
0.711	10.50	11.9	14.764	14.8
0.711	10.75	12.2	15.115	15.1
0.711	11.00	12.4	15.467	15.5
0.711	11.25	12.7	15.818	15.8
0.711	11.50	12.9	16.170	16.2
0.711	11.75	13.2	16.521	16.5
0.711	12.00	13.4	16.873	16.9
0.711	13.00	14.4	18.279	18.3
0.711	14.00	15.4	19.685	19.7
0.711	15.00	16.4	21.091	21.1
0.711	16.00	17.4	22.497	22.5

24-Gauge Wire (SWG)

WD (mm)	ID (mm)	OD (mm)	AR	Rounded AR
0.559	1.00	2.1	1.790	1.8
0.559	1.25	2.4	2.237	2.2
0.559	1.50	2.6	2.684	2.7
0.559	1.75	2.9	3.132	3.1
0.559	2.00	3.1	3.579	3.6
0.559	2.25	3.4	4.026	4.0
0.559	2.50	3.6	4.474	4.5
0.559	2.75	3.9	4.921	4.9
0.559	3.00	4.1	5.369	5.4
0.559	3.25	4.4	5.816	5.8
0.559	3.50	4.6	6.263	6.3
0.559	3.75	4.9	6.711	6.7
0.559	4.00	5.1	7.158	7.2
0.559	4.25	5.4	7.606	7.6
0.559	4.50	5.6	8.053	8.1
0.559	4.75	5.9	8.500	8.5
0.559	5.00	6.1	8.948	8.9
0.559	5.25	6.4	9.395	9.4
0.559	5.50	6.6	9.843	9.8
0.559	5.75	6.9	10.290	10.3
0.559	6.00	7.1	10.737	10.7
0.559	6.25	7.4	11.185	11.2
0.559	6.50	7.6	11.632	11.6
0.559	6.75	7.9	12.079	12.1
0.559	7.00	8.1	12.527	12.5

24-Gauge Wire (SWG) Cont'd.

WD (mm)	ID (mm)	OD (mm)	AR	Rounded AR
0.559	7.25	8.4	12.974	13.0
0.559	7.50	8.6	13.422	13.4
0.559	7.75	8.9	13.869	13.9
0.559	8.00	9.1	14.316	14.3
0.559	8.25	9.4	14.764	14.8
0.559	8.50	9.6	15.211	15.2
0.559	8.75	9.9	15.659	15.7
0.559	9.00	10.1	16.106	16.1
0.559	9.25	10.4	16.553	16.6
0.559	9.50	10.6	17.001	17.0
0.559	9.75	10.9	17.448	17.4
0.559	10.00	11.1	17.895	17.9
0.559	10.25	11.4	18.343	18.3
0.559	10.50	11.6	18.790	18.8
0.559	10.75	11.9	19.238	19.2
0.559	11.00	12.1	19.685	19.7
0.559	11.25	12.4	20.132	20.1
0.559	11.50	12.6	20.580	20.6
0.559	11.75	12.9	21.027	21.0
0.559	12.00	13.1	21.475	21.5
0.559	13.00	14.1	23.264	23.3
0.559	14.00	15.1	25.054	25.1
0.559	15.00	16.1	26.843	26.8
0.559	16.00	17.1	28.633	28.6

Imperial and Metric Conversion Charts

When determining aspect ratio, you may need to convert a fractional measurement to its metric equivalent before working through your calculations. For example, to determine the aspect ratio for a SWG 16g 7/32" jump ring, I would use the Inches to Millimeters chart to find the metric equivalent for 7/32: 5.56 mm. Then I would use the 16-Gauge Wire (SWG) aspect ratio chart to find the closest inner diameter to that measurement: 5.50 mm or 5.75 mm. Again using the chart, I now know that my ideal aspect ratio lies somewhere in between 3.4 and 3.5.

Inches to Millimeters

64ths	Fraction	Conversion	mm
1	1/64	25.4	0.40
2	1/32	25.4	0.79
3	3/64	25.4	1.19
4	1/16	25.4	1.59
5	5/64	25.4	1.98
6	3/32	25.4	2.38
7	7/64	25.4	2.78
8	1/8	25.4	3.18
9	9/64	25.4	3.57
10	5/32	25.4	3.97
11	11/64	25.4	4.37
12	3/16	25.4	4.76
13	13/64	25.4	5.16
14	7/32	25.4	5.56
15	15/64	25.4	5.95
16	1/4	25.4	6.35
17	17/64	25.4	6.75
18	9/32	25.4	7.14
19	19/64	25.4	7.54
20	5/16	25.4	7.94
21	21/64	25.4	8.33
22	11/32	25.4	8.73
23	23/64	25.4	9.13
24	3/8	25.4	9.53
25	25/64	25.4	9.92
26	13/32	25.4	10.32
27	27/64	25.4	10.72
28	7/16	25.4	11.11
29	29/64	25.4	11.51
30	15/32	25.4	11.91
31	31/64	25.4	12.30
32	1/2	25.4	12.70

Inches to Millimeters Cont'd.

64ths	Fraction	Conversion	mm
33	33/64	25.4	13.10
34	17/32	25.4	13.49
35	35/64	25.4	13.89
36	9/16	25.4	14.29
37	37/64	25.4	14.68
38	19/32	25.4	15.08
39	39/64	25.4	15.48
40	5/8	25.4	15.88
41	41/64	25.4	16.27
42	21/32	25.4	16.67
43	43/64	25.4	17.07
44	11/16	25.4	17.46
45	45/64	25.4	17.86
46	23/32	25.4	18.26
47	47/64	25.4	18.65
48	3/4	25.4	19.05
49	49/64	25.4	19.45
50	25/32	25.4	19.84
51	51/64	25.4	20.24
52	13/16	25.4	20.64
53	53/64	25.4	21.03
54	27/32	25.4	21.43
55	55/64	25.4	21.83
56	7/8	25.4	22.23
57	57/64	25.4	22.62
58	29/32	25.4	23.02
59	59/64	25.4	23.42
60	15/16	25.4	23.81
61	61/64	25.4	24.21
62	31/32	25.4	24.61
63	63/64	25.4	25.00
64	1	25.4	25.40

Millimeters to Inches

MM	CONVERSION	INCHES Fraction	Decimal
0.10	25.4	0	0.0039
0.20	25.4	0	0.0079
0.30	25.4	1/85	0.0118
0.40	25.4	1/63	0.0157
0.50	25.4	1/51	0.0197
0.60	25.4	2/85	0.0236
0.70	25.4	1/36	0.0276
0.80	25.4	3/95	0.0315
0.90	25.4	1/28	0.0354
1.00	25.4	3/76	0.0394
1.10	25.4	1/23	0.0433
1.20	25.4	1/21	0.0472
1.30	25.4	2/39	0.0512
1.40	25.4	1/18	0.0551
1.50	25.4	1/17	0.0591
1.60	25.4	1/16	0.0630
1.70	25.4	1/15	0.0669
1.80	25.4	1/14	0.0709
1.90	25.4	3/40	0.0748
2.00	25.4	3/38	0.0787
2.10	25.4	1/12	0.0827
2.20	25.4	2/23	0.0866
2.30	25.4	1/11	0.0906
2.40	25.4	5/53	0.0945
2.50	25.4	6/61	0.0984
2.60	25.4	4/39	0.1024
2.70	25.4	5/47	0.1063
2.80	25.4	1/9	0.1102
2.90	25.4	4/35	0.1142
3.00	25.4	2/17	0.1181
3.10	25.4	5/41	0.1220
3.20	25.4	1/8	0.1260
3.30	25.4	10/77	0.1299
3.40	25.4	2/15	0.1339
3.50	25.4	4/29	0.1378
3.60	25.4	1/7	0.1417
3.70	25.4	7/48	0.1457
3.80	25.4	3/20	0.1496

Millimeters to Inches Cont'd.

MM	CONVERSION	INCHES Fraction	Decimal
3.90	25.4	2/13	0.1535
4.00	25.4	3/19	0.1575
4.10	25.4	5/31	0.1614
4.20	25.4	1/6	0.1654
4.30	25.4	11/65	0.1693
4.40	25.4	13/75	0.1732
4.50	25.4	14/79	0.1772
4.60	25.4	2/11	0.1811
4.70	25.4	5/27	0.1850
4.80	25.4	17/90	0.1890
4.90	25.4	11/57	0.1929
5.00	25.4	12/61	0.1969
5.10	25.4	1/5	0.2008
5.20	25.4	17/83	0.2047
5.30	25.4	5/24	0.2087
5.40	25.4	10/47	0.2126
5.50	25.4	21/97	0.2165
5.60	25.4	15/68	0.2205
5.70	25.4	11/49	0.2244
5.80	25.4	21/92	0.2283
5.90	25.4	23/99	0.2323
6.00	25.4	13/55	0.2362
6.10	25.4	6/25	0.2402
6.20	25.4	21/86	0.2441
6.30	25.4	1/4	0.2480
6.40	25.4	1/4	0.2520
6.50	25.4	11/43	0.2559
6.60	25.4	20/77	0.2598
6.70	25.4	24/91	0.2638
6.80	25.4	15/56	0.2677
6.90	25.4	22/81	0.2717
7.00	25.4	8/29	0.2756
7.10	25.4	26/93	0.2795
7.20	25.4	19/67	0.2835
7.30	25.4	25/87	0.2874
7.40	25.4	7/24	0.2913
7.50	25.4	13/44	0.2953
7.60	25.4	3/10	0.2992

Imperial and Metric Conversion Charts

Millimeters to Inches Cont'd.

MM	CONVERSION	INCHES Fraction	Decimal
7.70	25.4	10/33	0.3031
7.80	25.4	4/13	0.3071
7.90	25.4	14/45	0.3110
8.00	25.4	23/73	0.3150
8.10	25.4	22/69	0.3189
8.20	25.4	10/31	0.3228
8.30	25.4	17/52	0.3268
8.40	25.4	1/3	0.3307
8.50	25.4	1/3	0.3346
8.60	25.4	21/62	0.3386
8.70	25.4	25/73	0.3425
8.80	25.4	9/26	0.3465
8.90	25.4	7/20	0.3504
9.00	25.4	28/79	0.3543
9.10	25.4	24/67	0.3583
9.20	25.4	21/58	0.3622
9.30	25.4	26/71	0.3661
9.40	25.4	10/27	0.3701
9.50	25.4	3/8	0.3740
9.60	25.4	17/45	0.3780
9.70	25.4	21/55	0.3819
9.80	25.4	22/57	0.3858
9.90	25.4	23/59	0.3898
10.00	25.4	37/94	0.3937
10.10	25.4	33/83	0.3976
10.20	25.4	2/5	0.4016
10.30	25.4	15/37	0.4055
10.40	25.4	9/22	0.4094
10.50	25.4	31/75	0.4134
10.60	25.4	5/12	0.4173
10.70	25.4	8/19	0.4213
10.80	25.4	37/87	0.4252
10.90	25.4	3/7	0.4291
11.00	25.4	13/30	0.4331
11.10	25.4	7/16	0.4370
11.20	25.4	15/34	0.4409
11.30	25.4	4/9	0.4449
11.40	25.4	22/49	0.4488

Millimeters to Inches Cont'd.

MM	CONVERSION	INCHES Fraction	Decimal
11.50	25.4	24/53	0.4528
11.60	25.4	21/46	0.4567
11.70	25.4	41/89	0.4606
11.80	25.4	46/99	0.4646
11.90	25.4	15/32	0.4685
12.00	25.4	43/91	0.4724
12.10	25.4	10/21	0.4764
12.20	25.4	12/25	0.4803
12.30	25.4	46/95	0.4843
12.40	25.4	21/43	0.4882
12.50	25.4	31/63	0.4921
12.60	25.4	1/2	0.4961
12.70	25.4	1/2	0.5000
12.80	25.4	1/2	0.5039
12.90	25.4	32/63	0.5079
13.00	25.4	22/43	0.5118
13.10	25.4	49/95	0.5157
13.20	25.4	13/25	0.5197

Index

aspect ratio (AR) 17, 30–31
awl, toothpick 12

block, bench 12; dapping 12

calipers 11
chain-nose pliers 11, 12
clasps 133–134, 140
closing weaves 16, 24–25

diameter, wire 30

ear wires 140
ending weaves 132–136

file, jewelry 12
findings 133–134, 140
finishing metal 141–142
flat-nose piers 11

glasses, magnification 11

hammer 12
hole punch 12

inner diameter (ID) 30

jump rings 11, 13–15, 16, 17, 21; closing 136–138; findings for 133–134, 140
jump ring opening tool 11

maintenance of chain maille 142
magnification glasses 11
mistakes, fixing 17

orientation of weaving 21, 35
outer diameter (OD) 30

paper clips 12
pins 12
pliers 11
projects:
  Beaded Linear Scale and Maille Collar 128–129; Colorful Scale and Box Chain Necklace 120; Dragonback Bracelet with Scales 123; Dragonback Ring 98–99; Elfweave Loop Earrings 76–77; Interwoven Stretch Cuff 100–101; Lightning Bolt Earrings 37; Linear Scale Maille Necklace with Crystal 117; Mixed-metal Claspless Viperscale Bracelet 58–59; Ombre Elfsheet Ring 78–79; Tapered Bronze Scale Maille Collar 124–127; Two-tone GSG Sheet Necklace 57
punch, dapping 12

round-nose pliers 12

safety 17
saw 12
saw blades 12
scales 14
sizing rings and bracelets 138–139
speed weaving 17, 21
storage of chain maille 142
tape 12, 21
tape measure 12

weaving large maille 16
weaving micro-maille 16
wire cutters 12
wire diameter 30
wire scale chart 30

Check out other ways to work with chain, metal, and wire
with these inspiring resources from Interweave

CHAIN MAILLE JEWELRY WORKSHOP
Techniques and Projects for Weaving with Wire

Karen Karon

ISBN 978-1-59668-645-8, $24.95

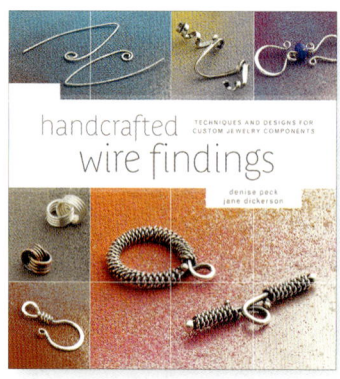

HANDCRAFTED WIRE FINDINGS
Techniques and Designs for Custom Jewelry Components

Denise Peck and Jane Dickerson

ISBN 978-1-59668-283-2, $22.95

ARTISAN FILIGREE
Wire-Wrapping Jewelry Techniques and Projects

Jodi Bombardier

ISBN 978-1-59668-635-9, $24.95

Available at your favorite retailer or

Jewelry Making Daily Shop

shop.jewelrymakingdaily.com

The only magazine on the market devoted to designing and making jewelry with wire, *Step by Step Wire Jewelry* magazine is packed with detailed and illustrated how-to projects. Each issue delivers easy-to-follow step-by-step jewelry projects for every skill level, plus tips, techniques, popular tools, advice drom the pros, and much more! **Stepbystepwire.com**

Jewelry Making Daily is the ultimate online community for anyone interested in creating handmade jewelry. Get tips from industry experts, download free step-by-step projects, check out video demos, discover sources for supplies, and more! Sign up at **jewelrymakingdaily.com**.